An OPUS book

A History of Western Philosophy: 4

THE RATIONALISTS

John Cottingham is Professor of Philosophy at The University of Reading, and author of numerous writings on early modern philosophy, including *Rationalism* (1984), *Descartes* (1986), and *A Descartes Dictionàry* (1993); he is co-translator of *The Philosophical Writings of Descartes* (1985–91), and editor of *The Cambridge Companion to Descartes* (1992), and of *Ratio*, the international journal of analytic philosophy.

OPUS General Editors

Christopher Butler
Robert Evans
John Skorupski

OPUS books provide concise, original, and authoritative introductions to a wide range of subjects in the humanities and sciences. They are written by experts for the general reader as well as for students.

A History of Western Philosophy

This series of OPUS books offers a comprehensive and up-to-date survey of the history of philosophical ideas from earliest times. Its aim is not only to set those ideas in their immediate cultural context, but also to focus on their value and relevance to twentieth-century thinking.

A History of Western Philosophy: 4

The
Rationalists

JOHN COTTINGHAM

Oxford   New York

OXFORD UNIVERSITY PRESS

This book has been printed digitally and produced in a standard specification
in order to ensure its continuing availability

OXFORD
UNIVERSITY PRESS

Great Clarendon Street, Oxford OX2 6DP

Oxford University Press is a department of the University of Oxford.
It furthers the University's objective of excellence in research, scholarship,
and education by publishing worldwide in

Oxford New York

Auckland   Cape Town Dar es Salaam   Hong Kong   Karachi
Kuala Lumpur Madrid Melbourne Mexico City   Nairobi
New Delhi Shanghai Taipei Toronto
With offices in
Argentina Austria Brazil Chile Czech Republic France Greece
Guatemala Hungary Italy Japan South Korea Poland Portugal
Singapore Switzerland Thailand Turkey Ukraine Vietnam

Oxford is a registered trade mark of Oxford University Press
in the UK and in certain other countries

Published in the United States
by Oxford University Press Inc., New York

ISBN 978-0-19-289190-7

For M. G. C. and J. L. C.

Preface

The philosophers who are the principal subjects of this book are beyond question three of the world's greatest thinkers, and to give a fully comprehensive account of their work is surely beyond the scope of a single volume—certainly one of this size. Even to claim to have outlined the most important topics would be rash, since we are dealing with writers whose ideas are extremely wide-ranging and opinions legitimately differ as to what is philosophically important. This book will have achieved its limited goal if at least some of the vital connecting links between the philosophies of Descartes, Spinoza, and Leibniz have been uncovered. But despite adopting a deliberately selective strategy, I have tried not to narrow the focus excessively; thus the reader will find that from time to time reference is made to less widely studied figures of the period, such as Malebranche and Arnauld, particularly where their ideas help to put the theories of the three great rationalists into perspective.

The very title which the editors of the Opus series have chosen for this volume may cause some hackles to rise, for the standard labels 'rationalist' and 'empiricist' have come in for a good deal of critical scrutiny in recent years. Much of this criticism seems to me well-taken, and some of the distortions which the traditional labels can encourage are touched on in Chapter 1. When the distortions have been removed, however, the term 'rationalist', if used with sufficient care, can still be of service. Moreover, irrespective of what classifications we use, there is still fascination and philosophical profit to be had in exploring the many common themes in the writings of Descartes, Spinoza, and Leibniz. If nothing else, such an exercise ought to serve as an antidote to the still frequent practice of analysing philosophers in isolation as if their ideas sprang into existence ready made, independently of the intellectual climate of their times. Yet for all that, the history of philosophy should never become a *purely* historical affair; part of the appeal of the great seventeenth-century rationalists is that by engaging with their arguments we are often able to gain insights into philosophical problems that continue to fascinate and perplex us today.

What follows is intended to be readily accessible to the non-specialist; in order to avoid interrupting the flow I have relegated many qualifications and matters of detail to the notes at the end of the book. I have also deliberately kept discussion of secondary material to a minimum, while providing extensive references to, and quotations from, the primary sources. Where standard translations are cited, I have occasionally modified or adapted the wording where this seemed desirable.

I am greatly conscious of the debts I have incurred in writing this volume, both to a host of previous interpreters and commentators and to the large number of friends and students with whom I have discussed many of the issues dealt with below. I should like to record my special thanks to Professor Harry Parkinson, whose erudition has saved me from many errors. The comments I received from the editor of the series and another press adviser have also been most helpful. Finally, I am once again grateful to Joan Morris for her marvellously cheerful and efficient work on the word-processor.

J. G. C.

Contents

List of Abbreviations

Descartes

AT   *Oeuvres de Descartes*, ed. C. Adam and P. Tannery, 12 vols. (revised edition, Paris: Vrin/CNRS, 1964–76).

CSM   *The Philosophical Writings of Descartes*, tr. J. Cottingham, R. Stoothoff, and D. Murdoch, 2 vols. (Cambridge: Cambridge University Press, 1985).

ALQ   *Descartes: Oeuvres Philosophiques*, ed. F. Alquie, 3 vols. (Paris: Garnier, 1963–73).

K   *Descartes: Philosophical Letters*, tr. A. Kenny (Oxford: Oxford University Press, 1970; reprinted Oxford: Blackwell, 1980).

CB   *Descartes' Conversation with Burman*, tr. with introduction and commentary J. Cottingham (Oxford: Clarendon, 1976). References to page numbers *not* section numbers.

Spinoza

G   *Spinoza, Opera*, ed. C. Gebhardt, 3 vols. (Heidelberg: Carl Winters, 1925; reprinted 1972).

C   *The Collected Works of Spinoza*, ed. and tr. E. Curley, Vol. I (Princeton: Princeton University Press, 1985).

W   *The Correspondence of Spinoza*, tr. A. Wolf (London: Allen and Unwin, 1928).

Leibniz

GP   *Die Philosophischen Schriften von G. W. Leibniz*, ed. C. I. Gerhardt, 7 vols. (Berlin: Weidmann, 1875–90).

L   *Gottfried Wilhelm Leibniz. Philosophical Papers and Letters*, tr. and ed. L. E. Loemker (2nd edn. Dordrecht: Reidel, 1969).

P   *Leibniz: Philosophical Writings*, ed. G. H. R. Parkinson (London: Dent, 1973).

R B *G. W. Leibniz: New Essays on Human Understanding*, tr. and ed. P. Remnant and J. Bennett (Cambridge: Cambridge University Press, 1981).

M *The Leibniz-Arnauld Correspondence*, tr. H. T. Matson (Manchester: Manchester University Press, 1971).

C O *Opuscules et fragments inédits de Leibniz*, ed. L. Couturat (Paris: Alcan, 1903).

G G *G. W. Leibniz, Textes inédits*, ed. G. Grua, 2 vols. (Paris, 1948).

References to these editions of the writings of Descartes, Spinoza, and Leibniz are by page number (preceded where appropriate by a volume number in roman numerals). From time to time, however, reference is also made to specific individual works, such as Descartes's *Principles* or Spinoza's *Ethics*, using the original subdivisions which are common to all subsequent editions and translations (for example, *Principles* II, 10; *Ethics* I, prop. 25).

Works by all other authors are referred to in the notes by the author's or editor's name followed by a page reference (preceded by a volume number where appropriate); full details may be found in the Reference List at the end of the book.

I

Background

> The human intellect understands some propositions,
> namely those of the mathematical sciences, quite per-
> fectly, and in these it has as much absolute certainty as
> Nature herself. Of course the Divine intellect knows
> infinitely more propositions than we do, since it knows
> all. Yet in respect of those few which the human intellect
> does understand, I believe its knowledge equals the
> Divine in objective certainty—for here it succeeds in
> understanding *necessity*, than which there can be no
> greater certainty (Galileo Galilei, *Dialogo sopra i due
> massimi sistemi del mondo, Ptolemaico e Copernicano*,
> 1632).[1]

Rationalists and empiricists

Confronted with the bewildering complexity and variety of
philosophical theories, the student turns with relief to labels and
pigeonholes. By classifying philosophers into 'movements' and
'schools of thought', we seem to have hope of discerning some
pattern in the tumultuous flow of ideas. But later, on closer
acquaintance with the texts, doubts creep in. Do the authors fit
the stereotypes? Have we achieved order only at the cost of
oversimplification or caricature?

The use of the label 'rationalist' is beset with many such
difficulties and dangers. None of the three great philosophers who
form the main subjects of this volume described himself as
'rationalist'; nor was the term 'rationalist' much in evidence in the
philosophical writings of the seventeenth century. But at the start
of the century, Francis Bacon articulated a contrast that will
strike a familiar chord for readers of many modern potted
histories of philosophy: 'empiricists are like ants; they collect and
put to use; but rationalists are like spiders; they spin threads out

of themselves.'² Though Bacon could not of course have foreseen it, and though he was using the labels in a very different context to that which has become common since,³ the philosophical history of the seventeenth and eighteenth centuries did come to be interpreted in terms of a conflict between two supposedly hostile armies: on the one side the 'empiricist' thinkers, led by Locke, Berkeley, and Hume, were seen as basing their philosophies on the foundation of sensory experience, while on the other side the 'rationalists', led by Descartes, Spinoza, and Leibniz, were seen as attempting to construct their philosophical systems purely a priori.

Although doubts about this model (which seems to be largely due to Kant⁴) have increasingly begun to surface in recent years, it continues to exert considerable influence on the way in which the philosophy of the seventeenth and eighteenth centuries is taught. So it will be as well to begin by indicating some of the ways in which the 'opposing armies' model is misleading. To begin with, the model may tempt us to project back on to the early-modern period contrasts and conflicts that are much more recent in origin. In present-day philosophy, there is a perhaps diminishing but still very wide gulf, in terms of style, methodology, and objectives, between 'Anglo-Saxon' and 'Continental' philosophers. In the seventeenth and eighteenth centuries, by contrast, there were no such fundamental differences of method or purpose between the so-called 'British empiricists' and their 'rationalist' counterparts in continental Europe. Despite the numerous and important issues on which they differed, it is probably fair to say that the six great philosophers mentioned in the preceding paragraph would all have seen themselves as engaged on a recognizably similar kind of enterprise.

If we move from the general conception of philosophy to its specific content, there is a further reason for mistrusting the model of two hostile armies, namely that it suggests a clash between two mutually exclusive sets of doctrines. But in fact the philosophical history of the period forms a complex pattern of constantly overlapping and criss-crossing influences and counter-influences. Thus, though Descartes undoubtedly had an important effect on the ideas of Spinoza and Leibniz, many of the doctrines of the two latter thinkers were developed through criticism of what they saw as weaknesses in the Cartesian system.[5] On the other side, John Locke, for all his supposed 'empiricism', was profoundly influenced, in much of his work, by Descartes's views on the nature of mind and the material universe.[6] Many elements in Berkeley's thought, too, can be seen as influenced by Descartes's ideas, mediated by his deviant disciple Nicolas Malebranche, while Malebranche also exerted influence, though in a different direction, on the work of Leibniz.[7] To try to separate out these interweaving strands into two wholly distinct structures labelled 'rationalism' and 'empiricism' would be fundamentally misguided.

Apart from questions of influence and cross-fertilization, there is another crucial respect in which the contrast between empiricism and rationalism may mislead. The 'ants and spiders' model suggests contrasting schools of philosophy, one based on careful observation, the other based on 'pure thought'. In the past, this contrast has worked to the detriment of the rationalists, implying that they were nothing but a priori web-spinners, building elaborate metaphysical systems 'from the armchair', and trying to settle by abstract theorizing questions about the nature of reality which ought properly to be determined by scientific experiment. This caricature of 'philosophical rationalism' involves more distortions than can conveniently be exposed in this brief introduction, but two particular points deserve a mention here. First, neither Descartes nor Spinoza nor Leibniz did in fact disdain the role of empirical investigation in achieving a proper understanding of the universe (see Chapter 2). Second, and irrespective of the role actually played by observation in the systems of Descartes, Spinoza, and Leibniz, the dismissive caricature of the rationalist as an 'armchair theorizer' presupposes an untenable contrast between, on the one hand, the supposedly down-to-earth observational methods of the scientist and, on the other hand, the purely aprioristic theorizing of the metaphysician. This contrast is untenable because it has become apparent in the latter half of our own century, first, that the reductionist programme of boiling down science to a set of down-to-earth observation-statements is unfulfillable; second, that the distinction between observation and theory is itself highly problematic; and third (and partly as a consequence of the first two points), that the distinction between the enterprises we call 'science' and 'metaphysics' is very far from being clear-cut. There may be many things wrong with the philosophical systems of Descartes, Spinoza, and Leibniz, but it is no longer possible to see it as a knock-down objection to those systems that they contain a substantial amount of speculative theorizing that is not directly testable against experience.

Reason, system, and necessity

Despite the caveats entered above, the very writing of this book presupposes that illumination is to be gained from grouping together the work of Descartes, Spinoza, and Leibniz. There is no quick and easy way of making good this claim: it is only by examining specific philosophical themes—knowledge, the nature of substance, mind and body, human freedom—that one comes to appreciate how an understanding of the ideas of any one of these philosophical giants enriches our understanding of the ideas of the other two. But it may be worth providing here, if only in a preliminary way, some general indications of the deep structural similarities to be found in the philosophies of Descartes, Spinoza, and Leibniz.

The term 'rationalist' comes from the Latin *ratio* ('reason'), while the term 'empiricist' with which it is so often contrasted comes from the Greek *empeiria* ('experience'). We have already noted that it is wrong to think of Descartes, Spinoza, and Leibniz as pure 'apriorists' who tried to dispense with sensory experience entirely; but it is none the less true that they shared a belief that it was possible, by the use of reason, to gain a superior kind of knowledge to that derived from the senses. Descartes saw it as one of the first steps in metaphysics to 'lead the mind away from the senses' (AT VII. 12; CSM II. 9); he believed that our inborn 'natural light' or 'light of reason' (*lumen naturale, lux rationis*) would enable us to 'penetrate the secrets of the most recondite sciences' (AT X. 495–6; CSM II. 400).[8] Spinoza, for his part, described cognition based on 'random experience' (*experientia vaga*) as the lowest grade of cognition—a 'mutilated and confused' kind of awareness that cannot provide an adequate representation of reality. For Spinoza, reason alone can perceive things 'truly, as they are in themselves' (G II. 122; C 477 and G II. 125; C 480). Leibniz, too, embraces the notion of an innate 'natural light' of reason which, he argues, enables us to know necessary truths: 'the senses can help us after a fashion to know what is, but they cannot help us to know what must be or what cannot be otherwise.' We need to go beyond the senses to gain knowledge of 'the universal and necessary truths of the sciences' (GP VI. 504–5; L 550–1).

The priority which Descartes, Spinoza, and Leibniz assigned to the deliverances of reason as against those of the senses is connected with their role in what is sometimes called the 'seventeenth-century scientific revolution'. The phrase is in some respects a misleading one, since the notions of 'science' and 'scientific inquiry' in the modern sense were still far from being explicitly formulated in the seventeenth century. But it is certainly true that the century witnessed the emergence and consolidation of a radically new world outlook, which came to be known by its supporters and its critics as the 'new philosophy' or the 'modern philosophy'. One of the central planks of the modern philosophy was a determined rejection of the medieval-scholastic reliance on qualitative descriptions and explanations, and an insistence that a proper understanding of the universe must be formulated in quantitative terms. The new creed is summed up in Galileo's famous pronouncement, in 1623, that the 'great book of the universe cannot be understood unless one can read the language in which it is written—the language of mathematics'.[9] The ˈ as conceived of by scholastic physics was in large part . 'common-sense' world as depicted by the five senses; explanations of the phenomena of nature were sought in terms of 'real qualities' (such as heaviness, lightness, moistness, and dryness) that were taken to 'inhere' in objects. A recurring complaint among progressive thinkers of the seventeenth century is that our understanding is not really advanced one bit when we are told that an object falls because of the 'real quality' of heaviness or dazzles because of the 'real quality' of whiteness; from Galileo onwards we find increasing demands for such qualitative approaches to be discarded in favour of a mathematical physics.[10]

It was a mathematical, and in particular a geometrical model, that was the inspiration behind the Cartesian programme for physics; Descartes firmly declared in his *Principles of Philosophy* (1644) that he recognized 'no matter in corporeal objects apart from what the geometers call quantity and take as the object of their demonstrations, i.e. that to which every kind of division, shape and motion is applicable' (AT VIII. 78; CSM I. 247). Echoing this, Spinoza took geometrical extension (in three dimensions) as the defining characteristic of matter; in his *Ethics* (*c.*1665) he argued that all the qualitative variety of the world which we perceive via the senses can be understood in terms of the motion and rest of such extended matter (G II. 97–102; C 458–62). And finally, in a letter written by Leibniz in 1702, we find clear allegiance to the central tenet of the 'new' philosophy— an insistence on the need to go beyond the obscure and imperfectly understood qualities perceived by the senses: '*sensible* qualities are in fact *occult* qualities, and there must be others *more manifest* which could render them more understandable' (L 541). Leibniz did not in fact believe that a satisfactory characterization of matter could be given in terms of extension alone; moreover, as will appear later, he maintained that certain aspects of scholastic philosophy could be salvaged (see below, pp. 104 ff.). But he held nevertheless that 'in order to understand sensible qualities distinctly one must always turn back to mathematical ideas, and these ideas always include magnitude or multitude of parts' (L 548).

Apart from their being inspired by the explanatory power of mathematics in respect of physical phenomena, the three great rationalists also saw mathematics as a kind of symbol of the unity and interconnectedness of all knowledge. This notion, Platonic in its origins, found no place in the Aristotelian-scholastic tradition which was still largely dominant in the universities of the seventeenth century, and which tended to conceive of human knowledge as a set of separate disciplines, each with its own methods and level of precision.[11] Descartes, probably the most influential pioneer of the new philosophy, proclaimed the ideal of systematic unification throughout his life. In one of his early notebooks he remarked that 'if we could see how the sciences are linked together, we would find them no harder to retain in our mind than the series of numbers' (AT X. 215; CSM I. 3); and in an unfinished dialogue found amongst his papers when he died we find the resounding declaration that 'all the items of knowledge that lie within the reach of the human mind are linked together with a marvellous bond, and can be derived from each other by means of necessary inferences' (AT X. 497; CSM II. 400). In his *Discourse on the Method*, in the course of describing his intellectual development, Descartes specifically remarks that it was the 'long chains of reasoning of the geometers' which provided the inspiration for this ideal of an interconnected system of knowledge (AT VI. 19; CSM I. 120). The same ideal is strongly in evidence in Spinoza, whose greatest work, the *Ethics*, deliberately follows a geometrical pattern, and attempts to provide a comprehensive account of the nature of substance, the relation between mind and body, and the formula for a fulfilled life, all within the structure of a single, closely knit system. As for Leibniz, though commentators have argued about the extent to which his philosophy was intended to form a tightly unified structure, there can be no doubt that he often presented it as hinging on a small number of fundamental and all-embracing principles.[12] One of Leibniz's continuing dreams was that of a *characteristica universalis*—a universal symbolic alphabet in terms of which the whole of human knowledge could be represented; and in an early paper entitled 'Of Universal Synthesis and Analysis' (*c*.1683) he speaks of a method of 'deriving the elements of eternal truth and proceeding in all things . . . in a way which is as demonstrative as that of geometry' (GP VII. 296; P 15).

Closely connected with this allegiance to the mathematical model of knowledge, and the ideal of knowledge as a unified system, is the rationalist doctrine, sometimes called 'necessitarianism', which implies that for any true proposition *P*, it can in principle be shown that *P* *must* be the case; the notion that something could merely 'happen' to be true, and 'might have been otherwise', is ruled out.[13] Spinoza should perhaps be regarded as the champion of this necessitarian view: 'if men clearly understood the whole of nature they would find that everything is just as necessary as the things treated of in mathematics' (G I. 266; C 332). The common notion of 'contingency'—the belief that there are truths which merely happen to be the case—is, for Spinoza, an illusion, which derives from the fact that our view of reality is often inadequate and incomplete. Thus the relation between a cause and its effect, for example, cannot be a matter of happenstance: causal relations cannot, as Hume was later to suggest, be mere contingent regularities or 'constant conjunctions'.[14] For if our perceptions were adequate we would be able to deduce the effect from the cause with the same kind of necessity that we can deduce, say, that certain properties must be true of a given triangle.[15]

In Descartes's writings there is very little explicit discussion of the distinction between 'necessary' and 'contingent' statements; but Descartes certainly articulated an ideal of scientific explanation in which the reasons for phenomena are 'deduced from indubitably true common notions'; the resulting self-evidence and necessity would enable such explanations to be regarded as having the same status as 'mathematical demonstrations' (AT VIII. 79; CSM I. 247). In Cartesian physics there are no 'brute facts'. In Leibniz's system, too, there is a powerful denial of the possibility of 'brute facts' in the shape of the celebrated 'principle of sufficient reason' which asserts that 'nothing happens without a sufficient reason why it should be thus and not otherwise' (GP VII. 363; P 211). Elsewhere Leibniz observes that in the case of any true statement, it must in principle be possible to reduce it by analysis to a 'primary truth'—one whose denial is self-contradictory (CO 518; P 87–8).

It is important *not* to interpret this necessitarian strand in rationalist thought as the implausible doctrine that one simply has to reflect on the laws of logic and mathematics in order to unravel an entire system of knowledge about the universe. The three great rationalists did certainly believe in a rationally ordered universe, such that every event finds its necessary place in the whole; but they were not so naïve as to suppose that human beings could automatically or immediately discern the necessary connections involved in any given case. Descartes explicitly pointed out that for many phenomena, we must be content with merely probable explanations, since we simply do not have sufficient information to determine which of several possible answers is the correct one (*Principles* III. 46). Spinoza, too, allows that there are elements of his system which fall short of absolute certainty (cf. *Ethics* II, prop. 17, schol.). And Leibniz makes it clear that though there is a set of sufficient reasons for each truth, the process of analysis which would uncover the chain of reasons in full detail may be far too long and complex to fall within the grasp of the human intellect (CO 17; P 97). These matters will be examined in more detail in Chapter 2.

In short, though the necessitarian view of truth involves a commitment to the ideal of an all-embracing rationally intelligible system such that nothing is in principle inexplicable, it need not involve, in the first place, excessive optimism about the powers of human reason; nor, in the second place, need it imply commitment to a naïvely aprioristic conception of science. On the first point, it is worth noting that the many thinkers who have been attracted by the necessitarian ideal include some who have taken a profoundly sceptical view about our ability to uncover necessary connections in the world; indeed their number includes philosophers who are normally not classified as belonging to the rationalist tradition at all:

I doubt not but if we could discover the Figure, Size, Texture and Motion of the minute Constituent parts of any two Bodies, we should know without Trial several of the Operations one upon another, as we do now the Properties of a Square or a Triangle ... The dissolving of Silver in *aqua fortis* and Gold in *aqua regia* and not *vice versa* would then perhaps be no more difficult to know than it is to a Smith to understand why the turning of one Key will open a Lock and not the turning of another.[16]

John Locke, from whose *Essay concerning Human Understanding* (1689) the above quotation is taken, doubted that humans would ever in fact discover the hidden structures that would give us 'certain knowledge of universal Truths concerning natural bodies'.[17] But in this passage he clearly declares his belief that there are such underlying structures, and that, could we but discover them, we would be put in touch with the necessary connections that do in fact obtain in nature. As to the second point (that necessitarianism need not imply apriorism), it is worth stressing that in our own day there have been scientists and philosophers who have taken a strongly necessitarian view of scientific truth without making any concessions whatever to apriorism. 'The scientist', we are told in one influential recent work, 'attempts by investigating basic structural traits to uncover the nature and thus the essence (in the philosophical sense) of natural kinds.'[18] This claim entails that the connections which the scientist uncovers—for example the connection between heat and molecular energy—are *necessary* connections, but it certainly does not commit its author to an aprioristic methodology of science; on the contrary, we find a firm insistence that such necessary truths have to be uncovered a posteriori, by empirical investigation.[19] In this connection it is interesting to see Leibniz suggesting that careful experimentation can often be of great value, along with abstract reasoning, in uncovering the real essences of things and the underlying causes of phenomena (GP VII. 265–9; L 173–6).

A prerequisite for a fruitful study of the rationalists, then, is a readiness to be open-minded, and a willingness to discard some of the caricatures from which 'rationalism' has suffered in our own time. Many of the distortions arise from a tendency to see rationalism as a kind of seamless web, so that any philosopher whose thought contains rationalist elements is seen as being committed to the wildest excesses of speculative metaphysics.[20] What should by now be starting to emerge is that 'rationalism' stands not for a monolithic philosophical doctrine, but rather for a *cluster* of overlapping views and ideas.[21] To recapitulate, one element in rationalist thought is a certain caution about the deliverances of the senses, and a belief that the correct use of reason will enable us to progress beyond the naïve, common-sense view of the world. Another is the vision of the universe as an ordered system, every aspect of which is in principle accessible to the human intellect. A further strand is a tendency to be impressed by mathematics both in virtue of its intrinsic clarity and certainty, and also because it is seen as a model for a well-founded and unified system of knowledge. And a final element (from many more which could no doubt be discerned) is the belief in necessary connections in nature, and, more generally, the view that scientific and philosophical truth must involve reference to what, in some sense, cannot be otherwise. None of these beliefs is self-evidently antiquated or absurd; on the contrary, they still have an important place in much present-day scientific and philosophical thinking. For this reason alone, a study of the seventeenth-century rationalists is by no means of purely histor-ical interest; the tradition which Descartes, Spinoza, and Leibniz helped to inaugurate is far from defunct, and many of the problems with which they grappled are of enduring concern today.

René Descartes

René Descartes was born on 31 March 1596, in the small town between Tours and Poitiers which now bears his name.[22] He was a sickly child: his mother died soon after his birth, and he was brought up by his maternal grandmother. He was educated at the newly founded Jesuit College of La Flèche, in Anjou, where, so his biographer Adrien Baillet reports, he enjoyed the privilege of 'lying in' in the mornings, as a concession to his frail constitution. The young René's poor health no doubt contributed to his lifelong interest in medicine as a means for improving the quality of human life. 'The maintenance of health', he was to write in 1637, 'is undoubtedly the chief good and foundation of all other goods in this life . . . and I am sure that we might free ourselves from innumerable diseases both of the body and the mind, and perhaps even from the infirmity of old age, if we had sufficient knowledge of their causes' (AT VI. 62; CSM I. 143. Cf. AT V. 179; CB 51).

This characteristic enthusiasm for the kind of knowledge that would yield practical benefits for mankind explains much about Descartes's attitude to the education he received at La Flèche. Although he had considerable respect for some of his teachers,[23] he took a distinctly sceptical view of the value of many of the subjects taught. The autobiographical section of the *Discourse on the Method* suggests that he was irked by the strong emphasis on classical learning ('one who is too curious about the practices of past ages usually remains quite ignorant about the present': AT VI. 6; CSM I. 114). As for 'philosophy' (as used in the seventeenth century, this term often referred principally to the study of the natural world), Descartes soon discovered that every question of substance was hotly disputed, and much of what was taught boiled down to little more than a set of exercises for the development of debating skills. He later formed the goal of developing a 'practical philosophy' that would supersede the 'speculative philosophy taught in the schools':

through this practical philosophy we could know the power and action of fire, water, air, the stars, the heavens and all other bodies in our environment as distinctly as we know the various crafts of our artisans; and we could use this knowledge as the artisans use theirs—for all the purposes for which it is appropriate, and thus make ourselves, as it were, the lords and masters of nature (AT VI. 62; CSM I. 142).

Descartes left La Flèche probably in 1614, and proceeded to study for his doctoral degree (in law) at Poitiers, which he completed in December 1616.[24] Not long afterwards, at the age of twenty-two, he left France and embarked on a series of travels, going first to Holland—the country which was eventually to be his home. He was not 'seeking his fortune'—throughout his life he enjoyed comfortable private means; rather (if the *Discourse* reports his intentions accurately) he was deliberately rejecting the conventional world of university learning, in order to seek the knowledge to be found in the 'great book of the world' (AT VI. 9; CSM I. 115). On this first visit to Holland he met the philosopher and mathematician Isaac Beeckman, to whom he dedicated his first work, the *Compendium Musicae* (written in 1618). The following year Descartes travelled to Germany with the forces of Maximilian of Bavaria, and it was in November 1619 (aged twenty-three) that he had the remarkable experience that was to set the future course of his life. As Descartes tells the story, he was 'shut up all day in a stove-heated room' (*poêle*), where he was completely free to 'converse with himself about his own thoughts'

(AT VI. 11; CSM I. 116). A day of intense solitary meditation, followed by a night of vivid and disturbing dreams, convinced Descartes that he had a mission to found a new philosophical system.[25]

In the early 1620s Descartes continued to travel in Europe, but he returned to France in 1625, and lived in Paris for three years. During this period, he composed his first major work, the *Regulae ad directionem ingenii* ('Rules for the guidance of our native intelligence'). Though never completed or published in Descartes's lifetime, this work is an important statement of his early views on knowledge and philosophical method; it is inspired by the model of mathematical reasoning as pointing the way to the development of an entire scientific system (see Chapter 2, pp. 36–7). Pure mathematics was a major preoccupation of the young Descartes, and much of the work for his *Geometry* was probably done at this time.[26] Eventually published in 1637 as one of the three 'specimen essays' of Descartes's new method, the *Geometry* contained procedures for treating geometrical questions algebraically, thereby laying down the foundations for what is now known as analytical or co-ordinate geometry. The other two specimen essays (on which Descartes began working in the late 1620s) were the *Optics* (*La Dioptrique*) and the *Meteorology* (*Les Météores*). Both of these works applied geometrical techniques to the solution of problems in the real world; they also purported to show how a variety of seemingly diverse phenomena could be explained by reference to a few principles of great simplicity and generality.[27]

In 1629 Descartes decided to make Holland his permanent home. He had a keen horror of public controversy ('shun publicity' was his motto[28]), and in the years that followed he was to find that the Dutch countryside suited his desire for tranquillity and solitude. Little is known of Descartes's private life during his years in Holland. His voluminous correspondence shows that despite his distaste for the public arena, he rapidly acquired a wide circle of correspondents, but he seems to have had few close personal friends. He never 'settled down' in one place (changing his place of residence over a dozen times in as many years) and he

never married—though he did have a liaison with his serving woman Hélène, which resulted in the birth of a daughter, Francine, who died tragically at the age of five.[29] By 1632 (the year of Spinoza's birth) Descartes was in process of completing his treatise *Le Monde* ('The World' or 'The Universe'), which had the ambitious aim of providing a comprehensive account of the whole of physics, applying the same general principles to the explanation of both terrestrial and celestial phenomena (a concluding section, now known as the *Traité de l'homme* ('Treatise on Man'), deals with the workings of the human body). The same year saw the publication in Florence of Galileo's *Dialogue on the two chief systems of the universe*, a work which, like Descartes's, took a unificatory view of the cosmos, rejecting the traditional Aristotelian thesis that the celestial and terrestrial worlds are entirely different in kind; it also vigorously defended the Copernican view (to which Descartes also subscribed, in *Le Monde*) that the earth rotates diurnally and revolves annually about a central sun.[30] When Galileo's work was formally condemned by the Inquisition in June 1633, Descartes at once decided to withdraw his own *Le Monde* from publication. 'Although my arguments were based on very certain and evident proofs,' he later wrote to his chief correspondent, Friar Marin Mersenne, 'I would not wish for anything in the world to maintain them against the authority of the Church. I desire to live in peace . . .' (AT I. 285; K 25).

Four years later, however, Descartes ventured to publish a sample of his work, consisting of the three specimen essays already mentioned (the *Optics*, *Meteorology*, and *Geometry*), and an extended introductory essay entitled *Discours de la méthode pour bien conduire sa raison et chercher la vérité dans les sciences* ('Discourse on the Method of rightly conducting one's reason and seeking the truth in the sciences'). The volume appeared anonymously in Leiden on 8 June 1637. The *Discourse* is an informal and wide-ranging work, designed for the general reader; it includes Descartes's reflections on his education, a cautiously conservative 'provisional moral code' for the conduct of life, and a lucid summary of Descartes's metaphysical views, which con-

tains the famous dictum 'je pense donc je suis'—'I am thinking therefore I exist'. In the latter part of the work Descartes alludes to some of the material from *Le Monde* and the *Traité de l'homme*, which he had withdrawn from publication, and unfolds a number of his scientific ideas—most notably, perhaps, the plan for a purely mechanistic science of physiology. Descartes compares the human body to an 'automaton' and argues that had we sufficient knowledge of the structure of its working parts we could explain even highly complex behavioural responses in purely mechanical terms. The exception is *thought*, and its external manifestation, language: this alone cannot be explained mechanistically—a thesis which leads Descartes to assert a fundamental divide between human beings and 'the beasts':

There are no men so dull-witted or stupid—and this includes even madmen—that they are incapable of arranging various words together and forming an utterance in order to make their thoughts understood, whereas no animal, however perfect, can do the like. This is not because they lack the necessary organs, for we see that magpies and parrots can utter words as we do, and yet cannot speak as we do (i.e. show that they are thinking what they are saying). By contrast, even men born deaf and dumb, and thus deprived of speech organs as much as the beasts, or more so, normally invent their own signs to make themselves understood . . . This shows that the beasts do not merely have less reason than man, but have no reason at all . . . (AT VI. 57; CSM I. 140).

By writing the *Discourse* in French, Descartes hoped to reach beyond the narrow audience of the academic world. But in 1641 he published, in Latin, a much more thorough and carefully wrought presentation of the metaphysical foundations of his philosophy, the *Meditations on First Philosophy* (*Meditationes de Prima Philosophia*). Though aimed at a more learned audience, the work is emphatically not an academic treatise. On the contrary, as the title suggests, it is a set of mental exercises; and Descartes insisted that in order to derive any benefit from the work, each reader must be prepared to 'meditate along with the author' (AT VII. 9; CSM II. 8), following the path from preconceived opinion, to doubt, to awareness—first of one's own existence, then of God—and finally to knowledge of the nature and existence of the physical world, and its relation to the mind. Although the *Meditations* is a comparatively short work, the size of the volume that appeared in 1641 was greatly increased by the addition of six sets of 'Objections' by various scholars, philosophers, and theologians, together with Descartes's Replies. This remarkable arrangement was largely engineered by Mersenne, in Paris, who had a prodigious circle of learned correspondents, and circulated Descartes's manuscript widely prior to its publication. The objectors included Thomas Hobbes (who had fled to Paris for political reasons in 1640), the brilliant theologian Antoine Arnauld (then still under 30), and the celebrated neo-Epicurean philosopher Pierre Gassendi. The second edition, which appeared the following year (1642), included a lengthy—and distinctly hostile—Seventh Set of Objections by the Jesuit Pierre Bourdin.[31]

By the mid-1640s Descartes had become an internationally known figure. Despite his desire to avoid academic and theological wrangles, he found that the *Meditations*—particularly the arguments for doubt which opened the work—provided ammunition for what he had long feared—the 'envy and hostility' of his opponents (cf. AT VII. 574; CSM II. 387). His most implacable enemy was Gisbertus Voetius, Professor of Theology at Utrecht, whose vicious attacks forced Descartes to publish an open letter of self-defence (*Epistola ad Voetium*) in 1643 (AT VIIIB). Despite such problems, Descartes hoped to get his philosophical system accepted and taught in the universities, and the following year saw the publication, again in Latin, of Descartes's *magnum opus*, the *Principles of Philosophy* (*Principia Philosophiae*). Designed as an academic textbook, this large volume comprises a detailed introduction to Descartes's metaphysics (in Part I), a full account of the principles of his physics (Part II), his theory of the structure of the universe and the solar system (Part III), and his explanation of the origins of the earth and of a wide variety of terrestrial phenomena such as tides, earthquakes, and magnetism (Part IV). Two further parts were planned, dealing respectively with plants and animals, and with man, but these were never completed; a brief section at the end of Part IV does, however, provide a summary of some of Descartes's views on physiology and psychology.

It was the nature of man—a creature that was on his own account a curious compound of two incompatible substances, an incorporeal spirit and a purely mechanical body—that came increasingly to preoccupy Descartes during the latter half of the 1640s. Some of his reflections on this topic are to be found in his philosophical letters (of which a very large number have been preserved), and in particular those written to Princess Elizabeth of Bohemia, with whom Descartes enjoyed a long and fruitful correspondence. Eventually, in 1649, Descartes released, in French, an extensive study of the aspects of human life pertaining to what he called the 'substantial union' of body and mind; entitled *The Passions of the Soul* (*Les passions de l'âme*), this was to be the last work published in his lifetime.

Earlier, Descartes had sent a draft of the *Passions* to Queen Christina of Sweden, who had read his *Principles* and expressed an interest in his philosophy; and in 1649 he accepted, after much hesitation, an invitation from her to visit the royal court at Stockholm. Descartes arrived in Sweden in September but, as he had feared, the queen had 'an infinity of other preoccupations' apart from philosophy (AT V. 327; K 247), and for the last four months of 1649 Descartes was employed in a series of uncongenial tasks such as the writing of verses for a ballet to celebrate Christina's birthday. In January 1650, the queen was ready to begin her course of instruction in philosophy, but she commanded Descartes to attend on her at five o'clock in the morning. For years Descartes had carefully cosseted his health; now the strain of interrupting his lifelong habit of rising late proved too great, and he became fatally ill with pneumonia. His dying thoughts must surely have dwelt on the folly of forsaking his 'beloved solitude'. 'Without my solitude', he had written only a few months earlier, 'I cannot without great difficulty make any progress in that search wherein consists my chief good in this life, the search for truth' (AT V. 430; ALQ III. 111). His search unfinished, Descartes died on 11 February 1650, a little over a month short of his fifty-fourth birthday.

Benedictus Spinoza

Spinoza was born in Amsterdam on 24 November 1632, only a
year before Descartes, then comparatively unknown, took up
residence in that city for a characteristically brief period.[32] When
Descartes died Spinoza was only seventeen, and had not yet read
any of his works; but had Descartes survived his visit to Sweden
and returned, as he had hoped to do, to the Netherlands, Spinoza
would almost certainly have tried to meet him in later life, since
he was to become a fascinated student of the Cartesian system.
Though Descartes and Spinoza came from very different
backgrounds—the one brought up as a Catholic in an ancient
and well-connected family, the other born into the insecure and
tense social setting of a colony of Jewish refugees—the lives of the
two philosophers nevertheless show some interesting parallels.
Both came to enjoy the seclusion of the Dutch countryside; both
shunned publicity (Spinoza's motto, even more wary than
Descartes's, was the single word *caute*—'cautiously'); both endeavoured, without success, to avoid the calumny of their less
talented contemporaries; both remained unmarried; and both
had their lives cut short by illness.

Spinoza's father was an influential member of the Jewish
community in Amsterdam, and the young Baruch (Spinoza's
given name, by which he was known until the age of 21) received
an education dominated by the traditional studies of the Torah
and the Talmud. Circumstances made him a polyglot: he learned
Hebrew at school; he spoke Portuguese at home with his family;
he knew Spanish, the language of many of the Jewish *émigrés* in
Amsterdam; and he naturally became fluent in Dutch. Latin came
later, and it was not until the age of twenty that Spinoza began
a serious study of the works of the scholastic philosophers. His
teacher was a Gentile, Francis van den Enden, a noted intellectual
who was well versed in scholasticism as well as being a keen
student of the 'new' Cartesian philosophy. Spinoza's eyes were
rapidly opened to a whole intellectual world that was anathema
to his rabbinical mentors, and he became increasingly alienated
from what he saw as the rigid dogmatism of orthodox Jewish
learning.[33] At the age of 22, after a legal wrangle with his half-

sister over a legacy from their father, Spinoza changed his name to Benedictus (a Christianized, or at least Latinized, version of his Hebrew given name). The intellectual gap between his views and those of the Jewish elders continued to widen, and two years later (1656) Spinoza was formally accused of heresy, and solemnly cursed and expelled from the synagogue.

During the years that followed his excommunication, Spinoza developed the skill of lens grinding, and his talent for this work provided his main source of income. His philosophical interests grew, and by 1660, when he moved to the village of Rijnsburg in the countryside near Leiden, he had acquired a close circle of friends and correspondents with whom he regularly discussed his ethical, metaphysical, and scientific ideas. These included a close contemporary, Simon de Vries, a wealthy Amsterdam merchant who had the highest regard for Spinoza and who tried more than once (without success) to persuade him to accept financial assistance, and another citizen of Amsterdam, Lodewijk Meyer, an enthusiastic Cartesian whose interests also included medicine, literature, and the theatre.[34] During this early period, Spinoza wrote an outline of his views on the nature of God and the means of attaining human fulfilment; this was the so-called *Short Treatise on God, Man, and His Well-Being*. The work was probably penned in Latin, but has survived in the form of two manuscript versions of a Dutch translation of the original; it was not published until the nineteenth century.[35]

Among the first of those who came to see Spinoza at Rijnsburg was a visitor from London, Henry Oldenburg, a member of the influential group of scientists that was shortly to be incorporated under public charter as the Royal Society.[36] 'When I visited you in your retreat at Rijnsburg,' wrote Oldenburg in August 1661, 'I found it hard to tear myself away . . . We talked about God, about infinite extension and thought, about the difference and agreement of these attributes, about the way the human soul is united with the body, and about the principles of Cartesian and Baconian philosophy . . .' (G IV. 6; C 163). Later that year, Oldenburg sent Spinoza a copy of a newly published volume of *Physiological Essays* by the celebrated English chemist Robert Boyle (1627–92). Though Spinoza was not a great experimental scientist, he took a keen interest in Boyle's experiments, offering detailed comments and criticisms on a number of points. Despite his criticisms, Spinoza was, like Boyle, committed to the (broadly) Cartesian programme for banishing occult qualities and 'substantial forms' from physics, in favour of explanations which, in Spinoza's words, invoked only 'motion, shape and the remaining mechanical affections' (G IV. 25; C 178).[37]

The early 1660s were a time of intensely productive activity for Spinoza, and he worked on several major projects during this period. The first was his *Treatise on the Purification of the Intellect* (*Tractatus de intellectus emendatione*), never completed or published in his lifetime—a work which has often been compared to Descartes's early unpublished treatise, the *Regulae*. It is largely methodological in character, describing how the mind must be directed in its search for the truth (see Chapter 2); it also includes an ambitious statement of the aims of philosophy. This is in one way typical of many of the grand programmes for the advancement of human knowledge that were mapped out in the seventeenth century, but at the same time shows a characteristically Spinozan perspective in its stress on the goal of achieving a mind 'united with the whole of nature':

> This is the end I aim at: to acquire knowledge of the Union of the mind with the whole of Nature . . . To do this it is necessary, first, to understand as much of Nature as suffices for acquiring such knowledge, and, second, to form a society of the kind that permits as many as possible to attain such knowledge. Third, attention must be paid to moral philosophy . . . Fourthly, because health is no small means to achieving this end, the whole of medicine must be worked out. And fifthly, . . . because it is possible to gain more free time and convenience in life, mechanics is in no way to be despised (G II. 9; C 11).

Some at least of these goals were the inspiration behind Spinoza's greatest work, the *Ethics demonstrated in geometrical order* (*Ethica ordine geometrico demonstrata*), which he also began working on at this time. The bulk of the work was finished by 1665. Later, in the early 1670s, Spinoza revised the manuscript, hoping to have it published, but he was earnestly advised by friends such as Oldenburg not to risk releasing any work 'which might seem, in any way whatsoever, to overthrow the practice of religious virtue' (Letter 62: G IV. 273), and he held back. The work eventually achieved publication only after Spinoza's death; together with the *Treatise on the Purification of the Intellect* it was included in the *Opera Postuma* which appeared in 1677. The only major work which Spinoza saw published under his own name during his lifetime was his exposition of Descartes's *Principles of Philosophy* (*Principia Philosophiae Renati Descartes*), which he completed at Rijnsburg, reportedly taking only two weeks over the writing. The book appeared in 1663. A preface by Lodewijk Meyer explained that Spinoza's own views did not necessarily accord in all respects with those of Descartes; and an appendix, the *Metaphysical Thoughts* (*Cogitationes Metaphysicae*), contains some distinctly unCartesian suggestions which foreshadow some of Spinoza's own doctrines in the *Ethics*.

In 1663, the year his study of Descartes was published, Spinoza moved from Rijnsburg to Voorburg, near The Hague. There he became friendly with a leading statesman of the day, Jan de Witt, who held the important post of Grand Pensionary of the Netherlands. Spinoza, partly as a result of this friendship, became increasingly interested in political theory—particularly the issues of tolerance, freedom of speech, and religious freedom—and in 1670 (at the age of 38) he published, anonymously, his *Tractatus Theologico-Politicus* ('Theologico-Political Treatise'). In a century marked by the violence of its religious hostilities, the book is a remarkably clear and forthright defence of individual liberty, and unusually free of the cautious circumlocutions and expressions of deference to established authority that are characteristic of so much writing of the period.[38] 'The Bible', asserts Spinoza in his outspoken preface to the work, 'leaves reason absolutely free and has nothing in common with philosophy . . . And as each man's habits of mind differ, so that some more readily embrace one faith and some another . . . everyone should be free to choose for himself the foundation of his creed, and his faith should be judged only by its fruits.'

The gap between the ideals he advocated and the harsh realities of the world in which he lived was brought home to Spinoza by the storm of protest which his book aroused; the work was widely condemned, and its critics eventually got it banned. For a time Spinoza continued to enjoy the patronage of de Witt (who arranged for him to receive a small pension in 1670), but in the riots that followed the French invasion of the Netherlands in 1672 both de Witt and his brother were lynched by an angry mob in The Hague. This appalling event took place not far from Spinoza's home (he had been living in The Hague since 1670), and apparently he had to be restrained forcibly from confronting the bloodthirsty crowd.[39] The following year Spinoza was invited to go to Utrecht to meet the Prince of Condé, commander of the French forces; his precise role is unclear but he may have hoped to act as an intermediary between the French general and the Dutch authorities. At all events, the visit was a failure, and on his return Spinoza was widely suspected of treason. Despite the threat to his safety, he remained at The Hague, declining the offer of a professorship at Heidelberg; his courteous letter of refusal, dated 30 March 1673, refers to his 'love of peace' and the fear that a public appointment would leave him even more open to having his views distorted and reviled by 'lovers of contradiction' (G IV. 236; W 267).[40]

Towards the end of 1676, Spinoza received a visit from a young German, whom one of his correspondents had described as 'a man of uncommon learning, well versed in many sciences, and free from the vulgar prejudices of theology' (G IV. 302; W 338).[41] The visitor was Leibniz, then aged thirty; he had written to Spinoza five years earlier enclosing a paper on optics[42] and he had recently been trying to gain access to Spinoza's (still unpublished) *Ethics*.[43] Leibniz had several lengthy discussions with Spinoza at The Hague and was able to question him in detail about his metaphysical views. The opinion Spinoza formed of his German visitor is not known.

By the time of Leibniz's visit, Spinoza was suffering from consumption, and the winter of 1676–7 was to be his last. He died on 21 February 1677, aged 44. At the time of his death, Spinoza had completed a substantial portion of a second major work on political theory, the *Tractatus Politicus* ('Political Treatise'), which, as he explained in a letter written shortly before his death, included a discussion of natural rights, a theory of the nature and limits of government, and an account of 'the ways in which monarchy ought to be constrained so as not to slide into tyranny' (G IV. 336; W 366). The treatise also refers back to some of the themes of the *Ethics*, including Spinoza's ambitious programme for the conquest of the passions. It is hard to say how far Spinoza himself achieved the tranquillity and detachment that his ethical system holds out as the highest human good. Though many of his letters have survived, like those of Descartes they reveal much about the writer's intellectual development but little of his emotional life. As far as can be gleaned from his last work, Spinoza came to have certain reservations about the feasibility of living free of the passions according to the 'bare dictates of reason'. He writes in one passage that though all may accept that the rights of others ought to rank equally with their own, the mere rational recognition of this truth is often of little avail, except 'in the hour of death, when disease at last subdues the passions, and man lies inert' (*Tractatus Politicus*, ch. I, sect. 5). When he came to face his own death, Spinoza seems to have done so with calmness and fortitude, true to his long-standing conviction that when dealing with human affairs, one should 'never mock, lament or execrate, but strive above all to understand . . .'.[44]

Gottfried Wilhelm Leibniz

Leibniz was born on 1 July 1646, at Leipzig in Saxony. He came from an academic family; his father (who died when he was only 6) was Professor of Moral Philosophy at the University of Leipzig. The young Leibniz appears to have had an eager appetite for learning, which he had ample opportunity to satisfy in his late father's extensive library. He entered the local university at the age of 15, where he continued the extensive study of the classics which he had begun as a young boy. At university Leibniz also acquired a detailed knowledge of the scholastic philosophy which still dominated European universities in the mid-seventeenth century; an early dissertation, *De principio individui* ('The Principle of Individuation'), written when he was still in his teens, was an exercise in scholastic metaphysics. But the intellectual climate in which Leibniz grew up was one in which scholasticism was under increasing attack and it was not long before he became dissatisfied with the traditional systems of learning. 'I had travelled far into the world of the Scholastics', he later wrote, 'when mathematics and modern writers lured me out while still a young man. I was charmed with their beautiful way of explaining nature mechanically, and scorned, with justice, the method of those who make use only of "forms" or "qualities", from which we learn nothing' (GP IV. 478; P 116).

Leibniz's university studies were wide-ranging in a way which prefigured the extraordinary breadth of his intellectual interests in later life. He had a semester at Jena, where he studied mathematics under a celebrated exponent of Greek mathematical systems, Erhard Weigel; returning to Leipzig he worked on an ambitious project—the developing of a scheme for translating logical combinations of ideas into a symbolic language—which led to the writing of his *Dissertatio de arte combinatoria* ('Dissertation on the Art of Combination').[45] Leibniz's main early ambition, however, was to gain an academic position in the field of law. He was unable to obtain a post at Leipzig, and moved to the small university of Altdorf, near Nuremberg, where in 1667 he submitted his doctoral dissertation *De casibus perplexis in jure* ('On Disputed Cases in Law'); the work was so well received that Leibniz was forthwith offered a professorship, at the age of 21. But in the summer of the same year Leibniz made the acquaintance of the Baron of Boineburg, former chief minister of the Elector of Mainz, who was impressed by Leibniz's energy and erudition, and offered him employment. In what was probably the most significant decision of his life, Leibniz resolved to abandon an academic career in favour of the more active and lucrative pursuits of the courtier and diplomat.

Under Boineburg's patronage, Leibniz was able to make contact with a wide variety of political thinkers, philosophers, and men of letters, and he began to build up a formidable circle of correspondents. He carefully preserved copies of most of the vast number of letters he wrote throughout his life, and these have become a valuable source for his philosophical, mathematical, and scientific views. The exchange and dissemination of ideas became one of Leibniz's major interests: apart from corresponding personally with over a thousand individuals, he was also actively involved in the launching of a seventeenth-century prototype of the learned journal, the *Acta Eruditorum* ('Proceedings of the Learned'), founded in Leipzig in 1682,[46] while in his later years he endeavoured to set up a number of scientific societies.[47] Much of Leibniz's time during his service with Boineburg, however, was devoted to more concrete political issues, in particular to the major problem troubling the German states at the time, the imperialistic designs of King Louis XIV of France. Among the many pamphlets and memoranda Leibniz composed during these years was the *Consilium Aegyptiacum* ('Egyptian Proposal'), whose aim was to divert the Sun King's expansionary energies from Europe to the Middle East.

A diplomatic initiative associated with this project led to Leibniz being sent to Paris in 1672, and he spent four exciting years in what was then the undisputed cultural capital of Europe. The 'Paris years' were a source of immense and fruitful intellectual stimulus for Leibniz. He met the great Cartesian Nicolas Malebranche (1638–1715),[48] and began a serious study of Descartes's philosophy; he also had discussions with the now famous logician and theologian Antoine Arnauld (1612–94), who had been one of Descartes's most searching critics.[49] Leibniz continued to correspond with Arnauld after he left Paris, and the letters they exchanged in the 1680s are a vital source for Leibniz's views on the concept of truth and the nature of substance. From Paris Leibniz visited London, where he met Henry Oldenburg and Robert Boyle; among the topics he discussed with the English scientists was his long-standing project for the construction of a machine for performing mathematical calculations. Mathematics remained Leibniz's chief interest during these years: on arrival in Paris he rapidly came to see that many of the mathematical techniques he had been taught at university were outmoded and inadequate, and under the stimulus of discussions with a number of brilliant mathematicians such as Christian Huygens, his own ideas developed at great speed. By the end of his time in Paris Leibniz had arrived at one of his most celebrated discoveries, the theory of the Infinitesimal Calculus. The fame of Leibniz's

achievement was later somewhat tarnished by a long and acri-
monious dispute with the friends of Newton over who had discovered the calculus first; though Newton arrived at the idea
some years before Leibniz, it is now generally accepted that
Leibniz reached his own results independently.[50]

Leibniz clearly wished to stay in Paris longer, but no suitable
employment was forthcoming.[51] In 1675 he accepted the post of
Court Councillor and Librarian at Hanover, in the service of
Johann Friedrich, Duke of Brunswick-Lüneburg. Leibniz returned
to Germany following a circuitous route which took him first to
London, then to Holland (where he had his meeting with
Spinoza—see above, p. 22), and finally to Hanover where he
arrived in January 1676; he was to remain in the service of the
ducal house for the remaining forty years of his life. A considerable portion of his energy was to be devoted to research for a
family history of the House of Brunswick, a project dear to the
heart of Ernst August, who succeeded to the dukedom on the
death of his elder brother in 1679. That Leibniz should have
squandered his intellectual talents on such a task has contributed
to the rather poor view of his character and personality which
some commentators have taken. Bertrand Russell, for example,
referred scathingly to Leibniz's 'undue deference to princes and
lamentable waste of time in the endeavour to please them'.[52] But
Leibniz's service to the Hanoverian dynasty provided him with a
comfortable income which left him free to travel extensively (he
made a grand tour of Bavaria, Austria, and Italy from 1687 to
1690), to pursue a wide variety of scientific and philosophical
interests, and to work on a number of technological projects.[53]
While it is no doubt true that his courtly commitments contributed to his failure to write a *magnum opus* comparable to
Descartes's *Principles* or Spinoza's *Ethics*, Leibniz did produce a
formidable number of shorter essays, articles, and pamphlets,
which taken together constitute a philosophical corpus that is
quite as impressive as the grander works of Descartes and
Spinoza. Among the most important of these writings were the
Meditations on Knowledge, Truth and Ideas, published in Latin in
1684; the *Discourse on Metaphysics*, composed in French in 1686;

the *Remarks on the General Part of Descartes's Principles*, a critical discussion of Descartes's system, written in the early 1690s; the *New System* and *Explanation of the New System*, published in French in 1695–6; the *New Essays on Human Understanding*, an extensive dialogue criticizing John Locke's *Essay concerning Human Understanding*, written in French in the early 1700s (but not published until 1765, long after Leibniz's death); the *Metaphysical Consequences of the Principle of Reason*, a short paper written in Latin around 1712; and a concise summary of Leibniz's metaphysics, the *Monadology*, written in French in 1714 (but first published posthumously, in a German translation of 1720).

To a far greater extent than is true of the philosophies of Descartes and Spinoza, Leibniz's philosophy has called forth a variety of competing interpretations—something which is partly due to the fact that Leibniz himself approached the subject from many different angles: epistemological, logical, metaphysical, and theological. He was fascinated by the concept of knowledge, and the distinction between what can be known a priori and what can be discovered by experience; he was preoccupied with the nature of truth, and with developing the kind of analysis that would reveal the logical structure of true propositions; and he was intent on exhibiting the universe as a harmonious system, created by a benevolent God. But perhaps his main concern, the theme to which he repeatedly returned throughout his life, was the nature of individual substance, and the problem of how the world can be described in a way which does justice to the individuality and unity of the entities which make it up. In Leibniz's many discussions of this issue there is a recurring tension between the terminology of the scholastics which he had imbibed in his youth, with its apparatus of substantial forms and qualities, and the influence of the new reductive systems like those of Descartes and Spinoza, which dispensed with the traditional apparatus and endeavoured to explain the universe in terms of supposedly simple and straightforward categories such as thought and extension. Leibniz's goal was to effect a kind of reconciliation between these approaches, as can be seen from the following extracts from his *New System*, written in his fiftieth year:

> To find the principles of true unity of things . . . I found it necessary to
> recall and in a manner to rehabilitate *substantial forms*, which are so
> much decried today . . . I found that their nature consists of force, and
> from this there follows something analogous to feeling and appetite; and
> that therefore it was necessary to form a conception of them resembling
> our ordinary notion of *souls* . . . I saw that these forms must be
> indivisible, like our mind . . . I am as ready and willing as any man to give
> the moderns their due; but I think they have carried reform too far [in
> taking a purely mechanistic view] confusing the natural with the
> artificial. For they have not had a sufficiently exalted idea of the majesty
> of Nature (GP IV. 478–81; P 116–20).

The majesty of nature was for Leibniz a reflection of the power
and goodness of its creator, and it is impossible to read many of
his writings without being struck by the sincerity of his religious
faith. But, like Descartes and Spinoza, Leibniz abhorred theological dogmatism, and towards the end of his life he gave considerable thought to devising possible ways of reconciling the
Catholic and Protestant Churches, whose followers had clashed
so repeatedly and bloodily during the seventeenth century. The
problems of religious faith were a major topic of conversation
between Leibniz and an influential friend of his latter years,
Sophie Charlotte, daughter of the Duchess of Hanover and
Electress of Brandenburg (later to be Queen of Prussia). Leibniz
acted as her tutor for a time, and their discussions were an
important stimulus for the composition of the *Theodicy* (that is, a
vindication of God's justice), the largest work Leibniz published
during his life (the book appeared in 1710).[54] Leibniz's concern to
defend the cause of religion also emerges in the important
exchange which he had in the last two years of his life with
the English cleric and disciple of Newton, Samuel Clarke
(1675–1729). As Leibniz wrote in his first letter to Clarke,

> It appears that natural religion is growing steadily weaker. Many hold
> that souls are corporeal; others hold that God himself is corporeal. Mr
> Locke and his followers are at any rate doubtful whether souls are not
> material and naturally perishable . . . Mr Newton and his followers have
> an extremely odd opinion of the work of God, according to which he is

obliged to wind up his watch from time to time to prevent its running down, and even mend it. According to my view, the same force and vigour goes on existing in the world always, and simply passes from one matter to another, according to the laws of nature and a beautiful pre-established harmony . . . (GP VII. 352; P 205–6).

Side by side with his philosophical pursuits, Leibniz's political and diplomatic activities continued unabated until he was in his late sixties. He had contacts with a number of royal and princely houses, including several audiences with Peter the Great of Russia, and he made frequent visits to Vienna (where both the *Theodicy* and the *Monadology* were written), attaining the distinction of being made a Privy Councillor at the Imperial Court in 1712. In 1714, the Elector Georg Ludwig (the nephew of Leibniz's original ducal patron) acceded to the British throne; though Leibniz hurried back to Hanover on hearing the news he found that the court had already left for England. For the remaining two years of his life Leibniz remained at Hanover labouring over the family history of the House of Brunswick, on which he had now been working, though very intermittently, for over thirty years. He died peacefully on 14 November 1716, at the age of 70.

Spinoza, whose views Leibniz mistrusted as 'dangerous',[55] had seen man's highest fulfilment in terms of an intellectual contemplation of his essential union with the whole of reality. Leibniz, in his *Principles of Nature and Grace*, written two years before his death, had come to a different, but not entirely dissimilar conclusion:

The beauty of the universe could be learnt in each soul, could one unravel all its folds; . . . each soul knows the infinite, but confusedly. Just as when I walk along the shore of the sea, and hear the great noise it makes . . . so our confused perceptions are the result of the impressions which the whole universe makes on us (GP VI. 604; P 201).

But unlike Spinoza, Leibniz was able to combine his grand metaphysical vision with an altogether simpler and more traditional piety—the piety he had learned as a boy from his family in Leipzig:

the love of God gives us here and now a foretaste of felicity to come . . . for it gives us perfect confidence in the goodness of our Author and Master, which produces a true tranquillity of mind, not as in the Stoics, who resolutely force themselves to patience, but by a present contentment which assures us of a future happiness (GP VI. 606; P 203).[56]

2

Method

On the tenth of November 1619, I went to bed full of mental excitement, wholly preoccupied with the thought that I had that day begun to discover the foundations of a wonderful system of knowledge (Descartes, *Early Writings*).

There are some who have taken pity on the wretched plight of philosophy and departed from the common way of treating the sciences. They have entered on a difficult new path, aiming to bequeath to posterity the other parts of philosophy, beyond mathematics, demonstrated by mathematical method and with mathematical certainty (Lodewijk Meyer, Preface to Spinoza's *Principia Philosophiae Renati Descartes*, 1663).

Scarcely any sane man will question many . . . arguments of Aristotle in his eight books on physics and the whole of his metaphysics, logic and ethics . . . The one question is whether in place of Aristotle's abstract theories of matter, form and change, there can be explanations involving only size, shape and motion (Leibniz, letter to Jacob Thomasius of 30 April 1669).[1]

Descartes's fresh start

In an open letter published in 1647, Descartes commented bitterly on the philosophical orthodoxy of his time:

The majority of those aspiring to be philosophers in the last few centuries have blindly followed Aristotle. . . . And those who have not followed Aristotle . . . have nevertheless been saturated with his opinions in their youth (since they are the only opinions taught in the Schools) and this has so dominated their outlook that they have been unable to arrive at knowledge of true principles (AT IXB. 7; CSM I. 182).

Since his early years, Descartes had seen it as his mission to replace the prevailing orthodoxy of his day with a new philosophical system.[2] The chief problem with the dominant Aristotelian-scholastic tradition, as Descartes saw it, was the weakness of its foundations or 'principles'. 'For every single problem ever solved by the principles distinctive of peripatetic [that is, Aristotelian] philosophy', Descartes wrote to Dinet in 1642, 'I can demonstrate that the supposed solution is invalid and false' (AT VII. 580; CSM II. 391). The term 'principle' had a more precise meaning in the seventeenth century than it does today, and was specifically used to refer to the starting points or fundamental axioms on which a philosophical or scientific system was based.[3] Descartes repeatedly complained that the 'schoolmen' had all been guilty of 'putting forward as principles things of which they did not possess perfect knowledge' (AT IXB. 8; CSM I. 182).

It soon becomes clear that Descartes was not just alleging that the scholastic philosophers had got their principles wrong. His more serious complaint about the philosophy that predominated in the schools was, in effect, that it lacked proper principles *entirely*—it failed to take seriously enough the need to push philosophical inquiry back to clear and self-evident starting-points. An example which Descartes often cites in this connection is that of 'gravity'. A commonly accepted explanation of why bodies fall was that they had the quality of *gravitas* or 'heaviness'; sometimes this was amplified by saying that it was 'of the nature' of terrestrial or earthly matter to find a place below that occupied by air (while, conversely, it was of the nature of airy particles to occupy a place above that of earthly). But, Descartes objected:

although experience shows us very clearly that the bodies we call 'heavy' descend towards the centre of the earth, we do not for all that have any knowledge of the nature of what is called 'gravity'—that is to say, the cause or principle which makes bodies descend in this way (AT IXB. 8; CSM I. 182).[4]

Descartes insisted that no concept should be allowed in a philosophical or scientific explanation unless it is either transparently clear or capable of being reduced by analysis to elements that are clear. Notions like 'gravity'—at least as used in scholastic physics—were, he believed, inherently vague. They might appear to correspond to something we experience every day, but if asked to analyse exactly what the supposed quality of 'heaviness' consisted in, the schoolmen were reduced either to silence, or to a barrage of jargon which would be no clearer (and often considerably more obscure) than what it was supposed to explain.[5] Complaints about the obscurity of scholastic jargon continued well after Descartes's death—indeed, as scholasticism came under increasing attack, the self-defensive jargon proliferated ever more vigorously. By the end of the century, we find Pierre Bayle, in his celebrated *Dictionnaire historique et critique* (first published 1697), commenting acidly on the 'public disputations where the Scholastics defend themselves with a jargon of distinctions that are suitable only for preventing the disappointment their relatives might have had in seeing them reduced to silence'.[6]

The obscurities of the schoolmen were diagnosed by Descartes as resulting from their failure to appreciate that 'certainty does not lie in the senses, but solely in the understanding, when it possesses evident perceptions'. Instead of uncritical reliance on sensory experience, Descartes proposed an ideal of 'perfect knowledge' which he defined as knowledge which is 'deduced from first causes': 'if we are to set about acquiring perfect knowledge (and it is this activity to which the term "to philosophize" strictly refers) we must start with the search for first causes or principles' (AT IXB. 2; CSM I. 179).

But how are we to discover such first causes or 'principles'? Descartes's striking claim—one that is reiterated many times throughout his writings—is that each of us possesses the innate power to uncover such principles, provided that our natural light of reason is directed aright.[7] This last proviso leads us to one of the best known features of Descartes's philosophy, and the feature that probably aroused the greatest interest in his own day, the idea of a distinctive *method* for reaching the truth. In his earliest major work, the *Regulae*, Descartes specifically addresses himself to this topic:

By a 'method' I mean reliable rules which are easy to apply and such that if one follows them exactly one will never take what is false to be true . . . but gradually and constantly increase one's knowledge till one arrives at a true understanding of everything within one's capacity (AT X. 372; CSM I. 16).

Crucial to Descartes's method is the notion of *order*. 'The whole method', he writes in Rule Five, 'consists entirely in the ordering and arranging of objects on which we must concentrate our mind's eye; we first reduce complicated and obscure pro-positions to simple ones, and then, starting with the intuition of the simplest ones of all, try to ascend through the same steps to knowledge of all the rest' (AT X. 379; CSM I. 20). The model on which Descartes explicitly relies here is that of problem-solving in mathematics. The solution of difficult questions in arithmetic and geometry, he explains, involves just such a process of reducing the problem to its simplest essentials, and then proceeding in a step-by-step fashion from simple self-evident starting points to knowledge of ever more complex conclusions. 'Arithmetic and geometry are concerned with an object so pure and simple that they make no assumptions that experience might render uncer-tain, and they consist entirely in deducing conclusions by means of rational arguments' (AT X. 365; CSM I. 12).

The *simplicity* of the starting-points in mathematics means, says Descartes, that the truths in question can be 'intuited'. This term can mislead the modern reader into supposing that some non-rational or non-cognitive faculty—a kind of 'hunch'—is involved. But Descartes's Latin term *intueri* carries, in its literal sense, the straightforward meaning of to 'look at' or 'look upon'; what Descartes is maintaining is that if an intellectual object (such as a triangle, say, or the number two) is sufficiently simple, then we can, with our mind's eye, just 'see' certain truths about that object (for example, that a triangle has three sides, or that two is one plus one) in a way that leaves no possible room for error:

> By 'intuition' I do not mean the fluctuating testimony of the senses or the deceptive judgement of the imagination as it botches things together, but the conception of a clear and attentive mind which is so easy and distinct that there can be no room for doubt about what we are

understanding. Alternatively, and this comes to the same thing, intuition is the indubitable conception of a clear and attentive mind which proceeds solely from the light of reason (AT X. 368; CSM I. 14).

In his more mature writings, Descartes speaks, instead of intuition, of 'clear and distinct perception', but the basic comparison with ordinary ocular vision is preserved. 'I call a perception *clear*', he writes in the *Principles of Philosophy*, 'when it is present and accessible to the attentive mind—just as we say that we see something clearly when it is present to the eye's gaze and stimulates it with a sufficient degree of strength and accessibility' (AT VIII. 22, CSM I. 207). A perception is *distinct*, Descartes goes on to explain, when, as well as being clear, it contains *only* what is clear. Descartes's point here is that although many of our perceptions have clear elements, they are often mixed up with elements that are not clear, so that the resulting judgement goes beyond what is directly present to the mind. Thus (to take Descartes's own example), if I report 'I have a pain in my leg', though the pain may present itself vividly enough to the mind, the judgement I make may none the less carry with it further implications which are not themselves clear: a certain kind of discomfort may be immediately present to my consciousness, but the implication that my leg is in a certain state goes beyond what I am immediately and directly aware of (*Principles* I. 46). (Such further implications can, moreover, turn out to be false, as Descartes shows by his favourite example of the 'phantom limb' syndrome: he cites the case of a young patient who continued to complain that her hand was hurting even though the arm had in fact been amputated.[8]) Just as with 'intuition', then, the crucial point about a 'clear and distinct perception' is the absolute simplicity of its content. A clear and distinct perception is self-evident because it is straightforwardly accessible to my 'mind's eye', and does not contain any extraneous implications which take me beyond that of which I am directly aware. Thus in the case of a simple mathematical proposition such as 'two and two make four', if I focus on the content of this proposition, I have right there, in front of my mind, all I need to be sure that the proposition is true.

Mathesis universalis

Descartes's method, then, consists in breaking a problem down and taking it back to its simplest essentials, until we arrive at propositions which are simple and self-evident enough to serve as reliable 'principles' or starting points, from which the answers to the questions that perplex us may eventually be deduced. Such eventual results may come only at the end of a long chain of deductive reasoning, but Descartes maintains that our conclusions can enjoy the same certainty and self-evidence as our starting points, provided we proceed slowly and cautiously, step by step, and provided we make sure that each step in our chain of reasoning is itself transparently clear. In his 1637 *Discourse on the Method*, Descartes presents the essentials of his method in a way that is designed to be accessible to the widest possible audience; in Part II of the work, he sums up his procedure in a famous passage which pays tribute to the mathematical model that inspired it:

> Those long chains, composed of very simple and easy reasonings, which geometers customarily use to arrive at their most difficult demonstrations, had given me occasion to suppose that all the things which come within the scope of human knowledge are interconnected in the same way. And I thought that provided that we refrain from accepting as true anything which is not, and always keep to the order required for deducing one thing from another, there can be nothing too remote to be reached in the end or too well hidden to be discovered (AT VI. 19; CSM I. 120).

What is remarkable about this passage is the confidence with which Descartes proposes to extend the methods of mathematics to 'all the things which come within the scope of human knowledge'. On the face of it, this seems a wildly optimistic proposal. For while the goals of absolute simplicity and self-evidence may seem appropriate enough (or at least not obviously out of the question) when dealing with a subject like Euclidian geometry where even the most complicated figure is constructed out of relatively few simple elements (such as the point, the line, and the curve), what reason is there for thinking that they are applicable to the seemingly vastly more complex and varied problems of, for example, natural science? Part of Descartes's answer is that there are certain very simple and general notions that may serve as the starting points for explaining whole classes of seemingly diverse phenomena:

The exclusive concern of mathematics is with questions of order or measure, and it is irrelevant whether the measure in question involves numbers, shapes, stars, sounds or any other object whatsoever. This made me realise that there must be a general science which explains all the points that can be raised concerning order and measure, irrespective of the subject matter, and that this science should be termed *mathesis universalis* (AT X. 378; CSM I. 19).

The term '*mathesis*' is derived from the Greek verb *manthanein*, to learn, and thus corresponds to the Latin *disciplina*, formed from the equivalent Latin verb for to learn, *discere*. Descartes's claim is that mathematics furnishes us with a 'universal discipline' or general science which will provide the key to a wide range of apparently distinct investigations, for example in such subjects as astronomy, music, optics, and mechanics.[9]

Descartes's early studies in mathematics seemed to him to provide support for the idea that apparently diverse subjects could be handled in terms of a simple template involving 'order or measure'. A notable success in this area was his *Geometry* (written in the 1630s and published with the *Discourse* in 1637 as one of the 'specimen essays' of the new method): here Descartes was able to demonstrate that the essential relationships characterizing the structure of geometrical figures could be expressed arithmetically or, more generally, algebraically—an achievement that laid the foundations for what is now known as analytic or co-ordinate geometry. Descartes's next step was to propose that the same reductionistic techniques that had succeeded in pure mathematics could be transferred to the applied sciences. In the *Optics* (another of the 'specimen essays') a precise geometrical model of the angles of refraction which obtain when light rays pass through various transparent mediums led Descartes to articulate the fundamentals of what is now known as Snell's 'law of refraction' (AT VI. 101; CSM I. 161). All this seemed to Descartes to point the way to a general programme for the 'mathematicization' of physics: light, heat, weight, magnetism, and all other properties of the physical universe were to be explained as arising from the interaction of portions of matter defined solely in terms of the geometrical properties of size and shape (AT IXB. 16; CSM I. 187). How this programme fared in practice, and some of the difficulties that Leibniz, in particular, was to raise in relation to it later in the century, will be examined in Chapter 4.

Metaphysical foundations

In a famous metaphor (which was also employed by other seventeenth-century writers, notably Francis Bacon[10]), Descartes compares philosophy to a tree: 'the roots are metaphysics, the trunk is physics, and the branches emerging from the trunk are all the other sciences' (AT IXB. 14; CSM I. 186). Now Descartes's programme for a *mathesis universalis* is evidently designed to encompass the whole of physics, together with its offshoots in so far as they can be reduced to quantitative terms. But what is the relation between this project and the search for truth regarding the metaphysical issues—concerning knowledge and certainty, mind and body, the nature of God, the existence of the world—which Descartes saw as the 'root structure', the essential base for a well-founded scientific system? In the intellectual autobiography that forms Part II of the *Discourse*, Descartes reports that as a young man he deliberately postponed embarking on such fundamental inquiries. Though recognizing that they constituted the 'most important task of all', he saw the need for a long period of mental preparation, to avoid 'precipitate conclusions' and falling prey to 'preconceived opinions' (AT VI. 22; CSM I. 122). Nevertheless, he was maintaining as early as 1628 that our natural light of reason enables us to intuit certain fundamental 'simple natures', and that these include not only the 'corporeal natures' that are the subject-matter of mathematics, but also 'intellectual natures', or items relating to the mind (such as knowledge, doubt, and volition (AT X. 419; CSM I. 44)). It was Descartes's hope that a clear and distinct perception of these items would ultimately enable him to arrive at the fundamental metaphysical truths which would form the foundations of a complete system of knowledge.

It seems clear, however, that a radically new technique is called for when we move from mathematical notions such as size and shape to 'mentalistic' items such as knowledge, volition, and doubt. The instruction to break the problem down to its simplest essentials until we reach self-evident intuitions may look plausible enough if we are dealing with triangles; but how can it be applied to questions about the existence of God, say, or the soul? Descartes himself insisted that the primary notions of metaphysics were 'as evident or even more evident than the primary notions which the geometers study'; but he went on to admit that in practice considerably more effort was needed to arrive at reliable starting points in metaphysics:

The difference is that the primary notions which are presupposed for the demonstration of geometrical truths are readily accepted by anyone . . . In metaphysics by contrast, nothing causes so much effort as making our perceptions of the primary notions clear and distinct . . . Only those who really concentrate and meditate and withdraw their minds from corporeal things as far as possible will achieve perfect knowledge of them (Second Set of Replies: AT VII. 157; CSM II. 111).

In order to lay the metaphysical foundations of his system, Descartes devised his celebrated meditative technique which has come to be known as the 'method of doubt'. Although Cartesian doubt is sometimes taken to comprise Descartes's entire philosophical method, it should be clear from what has already been said in this chapter that this is to mistake the part for the whole. What is true is that systematic doubt plays a central role in Cartesian metaphysics or 'first philosophy'; what is also true is that Descartes's arguments in this area have captured the imagination both of his supporters and of his critics to a degree which has never been the case with the other parts of his method.

Descartes's definitive presentation of his technique of philosophical doubt is to be found in his *Meditations on First Philosophy*, published in 1641. The aim of the project is to 'demolish everything completely and start again right from the foundations, so as to establish something firm and stable in the sciences' (AT VII. 17; CSM II. 12). The First Meditation ('What can be called into doubt') is specifically designed to take doubt to its limits. Descartes describes his aim here as that of 'freeing us from all our preconceived opinions by leading the mind away from the senses'; the eventual goal is to 'make it impossible for us to have any further doubts about what we subsequently discover to be true' (AT VII. 12; CSM II. 9).

Descartes's doubt comes in four successive waves, and each succeeding wave is designed to demolish an apparently secure area left standing by the preceding wave.

1. First, we are reminded that the senses sometimes deceive us (sense-based judgements such as 'that tower is round' can turn out, on closer scrutiny, to be mistaken); and 'it is prudent never to trust completely those who have deceived us even once'.

2. The argument so far has left unscathed a large number of seemingly quite unproblematic sense-based judgements such as 'I am holding my hand in front of my face'; these, it seems, I would be mad to doubt. But now the second wave of doubt arrives: it is possible that even the judgement that I am holding my hand up could be false; for I might at this very moment be dreaming—not holding my hand up before my eyes, but asleep in bed with my eyes closed.

3. The possibility that I am now dreaming leaves unscathed my belief in the existence of at least general kinds of things such as heads, hands, and faces (for though a particular judgement about this hand may be false if I am dreaming, dreams are presumably formed from ingredients taken from real life). But now the third wave of doubt arrives: a dream may be compared to an imaginative painting—and though some paintings are formed by rearranging ingredients taken from real objects, it seems possible that a painting could depict 'something so new that nothing remotely similar has even been seen before—something which is therefore completely fictitious and unreal'. Could it not be, then, that my dreams have no foundation in reality whatever? (Later this doubt is reinforced by the scenario of a malicious demon who has brought it about that 'the sky, the air, the earth, colours, shapes, sounds and all external things are merely the delusions of dreams which he has devised to ensnare my judgement'.)

4. Despite the disturbingly radical implications of the doubt so far raised, Descartes notes that it nevertheless leaves unscathed

at least his grasp of what he calls 'simple universals' such as extension, size, quantity, and number. These general categories appear unaffected by the possibility of wholesale deception about the external world; and they seem to provide the basis for reliable mathematical judgements that can be made regardless of what exists around me. For 'whether I am awake or asleep two and three added together are five, and a square has no more than four sides; and it seems impossible that such transparent truths should incur any suspicion of being false'. But now the final and most devastating wave of doubt arrives. If, as I have been taught, there is an omnipotent God, it may be, for all I know, that he makes me go wrong 'every time I add two and three or count the sides of a square'; while if, on the other hand, my existence is not due to God but to some random chain of lesser causes, then it seems even more likely that I am so imperfect as to go astray even in my intuition of the simplest and seemingly most transparent truths (AT VII. 18–21; CSM II. 12–14).

The barrage of doubt eventually exhausts itself at the start of the Second Meditation. If doubt is pushed to its limits and I imagine 'a deceiver of supreme power and cunning who is deliberately and constantly deceiving me', then in that case 'I too undoubtedly exist, if he is deceiving me':

> Let him deceive me as much as he can, he will never bring it about that I am nothing so long as I think I am something. So I must finally conclude that this proposition, 'I am, I exist', is necessarily true whenever it is put forward by me or conceived in my mind (AT VII. 25; CSM II. 17).

Elsewhere expressed in the famous dictum *Cogito ergo sum* ('I am thinking therefore I exist'),[11] this is Descartes's 'Archimedian point'—the firm and reliable base on which he proposes to build.[12] From here, by reflecting on his own existence as a 'thinking thing', and the ideas he finds within himself, Descartes will endeavour first to prove the existence of God, the perfect being who created him, and then to establish the nature and existence of the external world around him. From then on, his clear and distinct perceptions will enable him to construct an entire description of the physical world—'the whole of that corporeal nature that is the subject-matter of pure mathematics'

(AT VII. 71; CSM II. 49). In short, he will have constructed a system which is entitled to the accolade '*vera et certa scientia*'— 'true and certain knowledge'.[13]

Scientia comes near to being a technical term in Descartes's metaphysical writings. Literally it means simply 'knowledge' (from the Latin verb *scire*, to know), but in Descartes's philosophy it is marked off from other possible forms of cognition by several crucial features. First, *scientia* is *systematic*: it proceeds step by step via an unbroken chain of reasoning in the way described in the *Regulae* as being characteristic of the most reliable mathematical demonstrations. Second, it meets the Cartesian ideal standard of *clarity and distinctness*, of containing nothing that is not present and open to the attentive mind. Third, it is *underwritten* by the meditator's proof of the existence of a perfect God who would not allow his creatures' most transparent perceptions to be inherently distorted or erroneous.[14] Fourth, it is based on *sure and indubitable foundations* which have survived the most extreme barrage of doubt that can be devised. Lastly, it is *all-embracing*—a universal structure that 'can be extended to the discovery of truths in any field whatsoever' (AT X. 374; CSM I. 17). Descartes's ideal of *vera et certa scientia* thus represents a goal that is in many ways definitive of what has come to be thought of as the rationalist enterprise. As we shall see, neither Spinoza nor Leibniz followed the Cartesian model slavishly, and their conceptions of philosophical method diverge in many respects from that of Descartes. But the influence of Descartes's work on the way that they and many of their contemporaries thought about knowledge is pervasive and undeniable.

Analysis and synthesis

The phrase 'Descartes's method' is by no means confined to modern commentators. Descartes himself, in the title of the *Discourse*, advertised his discovery of a new method of 'rightly conducting reason'; and although the term is not used in the *Meditations*, contemporary critics of that work saw it as exemplifying Descartes's new 'method of analysis' (cf. Sixth Set of Objections: AT VII. 413; CSM II. 278). In some quarters the reaction to Descartes's announcement of a new procedure for reaching the truth was distinctly hostile; particularly strong criticism was reserved for what was seen as Descartes's claim to have arrived at a new logic, a new method of reasoning. The Jesuit Pierre Bourdin, author of the Seventh Set of Objections, condemned the Cartesian method as 'full of holes, leaking everywhere, and fit to be thrown on the rubbish heap' (AT VII. 535; CSM II. 365); he went on to suggest that at least some of Descartes's desired results could be established much more safely and reliably by using the traditional formal techniques of the syllogism—the set of universally accepted patterns of valid reasoning codified by Aristotle. A syllogism is a standard three-step argument consisting of major premiss, minor premiss, and conclusion (a typical example: 'All birds lay eggs (major); all swans are birds (minor); therefore all swans lay eggs (conclusion)'). Such reasoning can be seen to be logically watertight, since once the premisses are accepted the conclusion cannot be denied on pain of contradiction.

Descartes had earlier criticized the traditional reliance on the syllogism, observing in the *Discourse* that syllogisms are 'of less use for learning things than for explaining what one already knows, or for speaking without judgement about matters of which one is ignorant' (AT VI. 17; CSM I. 119). In his reply to Bourdin, however, Descartes makes it clear that he has no wish to impugn the validity of syllogistic reasoning as such, and is quite happy to use it himself when the occasion demands it (AT VII. 522; CSM II. 355). Traditional logic, Descartes later accepted in an interview with the Dutchman Frans Burman in 1648, does indeed provide 'demonstrative proofs on all subjects' (AT V. 175; CB 46); but he suggested that the techniques needed for *discovery* are very different from those required for mere *exposition* (AT V. 153; CB 12). A year earlier, in his preface to the French edition of the *Principles of Philosophy*, he had written that what was needed was a kind of logic which 'teaches us to direct our reason with a view to *discovering* the truths of which we are ignorant' (AT IXB. 14; CSM I. 186).

Descartes's fullest discussion of these matters occurs in the Second Set of Replies to the *Meditations* of 1641. Marin Mersenne, compiler of the Second Set of Objections, had suggested that Descartes might gain wider acceptance for his arguments if he presented them in a more formal fashion. Mersenne did not in fact suggest a syllogistic presentation—which Descartes would in any case have rejected, for in his reply to Mersenne he made it clear that the typical syllogistic procedure of deducing particular results from general premisses would not be a suitable way of representing the solitary meditator's discovery of his own existence.[15] What Mersenne did propose, however, was that 'the entire argument be set out in geometrical fashion (*more geometrico*), starting from a number of definitions, postulates and axioms' (AT VII. 128; CSM II. 92). Descartes replied that in the *Meditations* he had deliberately avoided the standard geometrical technique 'which ancient geometers usually employed in their writings'. This traditional method was known as the 'method of synthesis', and Descartes conceded that it had the advantage of providing rigorous demonstrations where 'each step is contained in what has gone before' so that 'the reader, however argumentative or stubborn he may be, is compelled to give his assent' (AT VII. 156; CSM II. 111). The virtues of such a method are vividly illustrated by a famous anecdote describing how Thomas Hobbes was introduced to geometry in the 1620s:

> Being in a gentleman's library, Euclid's *Elements* lay open, and t'was the 47 *El. libri* 1. . . . *By G——*, sayd he . . . *this is impossible!* So he reads the Demonstration of it, which referred him back to such a proposition; which proposition he read. That referred him back to another, which he also read. And so on, [till] at last he was demonstratively convinced of that truth. This made him in love with Geometry.[16]

But Descartes goes on to point out that though demonstration from axioms might be suitable for geometry, where the axioms or primary notions involved are 'readily accepted by everyone', it is not suited to metaphysics, because here the primary notions conflict with the preconceived opinions, derived from the senses, which we have got into the habit of holding from our earliest years. In order that we may rid ourselves of such prejudices Descartes insists that each individual must go through a set of therapeutic exercises or 'meditations':

this is why I wrote 'Meditations' rather than 'Disputations', as the philosophers have done, or 'Theorems and Problems' as the geometers would have done. In so doing I wanted to make it clear that I would have nothing to do with anyone who was not willing to join with me in meditating, and giving the subject attentive consideration (AT VII. 157; CSM II. 112).

The crucial point is the need for active and enthusiastic participation by the individual reader as he struggles to find the truth. And the way to encourage this, says Descartes, is to employ the 'method of analysis'. For the method of analysis shows the 'true way by means of which the thing in question was discovered methodically . . . so that if the reader is willing to follow it he will make the thing his own, and understand it just as perfectly as if he had discovered it for himself' (AT VII. 155; CSM II. 110).

Analysis, then, follows the way of discovery and enables each reader to 'make the thing his own'. But is this not just what Hobbes did when he sat down and eagerly yet methodically traced Euclid's forty-seventh proposition back to the relevant axioms until he was demonstratively convinced of its truth? Once one raises this question, the contrast Descartes wants to draw between traditional deductive reasoning and his own method starts to look a little blurred. It seems that for any argument one may proceed in two ways: start from basic axioms and work 'downwards', unravelling the consequences that follow, or, alternatively, start from some complex proposition, and ask how it can be proved, climbing 'upwards' until one reaches unassailable axioms. Yet this hardly shows that there are two logically distinct patterns of argument involved. What makes a given argument *valid* is the same in both cases, namely the fact that it follows necessarily from certain premises in accordance with the rules of logic. Indeed, if one looks at the work of the Greek geometricians such as Pappus of Alexandria, from whom Descartes took the distinction between 'synthesis' and 'analysis',[17] the distinction seems to boil down to nothing more than a contrast between moving 'downwards' from axioms to a desired result and moving 'upwards' from a given proposition until we reach the axioms that generate it.[18]

At this point one begins to suspect Descartes's triumphant proclamation of his 'new method' involves more than a small measure of window dressing, at least as far as his metaphysics is concerned. But the important point Descartes is concerned to stress nevertheless stands, namely that instead of being presented with a static deductive layout, the meditator must be encouraged to follow the hard upward path of discovery, to engage for himself in the taxing mental struggle whereby the relevant truths can be unearthed. Nothing should be taken for granted; no universal major premisses, no 'accepted definitions', no corpus of 'agreed axioms' should be taken on trust as the basis for a metaphysical system. In metaphysics, the basic task is not to unravel the consequences of a body of primary truths but to fight to discover what propositions, if any, unquestionably qualify for that status.

Our earlier summary of the opening arguments of the *Meditations* should make it clear what Descartes had in mind when he said that in his method of analysis the order followed is the 'order of discovery'. Descartes does not begin by asserting his first principle *cogito ergo sum*, or claiming for it the status of a self-evident axiom. Rather, he shows how each individual can discover, by subjecting all his beliefs to the successive waves of doubt, that at least one thing—his own existence—cannot be doubted. The Cogito is, as it were, 'extruded' from the method of doubt; the insight is not delivered ready-made, but is achieved at the end of a long meditative exercise. Only by 'meditating along with the author', and 'making the thing his own', will each reader be able to complete the voyage of discovery that Descartes has mapped out.[19]

Problems with the Cartesian method

Although it is possible to appreciate Descartes's pride in the distinctive features of his *Meditations*, his claim that the work as a whole exemplifies a reliable new method of discovery cannot in the end be made good. To the modern reader, indeed, the very idea of a canonical method for the discovery of the truth may seem to be something of a fantasy. The field of natural science seems today to provide the most obvious success story as far as 'discovering the truth' is concerned, but it has become plain that the activities of the scientist do not, and cannot, conform to any ideal 'logic of discovery'; there is simply no canonical set of investigative procedures that can guarantee progress. As for the metaphysical foundations of science, there is nowadays widespread scepticism about the prospects for finding an indubitable bedrock of certainty on which to base our philosophical and scientific theories; to many, indeed, the very notion that there could be such permanent and guaranteed foundations rests on a misconception. Any system, it seems, must be open to revisions and adjustments in the quest for a more coherent and workable body of knowledge, and these revisions and adjustments may well include truths previously taken to be fundamental, and will perhaps encompass even the very methodological rules that determine how we proceed in our investigations.[20]

Apart from this characteristically 'modern' worry about the general nature of Descartes's enterprise, there are other difficulties that arose even for those who accepted his general terms of reference. Descartes hoped, in writing the *Meditations*, to create a friendly audience among the leading theologians of the day. He knew, such was the power and influence of the theology faculties in the universities of the seventeenth century, that his metaphysical views, let alone his physics (most of which had yet to be released), stood little chance of a favourable reception without their approval. In the Dedicatory Letter to the Theology Faculty of the Sorbonne which was printed at the front of the first edition of the *Meditations*, in 1641, Descartes extols the virtues of philosophy as an instrument for defending the cause of religion, and instances the knockout blow to atheism which he hopes will be delivered by his own proofs in the *Meditations* of the existence of God and the 'real distinction' between the human soul and the body (AT VII. 2 and 6; CSM II. 3 and 6). It soon became all too clear, however, that the approval which Descartes sought was not to be forthcoming from the theologians. His proofs of the existence of God were widely attacked as inadequate or invalid (cf. AT VII. 206; CSM II. 145); almost every step of his route for establishing firm foundations for knowledge was criticized (AT VII. 413 ff.; CSM II. 278 ff.): and, worst of all, the very method of doubt which he had introduced as an instrument for uncovering certainty was itself attacked as deliberately subversive and damaging to the faith (cf. AT VII. 573–4; CSM II. 387).

Some of these criticisms, particularly the last, can be dismissed as unfair and maliciously motivated. But although Descartes's own intentions were to refute scepticism, the extreme or 'hyperbolical' doubt that he employed as part of his method for reaching the truth was something that many came to find genuinely alarming; it seemed to add fuel to the fires of radical scepticism that burned strongly in the latter half of the seventeenth century. In his *Pensées*, published posthumously in 1670, Blaise Pascal (1623–62) fiercely attacked Descartes's attempted validation of human knowledge and poured scorn on the whole process of hyperbolical doubt as a kind of wilful madness: 'What shall man do in this state? Shall he doubt everything? Shall he doubt if he is awake? If he is being pinched? If he is being burned? Shall he doubt if he doubts? Shall he doubt if he exists? It can never reach this stage . . .'[21]

Other critics of Descartes, including those who commented on the first edition of the *Meditations*, discerned serious structural problems in the logical plan of the work. One such difficulty is that as Descartes proceeds beyond the awareness of his own existence to the proofs of a perfect God which are needed to establish the basis for a reliable system of knowledge, he is increasingly forced to import into his argument premisses which, far from being methodically unearthed by the technique of systematic doubt, are simply declared to be true. In the Third Meditation, in arguing that the idea of God which he finds within him can only be explained by supposing that it was placed in him by a perfect being, Descartes baldly introduces, in the very first sentence of the proof, a complex and controversial causal maxim: 'It is manifest by the natural light that there must be at least as much reality in the efficient and total cause as in the effect of that cause' (AT VII. 40; CSM II. 28). It is interesting to note that when Descartes did eventually and somewhat reluctantly accede to Mersenne's request to provide a 'geometrical style' exposition of his reasoning, this maxim, or something very close to it, is simply listed without comment as having the status of an 'axiom or common notion'.[22]

A closely connected problem that worried many of Descartes's contemporary critics and has continued to vex commentators ever since is the notorious problem of the 'Cartesian circle'. The problem comes down, in its most general form, to this: if Descartes's programme is indeed the radical one of 'demolishing everything and starting again right from the foundations' (AT VII. 17; CSM II. 12), will he not inevitably be forced, in taking his first steps in reconstruction, to presuppose results on which, given his wholesale rejection of previous beliefs, he is not yet entitled to rely? How, for example, can the meditator prove God's existence from his clear and distinct perceptions, when it seems that the veracity of clear and distinct perception can be guaranteed only *after* God's existence is known? This issue was raised by several critics in the Objections published with the *Meditations* in 1641, perhaps most devastatingly by Antoine Arnauld in the Fourth Set of Objections (AT VII. 214; CSM II. 150); indeed the 'circle' objection was often referred to as 'Arnauld's circle' in the later part of the seventeenth century.

The young Dutchman Frans Burman, who interviewed Descartes in 1648, focused on Descartes's comment, in his reply to Arnauld, that 'the only reason we have for being sure that what we clearly and distinctly perceive is true is the fact that God exists' (AT VII. 245; CSM II. 171). How in that case, asked Burman, is Descartes entitled to presuppose the truth of the axioms he needs to prove God's existence (AT V. 148; CB 5). Descartes's reply suggests that at the time when I am actually attending to a proposition which is completely clear and distinct, no divine guarantee is needed; a clear and distinct proposition has no extraneous implications beyond what I am immediately aware of, so there is no sceptical scenario, however radical or extreme, that could possibly cast doubt on its truth.[23]

Many of Descartes's critics, notably Leibniz, were somewhat scathing about his reliance on the notions of clarity and distinctness. People may *think* something is clear and distinct, and yet be wrong, objected Leibniz; the principle that what we clearly and distinctly perceive is true is useless unless further criteria for clarity and distinctness can be specified (GP IV. 425; L 294). In fact, Descartes does supply a criterion of distinctness, namely that a distinct idea must contain *only* what is clear (so that my judgement does not involve any claim that goes beyond what I am directly aware of). But the trouble is that only exceedingly simple and uninformative propositions (such as 'I am thinking' or 'two plus two is four') seem able to meet this criterion. In order to build a substantive body of knowledge, Descartes needs to advance hypotheses which go beyond such thin and unexciting truths; he needs to run risks which his austere requirements for the foundations of knowledge do not strictly permit him to take.[24]

In view of the fierce criticisms which Descartes's procedures aroused, it is perhaps not surprising that neither Spinoza nor Leibniz modelled their philosophies on the Cartesian 'method of analysis'. Indeed, it is one of the ironies of philosophical history that Spinoza, whose metaphysics is deeply imbued with Cartesian language and Cartesian ideas, chose to present his own philosophical system in that very geometrical manner which Descartes had declared to be unsuitable for metaphysical enquiry.

Spinoza and the 'geometrical order'

Spinoza's fascination with the geometrical method of presentation is exemplified above all in his *magnum opus*, the *Ethics*, published after his death in 1677 but written in the 1660s. This remarkable work (it is the only major philosophical classic to follow such a pattern[25]) is divided into five parts dealing respectively with God, the human mind, the 'affects' (psychophysical states including emotions), human subjection, and human freedom. Each part typically opens with a numbered list of 'definitions' followed by a numbered list of 'axioms'.[26] There then follows a long sequence of numbered 'propositions' (there are over thirty for each part, 259 in all); after each proposition we find a demonstration showing how the proposition in question is derived either directly or indirectly (via previously demonstrated propositions) from the definitions and axioms.

Much less well known than the *Ethics*, but providing another illuminating illustration of Spinoza's attachment to the geometrical style, is the only major work he published under his own name in his lifetime, the *Principia philosophiae Renati Descartes ordine geometrico demonstrata* (1663), sometimes known in English as the 'Principles of the Cartesian Philosophy', though a better rendering would be 'Descartes's *Principia* demonstrated in geometrical order'. As its Latin title implies, the work attempts to provide a geometrical-style exposition of Descartes's *Principles of Philosophy*.[27] Some have seen it as curious that Spinoza thought it necessary to provide a 'synthetic' exposition of Descartes's *Principles*, since Descartes himself reportedly remarked that his *Principles* followed the 'order of exposition' rather than the 'order of discovery' and thus exemplified the 'synthetic' rather than the analytic method.[28] But although Descartes's *Principles* is divided into short articles, each consisting of a numbered proposition followed by an explanation or defence of that proposition, there is no attempt to provide formal deductions from axioms. In Spinoza's exposition, by contrast, the geometrical pattern of exposition is strictly ahered to throughout; thus Part I, after a short introduction, begins with ten numbered 'definitions' and eleven 'axioms'; twenty-one 'propositions' then follow, and for each of these Spinoza provides a demonstration showing how it follows directly or indirectly from the axioms or definitions. Propositions are often followed by 'corollaries' which spell out further logical implications of what has just been established.

The obvious inspiration for the pattern followed both here and in the *Ethics* is Euclid's *Elements* (*Stoicheia*), written in Alexandria around 300 BC, widely available in Latin translation in the seventeenth century, and universally admired as a paradigm of rigorous reasoning.[29] Book I of Euclid consists of thirty-five definitions (for example, 'An obtuse angle is that which is greater than a right angle': def. 11) and twelve axioms (for example, 'If equals be taken from equals the remainders are equal': ax. 3). There then follow forty-eight propositions, most of which are called 'theorems' (that is, results derived from the axioms or definitions).[30] Thus, Proposition 15 states that the opposite angles of two intersecting lines are equal:

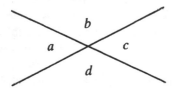

This is demonstrated by showing, first, that the adjacent angles *a*
and *b* equal two right angles (drawing on a previously established
result); and then, by similar reasoning, that *a* and *d* equal two
right angles. If we now subtract angle *a* from each of these two
aggregates, then by Axiom 3 the remainders *b* and *d* must be
equal. By similar reasoning it is shown that *a* and *c* are equal. In
Latin editions of Euclid the triumphant letters QED (*quod erat
demonstrandum*—'which was to be demonstrated') are placed at
the end of this and all the other demonstrations. One cannot but
be impressed by the compactness and simplicity of the reasoning,
and by the fact that each step in the argument is guaranteed either
by reference to a previously established result or by invoking one
of the initial definitions or by citing one or more of the
fundamental axioms of the system.

Some commentators have suggested that Spinoza's attachment
to the geometrical method was merely a matter of stylistic
preference, but it seems highly likely that what attracted him
about the Euclidian approach was its claim to offer logically
watertight demonstrative proofs. It is no accident that Spinoza's
demonstrations, like Euclid's, are always followed by 'QED'. It
has been objected that Spinoza could not have intended his
arguments to carry the same sort of irresistible conviction as
Euclid's unless he was wildly over-optimistic about the plausibility of his initial axioms and definitions.[31] But there are really
two quite separate features of the Euclidian system that we need
to distinguish: the deductive rigour of its demonstrations, and the
compelling self-evidence of its axioms. Spinoza could well have
believed that his philosophy could aim to match the former
feature without being naïvely optimistic on the second point. In
fact, though, Spinoza did unquestionably believe that his axioms

were self-evidently and necessarily true. The term 'self-evident' does, however, need to be used with caution. It was common in scholastic philosophy to distinguish two kinds of self-evidence, which we might label 'objective' and 'subjective' self-evidence respectively: a proposition could be objectively self-evident, or self-evident 'in itself', without being subjectively self-evident— that is, irresistibly obvious to anyone at first glance.[32] To a being of infinite intelligence *all* truths (on Spinoza's view) would be self-evidently manifest, since their truth is a matter of logical necessity. But from a human point of view there is room for debate about which truths are best suited for selection as the starting points for a deductive exposition. Spinoza acknowledges that there can be considerable flexibility here. Thus while Proposition 7 of Part I of the *Ethics* demonstrates that 'It belongs to the nature of a substance to exist', in one of his 'scholia' (the pieces of informal commentary that follow many of the demonstrations) Spinoza observes:

> I do not doubt that the demonstration of P7 will be difficult to conceive for all those who judge things confusedly, and have not been accustomed to know things through their first causes . . . But if men would attend to the nature of substance they would not at all doubt of the truth of P7. Indeed this proposition would be an axiom for everyone, and would be numbered among the common notions (G II. 49–50; C 413).[33]

Immediate self-evidence, then, at least as far as humans are concerned, is a relative matter and depends on the extent of our attentive reflection on the concepts involved.

It follows that Spinoza is not so sanguine as to expect that every reader will open the *Ethics* and be struck with the blinding conviction that all the opening axioms are true. Rather he expects that in practice the reader will often suspend judgement until he has read further. The scholium after Proposition 11 of Part II of the *Ethics* might well be a motto for the study of the *Ethics* as a whole:

> Here no doubt my readers will come to a halt and think of many things which will give them pause. For this reason I ask them to continue on with me slowly, step by step, and to make no judgement on these matters until they have read through everything (G II. 95; C 456).

In the light of such comments it is often said that Spinoza's system, despite its axiomatic structure, is meant to be evaluated as a whole. As one recent commentator has put it: 'Spinoza offered his axioms . . . not as immediately compelling but rather as the first bricks in an edifice to be tested as a whole.'[34] Certainly the axioms are often best understood in the light of what comes later, and Spinoza's own advice to 'read through everything before passing judgement' is indispensable for any student of the *Ethics*. Nevertheless, we should not forget that Spinoza had absolute faith in the truth and 'objective' self-evidence of his axioms. He certainly did not construe them as tentative hypotheses that might have to be revised in the light of later discoveries; rather he insisted, whenever his critics cast doubt on any of the axioms, that their self-evidence could always be appreciated provided the reader was prepared to devote sufficiently careful attention to the terms involved (cf. G IV. 13; C 171). There is thus nothing superficial about Spinoza's choice of the geometrical model; and we should resist the temptation to 'water down' his enterprise so as to make it more congenial to the lower-key philosophical aspirations of modern times. Spinoza's deductivism has a deep philosophical motivation—a motivation which links in with his commitment to the goals of self-evidence in our intellectual perceptions and demonstrative certainty in our reasonings. There are striking links here with Descartes's ideal of *vera et certa scientia*—the model of a true and certain system of knowledge 'deduced from first causes' (see above, pp. 33, 42). Despite the fact that Descartes himself was reluctant to use a geometrical presentation for his metaphysics, it seems probable that Spinoza saw the axiomatic method as being ideally suited to the 'foundational' project of establishing a reliable philosophical system, based on self-evident 'principles'. This is precisely the claim made for the axiomatic approach in the introduction, written by Spinoza's friend Lodewijk Meyer, which is prefixed to Spinoza's geometrical exposition of the Cartesian system:

The best and surest method of seeking the truth in the sciences is that of the mathematicians who demonstrate their conclusions from Definitions, Postulates and Axioms. For since a certain and firm knowledge of anything unknown can only be derived from things known certainly beforehand, these things must be laid down at the start as a stable foundation on which to build the whole edifice of human knowledge (G I. 127; C 225).

Definitions, essences, and apriorism

To give a fuller picture of Spinoza's geometrical method, something should be said of the other elements in his system, besides the axioms and the propositions derived from them. As already noted, in demonstrating his propositions Spinoza refers back not just to initial axioms but also to 'definitions'. The definitions to be found in Euclid are for the most part indications that a certain label will be used in a certain way: thus 'a *scalene* triangle is that which has three unequal sides'.[35] Spinoza's definitions, however, are far from being arbitrary stipulations about the use of terms; on the other hand, as Spinoza himself points out, they are not necessarily meant to reflect common usage (G II. 195; C 535). It is made clear in a letter of March 1663 that although some definitions may simply 'explain a thing as we conceive it or can conceive it', a definition is typically designed to explain a thing 'as it is in itself outside the intellect': 'then it ought to be true, and to differ from a proposition only in that a definition is concerned solely with the essences of things or of their affections (whereas an axiom or a proposition may extend more widely to eternal truths as well)' (G IV. 43; C 194).[36] The reference to 'essences of things' is crucial. In his early *Treatise on the Purification of the Intellect*[37] Spinoza argues that the intellect, if properly directed and freed from misleading external influences, can attain to 'the perception of a thing through its essence alone' (G II. 10; C 13). The right method in philosophy is to form 'perfect definitions' which 'explain the inmost essence of a thing' (G II. 34; C 39). The definition must not merely capture one true or essential property (*proprium*) of the thing in question; rather it must be such that 'when the definition is considered alone, without any others conjoined, all the thing's properties can be deduced from it' (G II. 35; C 40). Spinoza's definitions are thus supposed to have great generative power: they represent the 'seeds of knowledge' (*semina scientiae*—to use a metaphor of Descartes[38]) that each intellect may find within itself. And from these seeds an entire deductive explanation of all the properties of a thing may be unravelled:

> Just as men in the beginning were able to make the easiest things with the tools they were born with [*innatis instrumentis*] . . . so the intellect, by its own inborn power [*vi nativa*] makes intellectual tools for itself by which it acquires other powers for other intellectual works . . . and so proceeds by stages till it reaches the pinnacle of wisdom (G II. 14; C 17).

The examples Spinoza gives to illustrate how this process works are, not surprisingly, mathematical: a true definition of a circle will enable all that figure's properties to be deduced (ibid.). Spinoza is very close here to the mathematical intuitionism of the early Descartes in his *Regulae*: just as for Descartes knowledge is based on intuition of 'simple natures' or essences, so for Spinoza the purified intellect arrives at the definitions which capture the essences of things; and in each case this provides the foundation for a deductive system of knowledge.[39]

For the ordinary reader the most pressing worry in coming to terms with Spinoza's programme is likely to be just the one which Descartes raised against the 'method of synthesis': 'it is not as satisfying as the method of analysis, nor does it engage the minds of those who are eager to learn, since it does not show how the thing in question was discovered' (AT VII. 156; CSM II. 111). Descartes's *Meditations* have a compelling power even for those who are not normally attracted by philosophical inquiry; the reader is swiftly caught up in the individual drama of the lonely meditator as he struggles to reach some certainty. In the case of Spinoza's *Ethics*, by contrast, even the most enthusiastic beginner is liable to be daunted by the barrage of technical definitions that opens the work: 'By *cause of itself* I understand that whose essence involves existing'; 'That thing is said to be *finite in its own kind* that can be limited by another of the same nature'; 'By *substance* I understand that which is in itself and is conceived through itself' . . . and so on. Nothing could be further removed from Descartes's proclaimed strategy of starting from a consideration of the views of the person who is 'only just beginning to philosophize' (AT V. 146; CB 3).

To some extent, the initial disquiet felt by the reader of the

Ethics diminishes as the work unfolds. For although Spinoza sticks firmly to his austere deductive framework, he does render it less daunting by the addition of a large auxiliary apparatus of scholia, appendices, and prefaces. The scholia (or pieces of commentary) which follow many of the demonstrations of particular propositions, and the appendices and prefaces which follow or precede various parts of the book, are all couched in much less formal language. Their role is to support the demonstrations, to clarify the terminology, and to explain the philosophical background and motivation for many of the steps Spinoza takes. To a considerable extent these additions make good the gap Descartes saw in the 'synthetic method': they help the reader to 'make the thing his own', and at least provide some indication of 'how the thing in question was discovered'.

Apart from the question of the accessibility of Spinoza's method, there is an important point to be made about its logical structure. We noted above that in addition to his axioms, Spinoza lists a number of 'postulates'. The postulates to be found in Euclid have quasi-axiomatic status; indeed some editions of Euclid list as axioms what in other editions are listed as postulates, and vice versa. But Spinoza's postulates are rather different, as illustrated by some comments he makes on his account of sensory perception at Proposition 17 of Part II of the *Ethics*:

> This can happen from other causes also, but it is sufficient for me here to have shown one through which I can explain it as if I had shown it through its true cause. Still, I do not believe that I have wandered far from the true cause, since all the postulates I assume contain hardly anything which is not consistent with reliable experience . . . (G II. 105; C 464).

This is strongly reminiscent of a passage in Descartes which asserts that there are limits to the deductive method. We can deduce from the nature of God a certain number of general laws concerning the universe, says Descartes, but there are very many matters of detail which cannot be settled a priori, but where we are 'free to make any assumptions provided that all the consequences of our assumption agree with our experience' (AT VIII. 101; CSM I. 256).[40] Spinoza's 'postulates', then, are assumptions which are considered well supported if they can be shown to square with experience; they are not supposed to be intuited as self-evident. Thus even in the case of Spinoza, who of all the three rationalists is most strongly attracted to the deductive model, we do not find, at the level of detailed explanations of particular phenomena, the kind of rigid apriorism that figures so prominently in the common caricature of philosophical rationalism.[41]

The denial of contingency, and Spinoza's grades of cognition

Though Spinoza is not a rigid apriorist, he does nevertheless maintain that all truths are in principle demonstrable, even though this may not be achievable in practice. For Spinoza 'all things have been determined by the necessity of the divine nature to exist and produce an effect in a certain way' (*Ethics* I, prop. 29). It follows that a fully adequate grasp of the divine nature would enable us to demonstrate the inevitability of everything that happens. 'I have shown more clearly than the noon light, that there is absolutely nothing in things on account of which they may be called contingent' (G II. 74; C 436).

Without delving into the metaphysical background of all this (something that will be examined in the next chapter), we will simply attempt here to trace the way in which Spinoza's denial of contingency affects his view of philosophical method, and his account of how knowledge is to be achieved. It may seem at first sight that Spinoza's denial of contingency is out of tune with standard ways of thinking. For many tend to think of necessity as something which is rather special, which applies only to propositions such as those of logic and mathematics, which in some sense 'must' be true, or cannot be otherwise. But in the case of everyday statements about the world like 'it's raining in London', we take it that there is no necessity: things might, as we say, have turned out differently. (For David Hume, indeed, all matters of fact and existence have this essentially contingent character: every single thing we observe could have happened differently, and any generalization we make could break down at any moment.[42]) For Spinoza, however, the fact that we regard certain events as contingent happenings is a sign of a defect in our knowledge.

Thus if we knew the full causal background which had given rise to the present state of the weather, we would know that 'it's now raining in London' is not something that may merely *happen* to be true; either it *has* to be true (it is necessary), or else it *cannot* be true (it is impossible):

> A thing is called contingent only because of a defect in our knowledge ... when we can affirm nothing certainly about the necessity or impossibility of its existence, because the order of causes is hidden from us (*Ethics* I, prop. 33, schol. 1).[43]

It follows from Spinoza's position that anyone who is in the position of entertaining some proposition as a contingent fact automatically has an inadequate perception of reality. Suppose I believe that, as a matter of fact, the earth is flat. Then my ideas are, in Spinoza's phrase, 'mutilated and confused'; if I had a more adequate perception I would see that this proposition, when combined with others, leads to a contradiction and so cannot be true. But notice that Spinoza's strictures do not only apply to the entertaining of false propositions; they also extend to what would ordinarily be thought of as contingent truths. If I believe that the sun is, as a matter of fact, larger than the moon, but lack adequate perception of the reasons which make this proposition necessarily true, then on Spinoza's view my state of mind still involves a degree of error or falsity. Falsity can be avoided only if the mind possesses a clear awareness not just of a given truth, but of the necessity of that truth.[44]

This very austere view of what counts as true knowledge is clarified further in the course of Spinoza's account of what he calls the three 'grades of cognition' (*cognitionis genera*). (*Ethics* II, prop. 40, schol. 2). These are often referred to as Spinoza's three grades of *knowledge*, but this is a misleading translation. Descartes had allowed that there were certain kinds of *cognitio* ('cognition' or 'awareness') that were not entitled to the honorific label *scientia*—a label he reserves for properly grounded systematic knowledge.[45] Spinoza does not make the same distinction as Descartes, but he does use *cognitio* to cover a wide variety of states of awareness—the lowest variety of which is not strictly a kind of knowledge at all, since it involves falsehood.[46] The lowest grade includes mere secondhand opinion (for example, my belief that I was born on such and such a day: G II. 10; C 13); to this is added perception arising 'from signs, e.g. from the fact that having heard or read certain words we form certain ideas of them through which we imagine the things' (G II. 122; C 477).[47]

Perhaps the most important example of Spinoza's lowest level of cognition is what he calls 'cognition derived from shifting experience' (*cognitio ab vaga experientia*). What is represented to us in sense-experience, says Spinoza, is 'presented to the intellect in a way that is mutilated, confused, and without order'. To many of Spinoza's readers, the unsatisfactoriness of sensory experience as a basis for knowledge would have seemed a familiar enough theme. This talk of sensory representation as 'confused' would probably have called to mind, first, Descartes's revival of the well-known 'argument from illusion', which makes play with cases such as that of the stick that appears bent in water, where the information provided by the senses can be misleading (AT VII. 438; CSM II. 296). Second, the labelling of sensory experience as *vaga* ('fleeting', 'inconstant') might have evoked the argument (which originated with Plato[48]) that claims based on the senses that count as true at a certain time, or from a certain point of view, may turn out to be false at a later date, or from a different point of view. Descartes's famous discussion of the piece of wax in the Second Meditation is an exploration of this theme: as I examine the wax my senses tell me it has a certain taste and smell and colour and shape and that it emits a certain sound; but a moment later, as I move the wax to the fire, 'the residual taste is eliminated, the smell goes away, the colour changes, the shape is lost, and if you strike it it no longer makes a sound' (AT VII. 30; CSM II. 20). Apart from these familiar arguments, a third and much more pervasive reservation about sensory experience had been voiced by Descartes. Descartes maintained that even when the senses are in perfect working order, and even when the conditions of sensory observation are carefully fixed, there is still something inherently indistinct and confused about the information they provide:

If someone says he sees colour in a body . . . this amounts to saying that he sees . . . something there of which he is totally ignorant, or in other words, that he does not know what he is seeing . . . If he examines the nature of what is represented by the sensation of colour . . . what is represented as existing in the coloured body—he will realize that he is wholly ignorant of it (AT VIII. 33; CSM I. 217).

For Descartes, an accurate perception of the world as it really is involves confining ourselves to the clear and distinct concepts of pure mathematics: we need to abandon descriptions of the world in terms of sensory qualities, and substitute precise quantitative notions which capture the essence of 'extended substance' (AT VIII. 41–2; CSM I. 224).

All of these three lines of argument may have indirectly influenced Spinoza's attitude to 'inconstant experience' (cf. G II. 82; C 445), but the argument that is most characteristic of his thinking about sensory experience depends on his distinction between adequate and inadequate perception. An adequate perception, as noted above, involves not merely a perception that something is the case, but an appreciation of the necessity for its being true. Now clearly an isolated sensory perception will merely convey the information that something *is* the case; moreover, no series of such perceptions, however extended, can of itself be sufficient to establish that something *must* be the case (a point on which Leibniz was later to lay considerable stress; see below, p. 73). It follows that one who is in search of necessary truth must go beyond the immediate data of the senses, and attempt to discover some underlying chain of reasons or causes which will establish that a given phenomenon must of necessity come about. This is what Spinoza means when he contrasts *vaga experientia* with his second grade of cognition, 'reason' (*ratio*). Reason takes us beyond the sphere of the temporary and the contingent to the permanent underlying reasons or caues of phenomena: 'Reason perceives things truly as they are in themselves, i.e. not as contingent but as necessary' (*Ethics* II, prop. 44). In place of 'vacillating opinion', one who has attained the second grade of cognition will have a rational grasp of a stable network of causes which explain how any given phenomenon must be the way it is.

In a graphic and celebrated phrase, Spinoza expresses this by saying that it is of the nature of reason to contemplate things *sub specie eternitatis* ('under the form of eternity', ibid., cor. 2).

Above reason, his second grade of cognition, Spinoza places a third and highest grade which he calls *scientia intuitiva* ('intuitive knowledge'). The term *scientia* is, as we have seen, used by Descartes as a label for a specially privileged kind of cognition; and Spinoza and Descartes are on common ground with respect to the need to transcend sense-experience and strive for a clear and distinct intellectual cognition. But how exactly does Spinoza's *ratio* differ from *scientia intuitiva*? The contrast between necessary and contingent propositions will not help us here, since both the second and third grades of cognition are said to involve apprehension of what is necessarily true (II, prop. 41); and both are said to conceive things *sub specie eternitatis* (II, prop. 44, cor. 2; V, prop. 31, schol.).

Those of Spinoza's audience who had been trained in the scholastic tradition would have been aware of a standard Aristotelian distinction between *nous* (generally translated 'intuition') and *apodeixis* (generally translated 'deduction'). *Nous* is, according to Aristotle, the faculty whereby we apprehend the truth of the first principles or axioms of a demonstration; *apodeixis* enables us to deduce the consequences. Spinoza's use of this fundamental contrast between what is immediately apprehended and what has to be deduced emerges in the following illustration which he provides to explain his three grades of cognition. The example concerns the mathematical exercise of finding the 'fourth proportional':[49] given three numbers a, b, c, we are to find the number which stands in the same ratio to c as b does to a (thus, for the sequence 2, 4, 5 the answer is 10). Spinoza lists three ways of tackling the problem. The first is to do 'what merchants do' and mechanically apply a rule of thumb (for example, 'multiply the second number by the third and divide by the first'); those who follow this procedure have been taught the rule as children but (we are to suppose) have no real understanding of why it works. This corresponds to the lowest grade of cognition. The second way involves applying the rule, but being able to back it up with a rigorous demonstration, showing that it must work for any series of proportional numbers. This corresponds with *ratio*, the second grade of cognition. But the person who enjoys the highest grade of cognition, *scientia intuitiva*, is able to see the answer at a glance. 'Thus given the numbers 1, 2 and 3 no one fails to see that the proportional number is 6—and we see this much more clearly because we derive the fourth number from the very ratio which we see at one glance obtains between the first and the second' (G II. 122; C 478). Descartes, in his own account of intuition in the *Regulae*, stresses the fact that it is possible to intuit a chain of connections 'in a continuous and wholly uninterrupted sweep of thought . . . so swiftly that memory is left with practically no role to play, and I seem to intuit the whole thing practically at once' (AT X. 387–8; CSM I. 25). Spinoza is clearly following the central Cartesian analogy between simple vision and intellection; where something is clearly and straightforwardly presented to the mind, and contains nothing that is not clear, then the mind has the ability to 'see' the truth in a way which leaves no room for error (G II. 24; C 29).[50]

Though reason and intuitive knowledge work in different ways, they can both attain to the truth, since they both operate on the basis of what Spinoza calls 'adequate ideas'. The hallmark of falsity is, for Spinoza, inadequacy or incompleteness. Fictitious ideas, he argues in his early *Treatise on the Purification of the Intellect*, are never clear but always confused, and 'all confusion results from the fact that the mind knows only in part a thing that is whole' (G II. 24; C 29. Cf. G II. 117; C 473). On this conception of understanding—what may be called a 'holistic' conception— the search for truth is a search for an ever more complete and all-embracing set of ideas, from which, as we have seen, the necessity of all true propositions will be apparent. This does not mean that sense-experience can be ignored or dispensed with entirely (as noted above, it is important for Spinoza that his postulates should square with experience). But it does mean that the philosopher will always be required to incorporate the results of sensory experience into a wider framework. Only within that wider framework will the appearance of contingency dissolve and the necessity of the truth emerge. 'It is of the nature of reason', says Spinoza, 'to view things not as contingent but as necessary'

(*Ethics* II, prop. 44). It should be clear from this that one of Spinoza's most celebrated doctrines—that the truth is self-manifesting (the truth is *index sui*, its own sign, or *norma sui*, its own criterion[51])—is far from being a naïve piece of optimism about the ability of the human mind to distinguish the true from the false. The adequate ideas of reason and intuitive knowledge presuppose a coherent and all-embracing structure that is wholly absent in the deliverances of 'fleeting experience'. It is because of this that Spinoza is able to claim that 'he who has a true idea at the same time knows that he has a true idea and cannot doubt the truth of the thing' (II, prop. 43). Many critics asked Descartes how one could be sure that one's ideas were clear and distinct; and Descartes's answers were not always convincing (cf. AT VII. 146; CSM II. 104). Since Spinoza defined falsity in terms of failure to have an adequate perception of why a proposition must be true (or why it cannot be true), one can see why he thought that falsity must reveal itself without difficulty to a reflective intellect. Similarly, given the holistic and necessitarian character of Spinoza's account of knowledge, it is possible to see how he came to maintain that one cannot arrive at an adequate perception without knowing one has arrived: 'As the light makes both itself and the darkness plain, so truth is the standard both of itself and of the false (II, prop. 43, schol.).

Leibniz and the 'art of combination'

We have seen the crucial importance, in Descartes's thought, of the idea of a 'new method' for investigating the truth; and the goal of discovering such a method remained a major preoccupation of seventeenth-century philosophy. Leibniz's approach to the problem is apparent from one of his earliest papers, the *Dissertation on the Art of Combination*, published when he was only twenty (it was an expanded version of the thesis he had offered for his *Habilitationsschrift* at the University of Leipzig). Here he shows how complex concepts in arithmetic can be exhibited as combinations or 'complexions' of more elementary concepts (a classic example of this was his later discovery of a binary notation enabling all numbers to be expressed as combinations of the symbols for one and zero[52]).

The inspiration behind this work was mathematical, but echoing Descartes's advocacy of the notion of a *mathesis universalis*,[53] Leibniz argues that the method of combining complex ideas out of simple elements will serve as the key to understanding in a whole range of subjects. Thus the 'combinatory method' could be applied, Leibniz claimed, not just to arithmetic but to metaphysics, physics, and even such practical subjects as jurisprudence: 'the elements are simple—in geometry figures (a triangle, a circle, etc.), in jurisprudence actions (a promise, a sale, etc.). Cases are complexions of those which are infinitely variable in any field' (GP IV. 58; L 82).

In a later paper entitled 'Of Universal Synthesis and Analysis, or the Art of Discovery and Judgement',[54] Leibniz gives a more general presentation of what he has in mind. If we possessed the 'true categories for the simplest terms', then we should have a 'kind of alphabet of human thoughts' which would represent the *summa genera* (most general categories or kinds) 'from a combination of which inferior concepts could be formed' (GP VII. 292; P 10). The extreme generality of the concepts involved means, according to Leibniz, that the 'alphabet of thoughts' would operate at an even more simple and universal level than mathematics:

> The art of combination is . . . the science which treats of the forms of things or of formulae in general. That is, it is the science of quality in general, or of the like and the unlike, according as various formulae arise from the combination of *a*, *b*, *c*, etc., whether they represent quantities or something else. Consequently algebra (which is concerned with formulae applied to quantity) is subordinate to the art of combinations and follows its rules. These rules, however, are much more general, and can be applied not only in algebra but also in cryptography, in various kinds of games, in geometry itself . . . and in all matters where similarity is involved (GP VII. 297–8; P 17).

Referring back to Cartesian discussions of the 'order of discovery', and the distinction between the two 'methods' of analysis and synthesis, Leibniz seems to identify his own 'art of combination' with the method of synthesis; he refuses, however, to be dogmatic about a canonical route for finding the truth, observing that 'Of the minds able to make discoveries, some are more analytic, others more combinatory' (ibid.). The prevailing impression, nevertheless, is that Leibniz finds the Spinozan ideal of a deductive system of knowledge highly attractive. The philosopher, says Leibniz, should aim at 'adequate' or 'intuitive' knowledge expressed in terms of 'real definitions' (GP VII. 295; P 14).[55] As with Spinoza, these definitions are regarded as having generative power (P 13) and provide the foundations from which all truths can be demonstrated:

> And so a reason can be given for each truth; for the connection of the predicate with the subject is either self-evident, as in the case of the identical propositions [i.e. tautologies] or has to be displayed . . . From this there can be derived a method of proceeding in all things (provided they are understood) in a way which is as demonstrative as that of geometry (GP VII. 295–6; P 15).

Despite his attraction to the deductivist model, Leibniz is, however, very far from offering a dogmatically aprioristic account of human knowledge. Immediately after the passage just quoted, he makes it clear that what he has just said represents a kind of ideal which characterizes what it would be to have perfect understanding; it is not meant to describe how ordinary human knowledge is normally built up. God, says Leibniz, 'understands all things a priori as eternal truths', since he possesses fully 'adequate knowledge'. Human beings, by contrast, 'know scarcely anything adequately and only a few things a priori'. For us, it is necessary to rely on experience; we humans, says Leibniz, have to deal with 'matters of fact, i.e. contingent matters which do not depend on reason but on observation' (ibid.). This leads us straight into one of the most distinctive features of Leibniz's conception of philosophical inquiry—his theory of contingency.

Necessity, contingency, and Leibniz's 'rationalism'

The distinction between eternal, necessary truths and contingent truths or matters of 'fact' receives great emphasis in Leibniz. He did not of course invent the distinction; the contrast between what has to be true and what merely happens to be true can be found as far back as Plato and Aristotle, and plays an important role in scholastic philosophy. But Spinoza, as we have seen, challenged the notion of contingency, arguing that it arises simply from a 'defect of our understanding' (G I. 242; C 308). Leibniz was concerned to show that a perfectly proper employment can be found for the term 'contingent'; but despite this typical attempt at reconciliation, Leibniz's views in this area turn out to have a surprising amount in common with those of Spinoza.

Necessary truths, or 'truths of reason', depend, says Leibniz, on the 'principle of contradiction', which he described in a late summary of his views, the *Monadology* (1714), as 'one of the two great principles on which our reasoning is founded' (para. 31). According to this principle, we judge a proposition to be true when its opposite is self-contradictory. Thus in the case of what Leibniz elsewhere calls 'primary truths' (propositions of the form '*A* is *A*' or 'each thing is what it is'), anyone who attempted to deny them would simply be talking nonsense. In Leibniz's terminology, they are 'identical' propositions, or, as we should say nowadays, 'tautologies'; their opposite, says Leibniz, 'contains an express contradiction' (para. 35). Leibniz goes on to explain that there are other truths of reason which do not obviously have the form of 'identical' propositions. 'A part is less than the whole' does not directly exemplify the form '*A* is *A*'. None the less, says Leibniz, it may be reduced to a primary truth with the aid of definitions. ' "A part is less than the whole" is very easily demonstrated from the definition of "less" or "greater" together with the primitive axiom, that of Identity' (*Primary Truths*: CO 518; P 87).

From this account, the distinction between necessary and contingent might seem to be plain sailing: a necessary truth would be one expressed either by an 'identical' proposition, or by one that is reducible to an identical proposition, and which it is therefore self-contradictory to deny; a contingent truth, by contrast, would be one which is *not* either an identical proposition or reducible to one, and whose denial is therefore possible. In fact, however, things are rather more complicated than that. For, according to Leibniz's account of what it is for a proposition to be true, in *every* true proposition, whether necessary or contingent, the predicate is, as he puts it, 'contained' or 'included' in the subject: 'Always, in every true affirmative proposition whether necessary or contingent, universal or particular, the concept of the predicate is in some way included in that of the subject—*predicatum inest subjecto*; otherwise I know not what truth is' (GP II. 56; P 62. Cf. P 57 and 61).

The principle that the predicate is in the subject (often called the '*Inesse* Principle') was a commonplace of scholastic philosophy; Leibniz claimed that it was directly derived from Aristotle.[56] But its application was normally taken to be restricted to necessary truths (thus, in the case of the necessarily true proposition 'a triangle is three-sided', the concept of three-sidedness may be regarded as contained in the concept of a triangle). By extending the maxim to *all* truths, Leibniz seems to risk eradicating the very distinction between necessary and contingent propositions which he has set up. For if we say even of a proposition like 'Fido is barking' that the predicate is contained in the subject, then we seem to be saying that it would be possible, merely by analysing the proposition, to recognize its truth; but this seems to make its truth discoverable by reason alone. So, far from having a distinction between 'truths of reason' and 'truths of fact', we seem to be sliding into a completely necessitarian system, where all truths can be established merely by unravelling the definitions of terms.

In an important paper entitled 'Necessary and Contingent Truths' (written in the late 1680s), Leibniz does much to resolve the paradox. Picking up the contrast which had appeared in his earlier work between how things are for a perfect intellect and how things are for human beings, Leibniz remarks:

In the case of a contingent truth, even though the predicate is really in the subject, yet one never arrives at a demonstration of an identity, even though the resolution of each term is continued indefinitely. In such cases it is only God, who comprehends the infinite at once, who can see how the one is in the other, and can understand *a priori* the perfect reason for the truth. In created things this is supplied *a posteriori*, by experience (CO 17; P 97).

Leibniz's attitude to the necessitarian or deductive model can now be explained. He does certainly share the 'rationalistic' view of Descartes and Spinoza that the universe is a rationally ordered system determined by (and, for Spinoza, inseparable from) God; hence he maintains that 'every true predication has some basis in the nature of things' (GP IV. 432; P 18). 'In virtue of the general interconnection of things', Leibniz wrote in July 1686 to the distinguished philosopher and former correspondent of Descartes, Antoine Arnauld, 'there must always be some foundation for the connection of the terms [that is, the subject and predicate] of a proposition' (GP II. 56; P 62). Thus, from a God's eye view, as it were, there are no events that merely 'happen' to occur and might have been otherwise:

> God, seeing the individual notion of Alexander, sees in it at the same time the foundation of and the reason for all the predicates which can truly be stated of him—as for example that he is the conqueror of Darius ... even to the extent of knowing *a priori* and not by experience whether he died a natural death or died by poison (GP IV. 432; P 19).[57]

But the process of analysis which would uncover these necessary connections is an infinitely complex one, and therefore beyond the reach of the human intellect. *We* can know the fate of Alexander only by historical investigation.

One way of expressing this result would be to make a distinction between what one might call 'ideal rationalism' on the one hand and 'methodological rationalism' on the other. Leibniz, like Descartes and Spinoza, is an ideal rationalist: he believes in a structure of all-embracing necessary connections such that there is no room for 'brute facts'. This is expressed by Leibniz in the second of his 'two great principles on which our reasoning is based'—the 'principle of sufficient reason'. In virtue of this principle, says Leibniz, 'we consider that no fact can be real or existing and no proposition can be true unless there is a sufficient reason why it should be thus and not otherwise, even though in most cases these reasons cannot be known to us' (*Monadology*, para. 32). But the qualification at the end is crucial. Leibniz's belief in a foundation of necessary connections underlying all phenomena does not commit him to the implausible doctrine of 'methodological rationalism'—the unappealing view that we only have to indulge in abstract intellectual reflection in order to establish an entire system of knowledge.⁵⁸

Innate ideas

Our knowledge of necessary truths is closely linked in Leibniz to the doctrine of innate ideas—a doctrine he inherited from Descartes, though its roots go back to Plato.⁵⁹ In Descartes's Third Meditation, the meditator makes an inventory of the ideas he finds within him, and observes that some seem to be innate, some 'adventitious' (coming from an outside source), and some 'fictitious' (or made up) (AT VII. 38; CSM II. 26). The first class includes the idea we have of ourselves as thinking things, the idea of God, and basic mathematical concepts (like that of triangularity); also included are certain fundamental truths of logic (such as 'that it is impossible for the same thing to be and not to be at the same time': (AT VIII. 24; CSM I. 209). In his celebrated critique of the innateness doctrine, in his *Essay concerning Human Understanding* (1689), John Locke was to urge the objection that many people ('idiots and children', for example) seem quite unaware of the relevant truths; yet 'to imprint any thing on the Mind without the Mind's perceiving it', he wrote, 'seems to me hardly intelligible'.⁶⁰ In fact, Descartes is not committed to the thesis that we are automatically aware of all the ideas within us: 'When we say that an idea is innate in us, we do not mean that it is always there before us—which would mean that no idea was innate' (AT VII. 189; CSM II. 132). Obviously we can consciously attend only to a tiny fraction of the mind's ideas at any one time. But Locke's observations at least have the merit of requiring Cartesians to specify exactly what is meant by the claim that a given idea is 'within us' or 'inside' the mind.⁶¹

Descartes's answer appears to be (though he does not use the metaphor) that ideas are actually present in the mind in the way that information is present in a book—though the reader of course does not and cannot consult all of it all the time. 'The child has within itself the idea of God, itself and all such truths as are called self evident, in the same way as adult humans have when they are not attending to them; it does not acquire them later on as it grows older' (AT III. 424; K 111). But if these truths are actually 'there' waiting to be discovered, what stops us discovering them? Descartes's reply is that we are distracted, first by urgent bodily stimuli which swamp the mind in childhood, and second by a body of inherited 'preconceived opinions'—obscure and confused judgements that obstruct our perception of the truth. But if the intellect is guided aright, if it is wooed away from the senses and allowed to attend to the ideas that are present right from birth, it will be able to recognize the truth quite plainly.[62] The soul, removed from the body, would readily find these ideas present within it (AT III. 424; K 111). The task of metaphysics, then, is to 'direct the reason aright', so that we can free ourselves from the obstructions to truth, and make use of the God-given knowledge which is implanted within each of us (compare Spinoza's account of the purification of the intellect by means of its 'innate instruments'—see above, p. 56).

Perhaps the greatest source of the unease which most people nowadays feel on being confronted with the theory of innate ideas is that it does not seem to do justice to the way in which human beings appear to acquire knowledge via a gradual process of learning. Since Plato, innatists had commonly pointed to the fact that our mathematical knowledge does not seem to be, in any obvious way, a function of empirical observation.[63] But even in the case of mathematics, there is clearly a learning process in which the external senses appear to play at least some role: quiet internal reflection may be crucial, but so, surely, is the stimulation, via the senses, which a good classroom typically provides. Leibniz's main task, in developing and defending the Cartesian doctrine of innate ideas, was to do justice to the role of experience. 'It would indeed be wrong', he writes in the Preface to the *New Essays*, 'to think that we can easily read these eternal laws of reason in the soul as the Praetor's edict can be read on his notice board, without effort or inquiry; but it is enough that they can be discovered within us by dint of attention' (RB 51). In a famous and illuminating metaphor Leibniz compares the mind to a block of marble—not a uniform block, but one that is veined in a certain way, so that the blows of the sculptor serve to reveal the underlying shape. In like manner the 'blows' of ordinary sensory stimuli may be necessary to enable us to uncover the inner truths within us (RB 50–2).

In a much-quoted passage, Leibniz expresses his view of innateness by saying that the ideas and truths are innate in us as 'inclinations, dispositions, tendencies or virtualities' ('des inclinations, des dispositions, des habitudes, ou des virtualités': RB 52). There is a certain looseness in this stringing together of labels, but Leibniz seems to have in mind at least two ways in which humans may be said to possess genuine knowledge which none the less falls short of actual explicit awareness. The first involves the notion of *virtual* or *implicit* knowledge. Anyone can recognize when a liar contradicts himself, says Leibniz, and this shows that, though he may not be able to formulate it explicitly, he has implicit or virtual knowledge of the principle of non-contradiction (RB 76).[64] Second, Leibniz draws a contrast (one which in fact goes back to Aristotle[65]) between actual and *dispositional* knowledge. The young child may not have actual awareness of, for example, the properties of a square. But when suitable sensory stimulus is provided, then the type of understanding that is elicited shows, according to Leibniz, that the mind 'has a disposition, as much active as passive, to draw [certain truths] from its own depths' (RB 80). A much-quoted Lockean objection to this way of interpreting innateness is that it makes the doctrine of innate ideas trivial, or, as Locke puts it, 'frivolous':

if the Capacity of knowledge be the natural impression contended for, all the truths a Man ever comes to know will, by this Account be every one of them innate; and this great Point will amount to no more, but only to a very improper way of speaking; which whilst it pretends to assert the contrary says nothing different from those who deny innate Principles.[66]

But to say that the mind has a disposition to grasp certain truths is to make a stronger claim than saying merely that it has the capacity to learn them. Leibniz's point is that the mind does not merely passively receive sensory data, and then come to learn certain truths as a result; rather it is 'programmed', as it were, to interpret the data in a certain way. In particular, the mind is programmed to recognize the 'infallible and perpetual certainty' of certain truths of logic and mathematics. For 'however often one experienced instances of a universal truth, one could never know inductively that it would always hold unless one knew through reason that it was necessary' (RB 80).

Leibniz's development of the doctrine of innate ideas is not as original as is sometimes supposed. Both the notion of 'virtual' or 'implicit' knowledge and the 'dispositional' interpretation of innate knowledge are to be found in Descartes.[67] The particular value of Leibniz's contribution to this topic is twofold. First, he raises in a particularly vivid form the issue of necessary truths and their status; by questioning whether our grasp of such truths can satisfactorily be accounted for by a theory which construes human knowledge merely in terms of the receiving, comparing, and classifying of sensory ideas, he provides a direct challenge to empiricist theories of knowledge. Second, and perhaps more important, in his account of innate knowledge he manages to avoid the harsh and dogmatic rejection of the senses which is characteristic of Platonic rationalism[68] and which surfaces from time to time in Descartes too. In his programme for 'leading the mind away from the senses', Descartes comes near to suggesting that our inborn light of reason can operate quite on its own, so as to reveal the essential structure both of our own minds and of the physical universe.[69] In practice, Cartesian science rapidly departs from such rigid apriorism (see above, p. 9), but the initial inquiries that constitute 'first philosophy' and the setting up of the foundations of physics certainly operate in that way. Leibniz goes so far as to say that arithmetic and geometry could be constructed 'with one's eyes closed'; but adds that if one had not seen or touched anything one would not succeed in bringing to the mind the relevant ideas (RB 77). Human knowledge is very far from being constituted by 'pure thought' alone; indeed, without the stimulus of the senses, thought itself would not occur.

The debate over the respective roles of reason and experience is thus resolved in Leibniz in a sane and judicious compromise between extreme empiricism and extreme apriorism. For Spinoza the value of experience is strictly limited: it provides the basis for only a confused form of cognition, which human beings need only where they are dealing with those matters that cannot be inferred from the essences of things (G IV. 47; C 196). For Descartes, experience, if not exactly a *pis aller*, is at least a secondary resource: the scientist should aim at self-evidence and deductive rigour, only making use of observation to narrow things down when our principles, because of their simplicity and generality, allow for a number of possible explanations of a given phenomenon (AT VI. 64; CSM I. 144). Leibniz is as articulate as Descartes and Spinoza in stressing the vital importance of our innate powers of reasoning, without which, he says, we would be no better than the beasts, whose 'sequences of impressions' are no more than a 'shadow of reasoning', a mere 'passage from one image to another' (RB 51). But the exercise of our reason cannot be separated from the exercise of our sensory faculties: the senses 'provide the occasion for its use, and successful experiments serve to corroborate its findings' (RB 50). Leibniz, like Descartes and Spinoza, was searching for a rational understanding of reality which goes beyond mere experience; but it is Leibniz more than any other writer of the seventeenth century who makes it clear that faith in a universe whose processes are, in principle, transparent and accessible to reason need not imply any commitment to a dogmatically aprioristic view of human knowledge.

3
Substance

Just as there is no sunlight without the sun, so nothing can exist without the cooperation of God. Without that cooperation, all created things would go to nothing. But a created thing may still be called a *substance*; for by this . . . we mean only that it is the sort of thing that can exist independently of any other created thing (Descartes, Letter to 'Hyperaspistes', August 1641).

Spinoza taught (1) that there is only one substance in the world; (2) that this substance is God; and (3) that all particular beings—the sun, the moon, plants, animals, men, their ideas, their imaginings, their desires—are modifications of God . . . This is the most monstrous and absurd hypothesis that could be imagined . . . (Pierre Bayle, *Dictionnaire historique et critique*, 1697).

The result of each view of the universe, as seen from a certain position, is a substance which expresses the universe from this perspective . . . Each substance is like a world apart, independent of every other thing, except for God (Leibniz, *Discours de métaphysique*, 1686).[1]

The classical background

The notion of substance lies at the heart of rationalist metaphysics. The term has a faintly archaic ring: it is very unusual to find discussions about substance in modern philosophical work, and the notion plays no role in science any more—except in the informal sense, meaning 'a kind of stuff', as when a chemist says 'the substance changed colour on being heated'. But questions about substance, in the seventeenth century, were questions about the ultimate constituents of the universe, or the ultimate nature of reality; and though the term 'substance' has lost its appeal, these questions certainly have not.

The modern reader is nevertheless apt to be sceptical about the value of the seventeenth-century debate about substance. Some of our reservations may arise from seeing the very diversity of the theories which were put forward. As is well known, Descartes, the 'dualist', argued that there were two substances, or at least two fundamental kinds of substance; Spinoza, the 'monist', that there was, and could be, only one substance; and Leibniz, the 'pluralist', that there must be an infinite number of substances. If such radically incompatible answers could be so earnestly advocated, we may feel inclined to suspect that there was something wrong with the terms of the enquiry. This indeed was the conclusion reached by David Hume in the following century, when he roundly declared in his *Treatise of Human Nature* (1739) that the notion of material substance was an 'unintelligible chimera', while the whole question concerning the substance of the soul was 'absolutely unintelligible'.[2]

In order to be properly understood and evaluated, however, the theories of Descartes, Spinoza, and Leibniz need to be seen in context. The preoccupation with substance in the seventeenth century did not spring up out of nothing, but represented a continuation of a long philosophical tradition with its roots in Aristotle. For Aristotle, as for Plato, philosophical understanding was seen as dependent on the possibility of identifying something stable and permanent, despite a world of constant change and alteration.[3] One way in which Aristotle defined 'substance' was as that which endures through change: although something may be *F* today and not-*F* tomorrow, there is none the less an underlying subject which remains the same.[4] The permanent underlying properties of a thing were said to be its *essential* properties (as opposed to its *accidental* properties); the notion of substance was thus linked to the idea of a thing's enduring essence or 'essential nature'.

Aristotle also approached the concept of substance from a logical point of view. In the *Categories* he suggested that something counts as a substance if it is the subject of predicates, but cannot itself be predicated of something else. Thus, stripedness is not a substance, since it can be predicated of another subject (as when we say 'a tiger is striped'); but an individual tiger, which is the subject of which stripedness and other properties are predicated, would be, for Aristotle, a substance.[5] Further reflection on this led Aristotle to make a distinction between what exists *in* a subject (as stripedness exists in, or belongs to, a tiger) and what exists in its own right. A substance is thus regarded as that which exists on its own, or has independent existence.[6]

This cluster of notions—substance as the enduring subject of change, as essence or nature, as the subject of predication, and as that which has an independent existence[7]—had become deeply ingrained into the thought patterns of the sixteenth and seventeenth centuries, though different thinkers attached varying importance to difference elements of the cluster. It is thus no surprise, for example, to find the notion of that which is a 'subject of predication' playing a key role in Leibniz's theory of substance. In his *Discourse on Metaphysics*, Leibniz begins his inquiries with the observation that 'when several predicates are attributed to one and the same subject, and this subject is not attributed to any other, one calls this subject an individual substance' (GP IV. 432; P 18). Leibniz, it is true, saw himself as a reconciler of traditional and modern philosophies; but even those who saw themselves as radically opposed to the Aristotelian-scholastic world view often retained much of its intellectual furniture. This is fully apparent from the definition of substance which Descartes offers in the *Principles of Philosophy*—a definition which exactly reflects the concept of substance as that which has independent existence: 'By substance we can understand nothing other than a thing which exists in such a way as to depend on no other thing for its existence' (*Principles* I, 51). Or, as Descartes puts it elsewhere: 'the notion of a substance is just this—that it can exist by itself, i.e. without the aid of any other substance' (AT VII. 226; CSM II. 159). This notion of independence also plays a crucial role in Spinoza's account of substance and in his construction of a monistic theory of reality. Thus a substance, for Spinoza, cannot be causally dependent on anything else, but must be *causa sui*— its own cause (cf. *Ethics* I, prop. 6 and 7). This brief list of Aristotelian and scholastic echoes could undoubtedly be extended much further; and although by the end of this chapter we shall have traced the ways in which the views of Descartes, Spinoza, and Leibniz diverge on the question of what counts as a substance, what should also become clear is the extent to which these divergent views were developed from strikingly similar sets of conceptual equipment.

Descartes on substance: God, mind, and matter

In establishing his own existence, so long as he is thinking (see Chapter 2, p. 41), Descartes formed a conception of himself as a *res cogitans*, a thinking thing. Thought alone, of all the properties he has hitherto attributed to himself, cannot conceivably be separated from him in any sceptical scenario, no matter how 'hyperbolical', that he can invent. I may perhaps have other properties, says Descartes in the Second Meditation; but if I confine myself to what cannot conceivably be doubted I am left with the notion of a 'thing that thinks'. 'Thinking', Descartes explains, comprises the whole range of conscious activity: 'But what am I? A thing that thinks. What is that? A thing that doubts, understands, is willing, is unwilling, and also imagines and has sensory perceptions' (AT VII. 28; CSM II. 19).

In an attempt to break out of the enclosed realm of his subjective consciousness, Descartes proceeds, in the Third Meditation, to make a survey of the ideas he finds within his consciousness; the 'first and most important' idea he becomes aware of is the idea of God. By this term 'God', he tells us, he means 'a substance that is infinite, eternal, immutable, independent, supremely intelligent, supremely powerful, and which created both myself, and everything else (if anything else there be) that exists' (AT VII. 45; CSM II. 31).

Descartes's subsequent argument for God's existence, which has been exhaustively analysed by commentators, depends on a principle which he says is 'manifest by the natural light': '*there must be at least as much in the cause as in the effect*', or (as he later formulates it), 'there is nothing in the effect that was not previously present either in a similar or a higher form in the cause' (AT VII. 135; CSM II. 97). Thus all the reality which is present in a stone must, says Descartes, be present in some way in the cause of the stone, whatever it may be (AT VII. 41; CSM II. 28). This principle (which we may dub the 'causal adequacy principle') is taken by Descartes to apply not just to ordinary effects (such as stones), but also to ideas in the mind, and in particular to what we may call their 'representational content' (or what Descartes calls their 'objective reality'[8]). If I examine what is contained or represented in my idea of God I find that what is represented is a substance that is infinite, eternal, etc; and, according to the causal adequacy principle, these various perfections that are contained in the idea must be present in whatever caused the idea. Now I can hardly be the cause of this idea since I am certainly not infinite (as I know from many imperfections, such as my ignorance on many topics). 'I could not', says Descartes, 'have the idea of an infinite substance, when I am finite, unless this idea proceeded from some substance which really was infinite' (AT VII. 45; CSM II. 31). Hence this infinite substance necessarily exists.

There is of course much in this reasoning (even in the highly compressed summary just given) that might be debated. Nicolas Malebranche, writing some thirty years after Descartes's death, displays an interestingly ambivalent attitude towards proofs based on the idea of God. On the one hand he observes that 'of the proofs of God's existence, the loftiest, the most beautiful, the primary and most solid . . . is that which invokes the idea we have of the infinite'.[9] But Malebranche goes on to insist that when we are aware of God, we are directly united with God himself—we see God directly and immediately, and not through the medium of any representative idea of the kind Descartes posited. Descartes maintained that although I myself am an imperfect created being, I none the less find within my mind a representation of the infinite; Malebranche replied that it is inconceivable for a created thing to represent the infinite.[10]

This issue became a major bone of contention between Malebranche and Antoine Arnauld during the 1680s and 1690s. Arnauld had earlier criticized certain aspects of Descartes's proof (in his Fourth Set of Objections of 1641); but forty years later, in his 'True and False Ideas' (*Des vraies et fausses idées*, 1683), he launched a major attack on Malebranche in the course of which he supported the Cartesian notion of an idea as essentially representative of its object.[11] 'It is not true', he later wrote to Malebranche, 'that a modality of our soul, which is finite, cannot represent an infinite thing; on the contrary, however finite our perceptions may be, there are some which have to be understood as infinite in the sense that they represent the infinite' (letter of 22 May 1694).

The prolonged and complex debate between Arnauld and Malebranche over the status of the idea of God cannot be evaluated here. But two general aspects of it are worth underlining. First, the debate illustrates something it is easy to forget from a twentieth-century perspective: that Descartes's arguments for the existence of God generated as much, if not more, interest in the seventeenth century than his mathematics or physics or psychology. It is important to remember, moreover, that for Descartes the struggle to establish God's existence was not, so to speak, a self-contained problem, one which could be relegated, as it might be today, to a special compartment marked 'philosophy of religion'. On the contrary, without an effective proof of the existence of a creator who is all-perfect and the source of truth, the whole Cartesian strategy for escaping from the subjective world of doubt, and establishing a reliable system of objective knowledge, crumbles away.

The second important aspect of the Malebranche–Arnauld debate is the doubt it casts on the supposedly straightforward nature of Cartesian metaphysics. Descartes himself claimed that his arguments were so simple, so free of obscurities and preconceptions, that they could be followed by any attentive person of simple good sense (AT X. 502; CSM II. 403). But the exchange between Malebranche and Arnauld forcefully illustrates the extent to which even such a basic item of Descartes's vocabulary as the term 'idea' is fraught with problems. Even back in the 1640s Descartes had had trouble explaining exactly what he meant by this term. Thomas Hobbes, in his Third Set of Objections, had taken the term to refer to some kind of simple *image*—a suggestion that Descartes adamantly rejected (AT VII. 179; CSM II. 126). But if not an image, what exactly is an idea? Is it simply a mode of thought, a 'modality of perception' as

Arnauld interpreted it, or was it regarded by Descartes as some kind of intermediate mental entity (as Malebranche supposed)? What exactly does it mean to say that an idea 'represents' an object? And is it necessary to construe the representational relation in terms of some kind of resemblance?[12] The points of controversy which emerge between Malebranche and Arnauld give a vivid sense of just how difficult is the Cartesian project of describing with unassailable clarity, and in a way which is free from all taint of preconceived opinion, the mental acts and processes of the meditator as he searches for knowledge.

If we turn now to more specific problems concerning Descartes's proof of God's existence from the idea of God, it is the causal adequacy principle which seems to present the greatest difficulty. Part of Descartes's reasoning for holding to the maxim 'nothing in the effect which was not previously present in the cause' seems to have been a rather crude 'heirloom' view of causation—that the only way an effect can come to have some property is by having it passed on, heirloom fashion, from its cause. This is close to the view which Bishop George Berkeley referred to some seventy years later as the 'old known axiom', 'Nothing can give to another that which it hath not itself.'[13] Such a thesis would appear to deny the possibility of 'emergent' properties (for example, the properties which emerge when two elements are compounded, even though they were not present in either of the constituents). Descartes does not, however, insist that the features present in an effect should always be present in precisely the self-same form in its cause;[14] and elsewhere he accepts a rather more general formulation of the relation that must obtain between cause and effect: 'The effect is like the cause' (AT V. 156; CB 17). In its general formulation, this slogan seems to encapsulate Descartes's commitment to the notion of a rationally intelligible link between cause and effect. If an effect has some feature F, then that feature cannot (as he says elsewhere) have come from nothing; it must have been present, in some form, in the cause (AT VII. 135; CSM II. 97). It follows from this that causal relations cannot be reducible to mere regularity or a repeated conjunction of events (as Hume was later to propose); rather, there must be some necessary connection—some link in terms of shared or common features—between cause and effect.[15] We shall return to this thesis later in this chapter, and also in the next, when we come to discuss the view taken by Descartes and the other rationalists of the nature of the apparent causal interactions between mind and body.[16]

At this stage of his 'way of discovery', however, Descartes is not yet ready to make any assertions about the physical universe. He is simply aware first of himself as a thinking substance, and now, secondly, of God, the supremely powerful substance who created him and placed the idea of himself within him 'to be as it were, the mark of the craftsman stamped on his work' (AT VII. 51; CSM II. 35). But Descartes has noted along the way that in addition to himself and God, he also finds within him the idea of 'extended, corporeal substance' or matter—that which occupies space and can be characterized in terms of length, breadth, and depth (AT VII. 43; CSM II. 30).[17] Now the existence of an idea is no guarantee that anything corresponding to the idea actually exists; and the hyperbolical doubts of the First Meditation have raised the possibility that the whole external world is a 'chimera'. The situation is radically altered, however, once Descartes has (or takes himself to have) established the existence of a perfect God who is the source of truth and who would not allow him to be systematically deceived. Given this foundation of certainty, Descartes can proceed to invoke a fact that he was aware of all along, namely his strong propensity to believe that his ideas of corporeal objects come directly from external objects. In the light of this, he does not see 'how God could be anything other than a deceiver if the ideas were transmitted from a source other than corporeal things' (AT VII. 80; CSM II. 55). It follows, Descartes concludes in the Sixth Meditation, that the external world does indeed exist; and although many of his sensory impressions of that world may be confused and misleading, at least he has some prospect of developing a reliable physical theory, provided he confines himself to his clear and distinct ideas of corporeal substance, that is, 'all those which viewed in general terms are comprised within the subject matter of pure mathematics' (ibid.).

From this very brief résumé, it should at least be clear that by the end of his metaphysical meditations, Descartes has established the existence of three substances: first, himself, *res cogitans* or thinking substance; second, God, the infinite substance who created him; and third, matter or extended substance.[18] In the *Meditations*, which is designed to avoid technical language as far as possible, Descartes does not do very much to unpack the notion of substance; indeed, he prefers wherever possible to avoid the Latin term *substantia*, speaking instead of *res cogitans* and *res extensa* (literally 'thinking thing' and 'extended thing'. Cf. AT VII. 78; CSM II. 54).[19] But in his 1644 *Principles of Philosophy*, which was designed as an academic textbook, Descartes goes into much more detail. Starting from the scholastic idea that the term substance conveys the notion of something which 'depends on no other thing for its existence' (see above, p. 77), Descartes remarks that it is only God who qualifies as a substance in the strict sense of depending on 'no other thing whatsoever'. (The whole of Spinoza's metaphysics, as we shall see, can in a sense be seen as a meditation on this one thought.) But a created thing can, Descartes asserts, be considered as a substance in a secondary sense, in so far as, unlike qualities or attributes which can only exist 'in' something else, it can be said to exist 'on its own', needing nothing else (except of course for the continuous divine action of God which preserves it, or keeps it in existence: *Principles* I, 51–2).[20]

With regard to created substance, we can, Descartes asserts, have two clear and distinct notions or ideas—one of thinking substance, the other of extended substance. Extension and thought are the 'principal attributes' of matter and mind respectively:

Each substance has one principal property which constitutes its nature or essence and to which all its other properties are referred. Thus extension in length, breadth and depth constitutes the nature of corporeal substance, and thought constitutes the nature of thinking substance. Everything else which can be attributed to body presupposes extension and is merely a mode of an extended thing; and similarly whatever we find in mind is simply one of the various modes of thinking (*Principles* I, 53).

Here in a nutshell is Descartes's celebrated 'dualistic' theory of substance, according to which all the various features we attribute to things are reducible to 'modes' or modifications either of thinking stuff or of extended stuff. But on closer examination this apparently very tidy schema begins to lose some of its symmetry.

The asymmetry of Descartes's dualism

The first signs of asymmetry between *res cogitans* and *res extensa* emerge when one scrutinizes Descartes's account of the physical world. For in the case of what Descartes calls 'corporeal substance', it turns out that what is involved is not the common-sense (Aristotelian) world of a plurality of individual substances— horses and trees and stones—but rather a single, indefinitely modifiable, indefinitely extended stuff which is characterized simply by the fact that it is 'extended':

> When I examine the nature of matter, I find it to consist merely in its extension in length, breadth and depth, so that whatever has three dimensions is part of this matter, and there can be no completely empty space, that is space containing no matter, because we cannot conceive of space without conceiving in it these three dimensions and consequently matter (AT V. 52; K 221).

Matter, or 'body-in-general' as Descartes calls it elsewhere (*Principles* II, 4), is the universal corporeal substance that occupies all conceivable space. The fact that we divide the world into individual objects does not, according to Descartes, indicate that there is a plurality of independent substances. Although we may ordinarily divide the world up into distinct objects, all that is really happening is that portions of universal 'body' or corporeal substance are moving at different speeds and in different directions:

> I regard the minute parts of terrestrial bodies as being all composed of one single kind of matter, and believe that each of them could be divided repeatedly in infinitely many ways, and that there is no more difference between them than there is between stones of various different shapes cut from the same rock (*Meteorology*: AT VI. 239; ALQ I. 726).

Descartes's language when discussing the physical world is not entirely consistent, and sometimes he slips into conventional talk of ordinary objects as 'substances'.[21] But it is clear from his work as a whole that as far as the physical universe is concerned, Descartes has a monistic theory of substance, regarding all the variety of terrestrial and celestial phenomena as resulting from nothing more than local variations in the universal plenum he calls *res extensa* or 'extended stuff'.

In the case of *res cogitans* or 'thinking stuff', matters seem to be quite different. For in becoming aware of myself as a thinking thing, I am not merely becoming aware of some local modification of a universal 'thinking stuff'; on the contrary I am, according to Descartes, aware of myself as a unique particular substance—a truly individual thinking thing. Some of Descartes's critics questioned whether he was entitled to this conclusion. 'How do you know it is you that thinks, and not the world soul that thinks in you?' wrote one objector (AT III. 403; cf. K 114). More recently, critics have suggested that the famous Cogito argument might more aptly be phrased *cogitatur ergo est* ('there is thought going on, therefore [something] exists').[22] Admittedly, when Descartes describes the process of becoming aware of his existence, in the Second Meditation, he does not claim to employ the term 'I' as anything more than a convenient label: 'I do not yet know what this "I" is that thinks; it may be that other things which are unknown to me are in reality identical with the "I" of which I am aware' (AT VII. 27; CSM II. 18). None the less, by the time he reaches the Sixth Meditation he takes himself to have established the existence of an individual thinking substance that is distinct from any other substance. The point is reiterated in the *Principles*:

> From the mere fact that each of us understands himself to be a thinking thing, and is capable, in thought, of excluding from himself every other substance, whether thinking or extended, it is certain that each of us, regarded in this way, is really distinct from every other thinking substance and from every corporeal substance (*Principles* I, 60).

Descartes at least has the beginnings of an argument for maintaining that he must be distinct from anything corporeal, since he claims he can clearly and distinctly separate the idea of himself from the idea of anything extended (though there are problems

even here, as we shall see in Chapter 4). But the only support for
the claim that I am distinct from every other *thinking* substance is
the alleged mental act whereby I am aware of myself as a distinct,
thinking individual. Descartes's intuition about the uniqueness of
each individual centre of consciousness—his claim that each of us
has direct awareness of himself as an individual 'thinking thing'—
is one which many people might feel intuitively inclined to accept;
but it is not in fact clear just how introspection is supposed to
support this claim. The fact remains that Descartes gives no clear
criterion for individuating mental substances, and this is a gap
which none of his writings on the subject of the mind do anything
to fill.[23]

The radical asymmetry that exists, in Descartes's view, between
mental and physical substance is well illustrated by some remarks
on immortality in the Synopsis which was prefixed to the first
edition of the *Meditations*:

> The human body, in so far as it differs from other bodies [is not a
> substance but] is simply made up of a certain configuration of limbs and
> other accidents of this sort, whereas the human mind is not made up of
> any accidents in this way, but is a pure substance. For even if all the
> accidents of the mind change, so that it has different objects of the
> understanding and different desires and sensations, it does not on that
> account become a different mind; whereas a human body loses its
> identity merely as a result of a change in the shape of some of its parts.
> And it follows from this that while the body can very easily perish, the
> mind is immortal by its very nature (AT VII. 14; CSM II. 10).

A particular body is merely a modification of that universal
extended stuff of which the entire physical universe is composed;
it has no distinct nature of its own. But each human mind is a
distinct substance—an immortal soul.

Though this latter thesis might have won approval from some
of Descartes's audience for being comfortably in tune with
Christian doctrine, it would be wrong to suppose that it was a
thesis that was blandly and universally accepted in the intellectual
climate of the seventeenth century. On the contrary, those who
had been educated in the orthodox Aristotelian tradition were
well aware that in Aristotle's view, to talk of a body having a

mind, or a soul, is simply to say that the matter of which it is composed is organized in such a way as to enable it to perform its various functions; thus when the particular organization disintegrates (as in death) it would not make any sense to suppose that the 'soul' could somehow survive as a separate entity.[24] Admittedly Aristotle had, in one strange and furiously debated passage, introduced the concept of an 'active intellect', which, being defined in terms of 'pure activity', was supposed to be by nature incorruptible; but this curious notion could not be taken as providing unambiguous support for anything approaching personal or individual immortality.[25] However that may be, Descartes's assertion that each individual mind is a genuine independent substance which is 'by its very nature immortal' is not something for which he at any point produces any real argument. And this is but one manifestation of a major lacuna in the Cartesian philosophy: the rationalist programme for complete and transparent explanation of the principles underlying all phenomena—a programme which Descartes could claim to have worked out in some detail in his account of the material world—all too often breaks down when it comes to the realm of the mental. Despite Descartes's frequent claim that we have a clear and distinct idea of thinking substance or mind, he offers, as we have seen, no convincing account of how minds are individuated; and when it comes to his account of the operations of the mind, there are (as we shall see in the next chapter) large areas of our human experience which remain, in the Cartesian system, ultimately mysterious.

Spinoza and independent substance

Summarizing his views in the *Principles*, Descartes speaks of three notions of substance: in addition to ordinary 'thinking substance' (*substantia cogitans*) and 'corporeal substance' (*substantia corporealis*), we can also have a 'clear and distinct idea of uncreated and independent thinking substance, that is, of God' (*Principles* I, 54). But he had earlier admitted that the term 'substance', in so far as it implies complete independence, should strictly speaking be applied to God alone:

There is only one substance which can be understood to depend on no other thing whatsoever, namely God . . . Hence the term 'substance' does not apply *univocally*, as they say in the Schools, to God and to other things; that is, there is no distinctly intelligible meaning of the term which is common to God and his creatures (I, 51).

At the heart of Spinoza's metaphysics is this 'strict' notion of substance as that which has completely independent existence; indeed, Spinoza leaves no room at all for the Cartesian way of talking, which allows created things to be spoken of as 'substances' in a secondary sense. The uncompromising and radical nature of Spinoza's position is not immediately apparent from the definition of substance which is to be found at the start of the *Ethics*. *Substantia* is there defined as *id quod in se est et per se concipitur*—literally 'that which exists in itself and is conceived through itself' (*Ethics* I, def. 3). To most of his readers, the first part of the definition would probably have called to mind the Aristotelian distinction (referred to above, p. 77) between what exists in, or can be predicated of, a subject, and what is not predicated of anything else but can, so to speak, stand 'on its own'. Thus, although the monistic theory which Spinoza begins to unravel struck most of his readers as highly unorthodox, they would readily have accepted this initial notion of a substance as that which stands on its own or 'exists in itself' as quite uncontroversial.

It might be thought that the whole of Spinoza's metaphysics depends on an illegitimate slide between something's standing on its own in this weak sense of being a subject of predication (and not needing to exist 'in' anything else), and something's standing on its own in the strong sense of being wholly self-sufficient and independent. The two senses are in fact quite distinct: a cat could be regarded as a substance in the weak sense, since it can stand on its own as a subject of predication (unlike, say, furriness, which can only exist as a predicate of a cat or some other animal); but it is not a substance in the strong sense, since it is far from being wholly self-sufficient and independent (it needed a cause or causes to bring it into existence, and it requires external things, like oxygen, to sustain it). It would probably be unfair to suggest that Spinoza deliberately equivocated between these two senses in which something may be said to stand on its own, or exist 'in itself'. But it is true to say that Spinoza's definition of substance is unproblematic only if taken in the first sense; whereas the monistic metaphysics he is aiming for—a metaphysics that struck many of his contemporaries as highly controversial—can be constructed only if it is taken in the second sense.

As for the second part of Spinoza's definition—a substance is that which is 'conceived through itself'—this has been exhaustively analysed by commentators, and several different interpretations have been offered of what is meant. Spinoza himself, however, supplies a reasonably clear gloss on what he has in mind. *S* is conceived 'through itself' means, we are told, that *S* is such that a concept of it can be formed without the need for the concept of any other thing.[26] Spinoza s thought here seems to be that since a substance is wholly independent and self-sufficient, and since 'A true idea must agree with its object' (*Ethics* I, ax. 6), the corresponding idea or concept of that substance must similarly be independent and self-sufficient; in other words, it cannot be the case that forming a concept of *S* obliges us to think of some other thing apart from *S*. A good example of the use to which Spinoza puts this part of his definition of substance is to be found in his demonstration that a substance cannot be produced by something else: 'If a substance could be produced by something else, the knowledge of it would have to depend on the knowledge of its cause; so (by def. 3) it would not be a substance' (I, prop. 6, cor.).

Despite the unorthodox destination which Spinoza has in prospect, the first few propositions concerning substance and attributes which are demonstrated in the *Ethics* would have seemed, to readers who were aware of the standard Aristotelian notion of substance, and of the use which the Cartesians had made of that notion, to be covering familiar territory. On the standard Aristotelian-scholastic view, a substance has an essential nature or 'essence' that makes it what it is. Descartes followed this terminology, but added the thesis that each substance is defined by a 'principal attribute' which 'constitutes its essence'; he further argued that all the other properties of a substance are to be analysed as 'modes' or modifications of this principal attribute (*Principles* I, 53). Spinoza follows this line, laying it down in Definition 4 that an attribute is 'what the intellect perceives of a substance as constituting its essence'.[27] Given this apparatus, Spinoza is able to show quite straightforwardly that, for example, 'two substances having different attributes have nothing in common with one another' (*Ethics* I, prop. 2). There is some basis for this in Descartes: given that mental substance and physical substance are defined in terms of different attributes of thought and extension, since every property of a mind must be a mode of thought, and every property of a body must be a mode of extension, there can, in the Cartesian system, be no scope for any 'overlapping' properties.[28]

After this groundwork, Spinoza is able to proceed to a more controversial claim: that there cannot be two distinct substances of the same nature. It should be clear from the discussion earlier in this chapter that Descartes would have strongly rejected this, since he maintained that there was a plurality of minds, each defined by the same essential attribute, thought (though as we have noted he had trouble providing a satisfactory way of individuating these minds). Spinoza puts his objection to a plurality of substances of the same nature somewhat as follows: since a substance is identified in terms of its defining nature or essence, then if we suppose there are two substances of exactly the same nature, there would be no way of distinguishing them as separate things: 'one could not be conceived to be distinguished from another' (prop. 5, dem.).[29]

An obvious 'common-sense' question that comes to mind here is: why should there not be several substances which are *numerically* distinct, even though they share the same essential nature— just as, for example, there can be many examples of a particular model of automobile, all sharing the same essential design and structure? Spinoza's answer to this hinges on his remarkable claim (to be discussed later on) that *existence* is part of a substance's essence: since a substance is independent and self-sufficient, it is *causa sui*—its own cause—and hence it 'pertains to its nature to exist' (prop. 7). Now let us suppose, to pursue our modern example, that there are twenty examples of a certain model of car in existence. Spinoza would argue that the reason for this number cannot be contained in the essence or definition of the model in question. 'No definition', he insists, 'involves or expresses any given number of individuals.' He goes on: 'A definition expresses nothing other than the nature of the thing defined. For example, the nature of a triangle expresses nothing but the simple nature of the triangle, but not any specific number of triangles' (prop. 8, schol. 2). It follows from this that the cause or reason why there are twenty, or thirty, or a hundred examples of our model of car must lie somewhere outside the definition or essence of the model in question. But in that case, our plurality cannot be a plurality of *substances*, since in the case of a substance the cause of its existence must be contained in its very nature or essence. There cannot, therefore, be a plurality of substances sharing the same essence.[30]

The proposition 'there are no two substances of the same nature' marks a crucial stage in the development of Spinoza's system. In putting this proposition forward Spinoza is taking a decisive step down a road which will take him far away from the common ground, familiar both to the traditional Aristotelians and to the 'modern' Cartesians, from which he began. Interestingly enough, the claim that there cannot be two substances which are essentially the same (and only numerically distinct) is one which also finds a central place in Leibniz's metaphysical system, though both the rationale offered for it by Leibniz, and the use which he makes of it, are, as we shall see, very different from anything to be found in Spinoza.

'God or nature'

The proposition that 'there cannot be two substances of the same nature' (*Ethics* I, prop. 5) enables Spinoza to proceed forthwith to a demonstration of the proposition that 'one substance cannot be produced by another substance' (prop. 6). In establishing this, Spinoza relies on a previously established result, namely that there must be something in common between an effect and its cause (prop. 3). As far as his allegiance to this latter thesis is concerned, Spinoza is on common ground with the Cartesians (see above, p. 81). What Spinoza's 'causal similarity principle' (as we may call it) comes down to is that causes and effects cannot be mere sets of correlated phenomena; they must share some common feature which provides a rationally accessible *link* between them. There is some analogy here between the 'link' that obtains between the premisses and conclusion of a valid argument; indeed, there is a general tendency in rationalist thought to assimilate what we nowadays often think of as the two distinct notions of 'logical necessity' and 'causal necessity'.[31] For a syllogistic argument to be valid, the terms that are present in the conclusion must be contained in the premisses; we are thus able to see where the result 'came from'—the result is, as it were, generated by, or extruded from, the premisses. In like manner, the rationalist view of causation takes it that to make effects intelligible, it must be shown that they are in principle deducible from their causes; and for that to be the case the phenomena involved cannot be completely heterogeneous: there must be some rationally accessible similarity between the causes and effects.[32] Spinoza is thus able to take it as axiomatic that 'knowledge of an effect depends on, and involves, knowledge of its cause' (ax. 4). If we now return to the demonstration under discussion, given Spinoza's previous proof that there cannot be two substances which share the same nature, it follows that if two substances are distinct, they will not have anything in common; hence, given the causal similarity principle, there can be no basis for a causal connection between them.

A substance, then, is independent of any other causes, and thus must be regarded as *causa sui*, its own cause. Spinoza now moves on to demonstrate that a substance so defined cannot be finite, since 'finite' has been defined as that which can be 'limited by something else of the same nature' (def. 2), and it has already been shown that there cannot be two substances of the same nature. A substance, then, is necessarily infinite (prop. 8). Henceforth, this self-causing infinite substance is identified with God, previously defined as an 'absolutely infinite being' (def. 6); and it is further shown that this being is indivisible (prop. 13), unique (prop. 14), eternal (prop. 19), and all-inclusive (prop. 15). From this last proposition, which Spinoza expresses by saying 'whatever is, is in God' (*quidquid est, in Deo est*), there follows a strikingly unorthodox thesis which was seen by many as taking the author of the *Ethics* perilously close to atheism. God, we are told in Proposition 18, cannot be regarded as the '*transeunt*' cause of the universe (i.e. a cause operating beyond itself), but must be the 'immanent cause of all things'. So far from being something outside the universe, God is in a sense identical with the universe; he is 'that eternal and infinite Being we call God or Nature—*Deus seu Natura*' (*Ethics* IV, Preface: G II. 206; C 544).

Spinoza's conclusions here may seem idiosyncratic, but in fact they represent the logical endpoint of various lines of thought that were part of his intellectual heritage. The idea of the immanence of God, the identity of creator and creation, was one he would have encountered in the Jewish cabbalistic teachings to which he was exposed in his early years.[33] A fact less often noticed is that there are immanentist tendencies, or at least hints of immanentism, in a number of seventeenth-century philosophers raised in the Christian tradition. The phrase 'God or Nature' was not invented by Spinoza: it comes in Descartes's *Principles*;[34] and although Descartes uses the orthodox language of creation, he is reported to have observed that an 'immeasurable and omnipotent' God cannot but be present within the world (AT V. 171; CB 40). Again, Nicolas Malebranche, though he never departs from creationist orthodoxy, asserts in one of the most celebrated theses of the *Recherche de la vérité* that 'we see all things in God'. And by this he means not just that our minds are enlightened by divine wisdom (though he does stress this) but also that 'all creatures, even the most material and terrestrial, are in God, though in a wholly spiritual way that is incomprehensible to us'.[35] The importance of these parallels should not be overstressed, but they do show that in the seventeenth century the concept of God was not (as we may be inclined to suppose today) a fixed and unalterable package, but was constantly evolving. Spinoza was by no means alone in struggling to find a coherent philosophical answer to the problem of how an all-embracing and all-pervasive God could be related to the material world. But his solution was more radical and uncompromising than anything that had gone before; and the immediate banning of the *Ethics* on publication is testimony to how far it exceeded the limits of permissible orthodoxy.

The existence of uncreated substance in Descartes and Spinoza

Spinoza's theory of substance can be regarded as an elegant unravelling of the concept of a wholly independent, self-sufficient, all-embracing being; but his long chain of demonstrations will remain no more than an abstract and ultimately sterile exercise unless it can be shown that the substance he describes actually exists. One might be tempted to suggest that this is no problem, since we know the universe exists, and Spinoza's substance is not distinct from the universe. But that would be too simple; for there are many properties that are supposed to be necessarily true of Spinozan substance, but which certainly do not seem to be necessarily true (or indeed true at all) of the universe—for example that it is infinite, self-causing, eternal and, moreover, something which is not only extended but also conscious (*Ethics* II, prop. 1 and 2). The paradoxical nature of Spinoza's view that there is but one single substance having the attributes both of extension *and* of thought was strongly underlined by Pierre Bayle, writing some twenty years after Spinoza's death: Spinoza's hypothesis, asserted Bayle, is 'diametrically opposed to the most evident notions of our mind'.[36]

In establishing the existence of the unique, infinite, and all-embracing substance Spinoza relies heavily on the proposition that substance, as defined, is *causa sui*, the cause of itself. The notion of something's being self-causing may strike the modern reader as exceedingly strange; indeed, it has appeared to some to border on the absurd. But here, as so often, Spinoza's ideas did not burst forth out of nothing; the question of whether God could be regarded as *causa sui* had in fact received extensive discussion from theologians and philosophers in the preceding centuries. Aquinas had argued that if 'cause' were taken in the sense of an 'efficient' cause (that is, the productive agency that generates some effect or brings it into being), then nothing could be said to be *causa sui*; for an efficient cause must be prior to its effect, and nothing can be prior to itself.[37] Descartes, however, took issue with the Thomists, arguing that there is a real and positive sense in which God can be said to be the cause of himself; in the second of his proofs of God's existence in the Third Meditation he argued that since we do not derive our existence from ourselves, we must ultimately have been produced by a self-causing being—a being that has the power of existing through its own might, or existing 'through itself' (*per se*) (AT VII. 50; CSM II. 34).[38] Commenting on this argument, he wrote:

> There is no need to say that God is the efficient cause of himself, since this might give rise to a verbal dispute. But the fact that God derives his existence from himself, or has no cause apart from himself, depends not on nothing but on the real immensity of his power. Hence, when we perceive this, we are quite entitled to say that in a sense he stands in the same relation to himself as an efficient cause does to its effect, and hence that he derives his existence from himself in the positive sense (AT VII. 111; CSM II. 80).

The celebrated theologian Antoine Arnauld objected to this talk of God's deriving existence from himself in a causal sense. 'If anyone asks why God exists,' he wrote in the Fourth Set of Objections in 1641, 'we should not try to find in God some efficient cause, or quasi-efficient cause; instead we should confine our answer to saying that the reason lies in the nature of a supremely perfect being' (AT VII. 213; CSM II. 149).

When Spinoza talks of God as *causa sui*, what he has in mind is something closer to the notion referred to by Arnauld—that the *reason* for God's existence lies in his nature or essence. Something is *causa sui*, we are told, when 'its essence involves its existence, or its nature is such that it cannot be conceived of except as existing' (*Ethics* I, def. 1). Modern readers may find this a curious sense of 'cause', but it needs to be remembered that in the philosophical Latin of the seventeenth century the term *causa* was still used in a very wide sense, often encompassing what we should nowadays call reasons rather than causes.[39] It is striking that when he comes to demonstrate the existence of God (or substance) Spinoza actually uses the terms 'reason' and 'cause' more or less interchangeably:

For each thing there must be assigned a cause or reason [*causa seu ratio*] for its existence or non-existence. . . . And this reason or cause [*ratio seu causa*] must be taken to be contained either in the nature of the thing or outside it. For example in the case of a round square, the very nature of the thing provides a reason why it does not exist (namely because it involves a contradiction). In the case of substance, by contrast, the reason for its existence follows from its nature alone, since that nature involves existence (*Ethic* I, prop. 11, dem.).

It is clear, then, that Spinoza proposes to demonstrate God's existence purely a priori, from a consideration of the nature or essence of God.[40] This approach to proving God's existence was far from new. Descartes, as we have seen, took an a posteriori route in the Third Meditation: starting from perceived effects (first, the idea of a perfect being; second, his own existence as a dependent being), he went on to infer the existence of God as the cause of these things. But later on, in the Fifth Meditation, he produced a completely different type of argument that proceeded purely a priori and invoked precisely the idea that Spinoza introduces in the above quotation: that God's essence or nature implies his existence. 'Existence', wrote Descartes, 'can no more be separated from the essence of God than the fact that its three angles equal two right angles can be separated from the essence of a triangle' (AT VII. 66; CSM II. 46).[41]

Since the time of Kant, this type of proof of the existence of God has been known as 'the ontological argument', though talk of *the* argument is perhaps misleading, since there are in fact several different versions involving rather different lines of reasoning. The earliest known version, that of St Anselm of Canterbury, argues that if God is defined as 'a being than which nothing greater can be conceived', then such a being must really exist (since there would be a contradiction in supposing the greatest conceivable being to exist only in the mind). By the late Middle Ages this argument had few supporters, mainly as a result of the searching critique to which Thomas Aquinas had subjected it in the thirteenth century. There was therefore widespread surprise that Descartes should have chosen to adopt a line of reasoning whose invalidity was taken to have been decisively established centuries before.

Descartes's version of the argument is more straightforward than Anselm's, and for that reason its flaws are perhaps all the more glaringly obvious. Quite simply, God is defined by Descartes as a 'supremely perfect being', and he then argues that 'it is a contradiction to think of God (that is a supremely perfect being) lacking existence (that is, lacking a perfection)' (AT VII. 66; CSM II. 46). The problem here is that, even if we accept the curious premiss that existence is a perfection,[42] the most the argument seems to establish is the hypothetical result that *if* there is a being who qualifies for the title of 'supremely perfect' (so defined) then such a being cannot but exist. This, essentially, is the Thomist critique of Anselm's version of the argument. Descartes's critic Johannes Caterus, who was a priest trained in the Thomist tradition, exposed the weakness of Descartes's reasoning very clearly, as follows:

> Even if it is granted that a supremely perfect being carries the implication of existence in virtue of its very title, it still does not follow that the existence in question is anything actual in the real world; all that follows is that the concept of existence is inseparably linked to the concept of the supreme being. So you cannot infer that the existence of God is anything actual, unless you suppose that the supreme being actually exists; for then he will contain all perfections, including the perfection of real existence (First Set of Objections: AT VII. 99; CSM II. 72).

Despite the heavy criticism that Descartes incurred for including the ontological argument in his *Meditations*, he refused to abandon it. Indeed, in the *Principles of Philosophy* he not only retained the argument but gave it pride of place, reversing the order of the *Meditations* and presenting it as the first argument for God's existence. 'The existence of God', he asserts, 'is validly inferred from the fact that necessary existence is contained in our concept of God' (*Principles* I, 14). Spinoza was, of course, heavily influenced by Descartes's *Principles*; but even without that influence the geometrical style chosen for the *Ethics*, with its method of deducing propositions from initial definitions, must have seemed specially suited for an attempt at demonstrating God's existence purely a priori.

Rather than relying on the notion of perfection, as Descartes does for his ontological proof, Spinoza bases his own argument directly on his central notion of substance.[43] He argues in the *Ethics* (I, prop. 7) that since a substance cannot be produced by anything else (see above, p. 91), it must therefore be *causa sui*; and if something is *causa sui*, then, by Definition 1, its essence involves its existence. Therefore it must exist (G II. 49; C 412). The argument is almost embarrassingly brief, and needless to say is subject to exactly the same strictures that were raised against Descartes by Caterus: all that seems to follow is that *if* there is anything that counts as a substance and therefore as *causa sui*, it must exist; but it still remains to be shown that there is anything that qualifies for this title in the first place.

Spinoza, however, has a second demonstration up his sleeve; and although it is presented as a kind of back-up or 'alternative' proof, it is in fact far more interesting than the first, since it takes us deep into Spinoza's necessitarian theory of truth. The key to this second argument is the Spinozan denial of contingency, a thesis which emerges progressively as one reads through Part I of the *Ethics*, and which is eventually asserted explicitly at Proposition 29: 'In nature there is nothing contingent' (*In rerum natura nullum datur contingens*) (see Chapter 2, p. 59). Given that there is, for Spinoza, no room for something's merely happening to be the case, it follows that he will allow only two possibilities regarding the existence of any X: either its existence is impossible or else it is necessary. The reason for this necessity or impossibility, says Spinoza, will either be contained within the nature of X, or be outside it. Thus in the case of a round square, the reason why it cannot exist is contained within the thing itself: its nature is self-contradictory. In the case of a triangle or a circle, by contrast, we cannot deduce the necessity or impossibility of their existence from the definitions of the things themselves. But Spinoza insists that there is none the less a reason why they must or cannot exist. If we had full enough knowledge of 'the order of corporeal nature in its entirety', then we would be able to deduce 'either that the triangle now necessarily exists or that it is impossible for it now to exist' (G II. 53; C 417). The upshot is that the kind of objection that was raised against Descartes's version of the ontological argument—'granted your supremely perfect being would have to exist, how do we know that there *is*, as a matter of fact, anything which meets this definition?'—cannot arise for Spinoza. Since all existential statements (and indeed all other statements) are either necessarily true or necessarily false, Spinoza is able to argue as follows: If God does not exist, then his non-existence must be necessitated. But it cannot be necessitated by something outside the divine nature, since any supposed substance other than God could not possibly have anything in common with God, and hence could not prevent his existing.[44] So if God does not exist, his non-existence would have to be necessitated by his own nature—in other words his nature would have to involve a contradiction (like the round square). To suppose this of God, says Spinoza, is absurd. And therefore God must exist (G II. 53; C 417). God's existence, in short, is either necessary or impossible (premiss 1); it is not impossible (premiss 2); hence it is necessary. So God necessarily exists. QED.

Leibniz's critique of the ontological argument

The revival of the ontological argument first by Descartes and then by Spinoza (it had also been vigorously defended by Descartes's disciple Nicolas Malebranche in his *Recherche de la vérité*[45]) aroused considerable controversy in the late seventeenth century. Leibniz criticized the argument on several occasions, both in letters and in published papers; and though his criticisms are officially presented as objections to Descartes's views, they are equally if not more aptly applicable to Spinoza's way of formulating the argument (it is known that Leibniz visited Spinoza in Holland in 1676, and discussed the ontological argument with him). Premiss one of the argument as summarized above Leibniz had no difficulty in accepting. 'God alone', he later wrote in the *Monadology*, 'has the privilege that he must exist if he is possible' (GP VI. 614; P 186). It was the second premiss, that God's existence is possible, that Leibniz regarded as problematic. 'It may be asked', he wrote, 'whether it is in our power to set up such a being, or whether such a concept has reality and can be conceived clearly and distinctly, without contradiction. For opponents will say that the concept of a being . . . which exists through its essence is a chimera' ('Notation for Discussion with Spinoza': G P VII. 262; L 168).

Spinoza's ontological argument thus cannot go through unless it can be shown that the concept of a necessarily existing being is possible (that is, free from incoherence). And a similar stricture will apply to the Cartesian version of the argument, since Descartes presupposes that the concept of a 'supremely perfect being' is one which can be clearly and distinctly perceived—that is, which does not involve any hidden contradictions. The point that Leibniz is making here is a valuable one, and has a philosophical importance which goes far beyond the question of whether the ontological argument is sound. Both the Cartesian theory of clear and distinct ideas, and the Spinozan notion of adequate ideas that are self-manifestingly true, seem to rely on the claim that we can, by the light of reason alone, determine whether or not a concept is coherent.[46] Leibniz's point is that matters may not be this simple: you may think you have an idea of X, but X may in fact be an incoherent notion. In a short paper published in 1684, Leibniz put the point neatly as follows:

> We cannot safely draw inferences from definitions until we know that they are real, or that they involve no contradiction. . . . Consider the idea of *the most rapid motion*, which at first sight we seem to have an idea of, since we understand what we are saying. But in fact this involves an absurdity. For suppose a wheel turns at the most rapid rate. Then anyone can see that if a spoke of the wheel is extended beyond the rim, its extremity will move more rapidly than will a nail in the rim itself (*Meditations on Knowledge Truth and Ideas*: G IV. 424; L 293, slightly adapted).

On the Leibnizian view, then, 'it is not enough to think of something in order to assert that we have an idea of it' (ibid.)—a point which could well be heeded today since it is still by no means unknown for philosophers to argue that a given phenomenon must at least be *possible* (or, as is sometimes said, at least *logically* possible) simply on the basis of their (alleged) ability to conceive of its being instantiated.[47]

Despite his acute criticisms of the ontological argument, Leibniz believed, on reflection, that it could be repaired. One line he suggested was that, since the divine essence is by definition supremely simple, indivisible, and unified, there can be no room here for any contradiction or incoherence (since all contradiction implies a clash between separate elements of a complex entity).[48] By the time he came to write the *Monadology*, Leibniz seems to have accepted Spinoza's implicit defence of the coherence of the concept of God, namely that an absolutely infinite and supremely perfect being could not contain any contradiction (G II. 53; C 417). 'Nothing', wrote Leibniz, 'can prevent the possibility of that which has no limits, no negation, and consequently no contradiction' (*Monadology*, para. 45). This claim seems far from decisive; indeed it appears vulnerable to the objection that Leibniz himself had raised earlier: 'how do we know that the thing does not imply some hidden contradiction, so that something absurd may be deduced from it?' (G IV. 359; L 386). However that may be, Leibniz's eventual acceptance, along with Descartes and Spinoza, of the ontological route to God's existence does provide at least some support for the standard charge against the 'rationalists' of attempting to establish substantive truths about the universe by rational reflection alone; this is one area where all three philosophers seem vulnerable to the challenge that Hume was to press so forcefully later in the eighteenth century—the challenge of showing how 'relations of ideas' can possibly serve to establish 'matters of fact or existence'.[49]

Leibniz and individual substance

The second half of the seventeenth century saw many attempts to defend traditional scholastic doctrines from the onslaught of Descartes and other 'modern' thinkers, and it is against this background that the distinctive theory of substance which Leibniz developed needs to be understood. Leibniz was educated in the scholastic tradition, but soon 'threw off the yoke of Aristotle' and for a time was drawn to the mechanistic atomism that had been put forward, amongst others, by Pierre Gassendi.[50] But during his four and a half years in Paris (from March 1672 to September 1676), Leibniz made a detailed study of Descartes's philosophy and met some of the leading exponents of Cartesian

ideas such as Nicolas Malebranche.[51] Leibniz admits that he
came to Descartes late ('it happened that I read almost all of the
other modern philosophers before I read him'—letter to Foucher
of 1675; GP I. 371; L 152), and from the start he was highly critical
of much of Descartes's reasoning. But it is quite clear from his
correspondence during these years that his exposure to Cartesian
ideas was an enormous source of intellectual stimulus.

One of the reasons for the appeal of the Cartesian system
among the 'progressive' thinkers of the seventeenth century was
its strongly reductionistic programme. Descartes had offered the
hope that all mental and physical phenomena could be explained
in terms of just two kinds of substance, characterized solely in
terms of the 'principal attributes' of thought and extension.
Especially as regards the physical universe, Descartes felt he had
done a great service to philosophy by sweeping away the
unhealthy plethora of 'substantial forms' and 'real qualities'
which the scholastics habitually invoked. Quite apart from
challenging the scholastics to specify clearly and distinctly exactly
what was *meant* by the 'substantial form' of water or the 'real
quality' of liquidity, the Cartesians condemned such notions as
explanatorily redundant, since all the properties of water (and all
other features of the natural world) could on their view be
explained using only modifications of the simple geometrical
attribute of extension. Descartes's own confidence in the explanatory economy of his system can be seen from the following
olive branch which (with studied irony) he holds out to the
scholastics:

> To keep peace with the scholastic philosophers, I have no wish to deny
> any further items which they may imagine in bodies over and above what
> I have described, such as their 'substantial forms' and 'real qualities' and
> so on. It simply seems to me that my arguments will be all the more
> acceptable in so far as I can make them depend on fewer entities (AT VI.
> 239; ALQ I. 726).

Spinoza, in limiting the number of substances to just one
(though he retained the two distinct *attributes* of extension and
thought[52]), pushed the reductionist programme even further, and
thus in a certain sense could be regarded as more Cartesian than

the Cartesians themselves. But in the course of his argument that there could be only one substance, Spinoza did, as we have seen, highlight a special problem for the Cartesian theory of mental substance, namely whether it could cope with the notion of *individuality*. If mind, or *res cogitans*, was to be characterized solely by the essential attribute of thought, how could there be a plurality of distinct substances? In virtue of what were they supposed to be distinct? (see above, p. 90). The Cartesians could claim that this problem did not arise in the case of matter, since particular objects, in Descartes's system, are not regarded as having any distinct individuality: they are no more than temporarily associated portions of universal extended stuff. But in the case of minds, it was not clear how two thinking substances defined in terms of the same essence could be individuated. Leibniz's general view on this matter was that (despite the difficulties of individuating minds on the Cartesian system) common sense strongly supported the view of Descartes, as against Spinoza, that there is a plurality of individual thinking substances:

> If anyone tries to maintain that there are no particular souls at all . . . he is refuted by our experience, which teaches that we are in ourselves something particular which thinks, perceives and wills, and that we are distinguished from another being who thinks and perceives and wills something else. Otherwise we fall into the opinion of Spinoza who holds that there is only one substance, God, who thinks, believes and wills one thing in me, but who thinks believes and wills an entirely contrary thing in someone else . . . ('Reflections on the doctrine of a single universal spirit': G P VI. 537; L 559.)

Leibniz was not content, however, to rest his case on an appeal to common experience. His aim was to provide a theoretical account of the nature of individuality, which would yield a 'demonstrative argument compelling us to admit individual souls' (ibid.).

The problem of individuation was one which had preoccupied Leibniz from his earliest years. It was the subject of a dissertation he wrote as a student,[53] and it formed a major theme of the first systematic exposition of his views on substance, the *Discourse on Metaphysics*, written in French in 1685. In the *Discourse*, Leibniz refers to a celebrated thesis which Thomas Aquinas had proposed in the thirteenth century in order to solve the problem of how disembodied intelligences (such as angels) were to be individuated: *omne individuum est species infima*—every individual is a 'lowest species', a distinct *kind* of being.[54] This may seem a quaint piece of theology, but it is based on inexorable logic. Since an angel, being purely spiritual, cannot be individuated spatially, it must be individuated by reference to its nature or essence; so if two angels were of an identical essence, there would be nothing to distinguish them. The upshot is that on Aquinas's view, no two angels can differ '*solo numero*': they cannot be the same in every essential respect and yet still be numerically distinct individuals.

Leibniz not only accepts this Thomist argument, but, remarkably, extends it to all substances whatsoever. 'No two substances can resemble each other entirely and differ *solo numero*', he wrote, 'and what St Thomas assures us regarding angels—*quod omne individuum sit species infima*—is true of all substances' (GP IV. 432; P 19). Part of Leibniz's rationale for extending Aquinas's reasoning to all substances may be seen in the light of his allegiance to the *Inesse* principle (discussed in Chapter 2, p. 68). Whatever is predicated of a subject, says that principle, is 'in' the subject, which Leibniz interprets as meaning that whatever can truly be said of a substance is contained in the concept of that substance. Notice that this means there cannot be, in scholastic jargon, *accidental* properties of things (in the sense that, for example, one might say that it is accidentally, or non-essentially, true of Jethro Tull that he lived in Berkshire—he might well have lived somewhere else). The *Inesse* principle means that whatever is true of something is *essentially* true of it; it is contained within the concept of that thing. Thus, says Leibniz, 'God seeing the individual notion or *haecceitas* ['thisness'] of Alexander sees in it at the same time the foundation and reason for all predicates which can truly be stated of him' (GP IV. 432; P 19). Now if *all* Alexander's properties are essentially true of him, then there cannot be another individual who has all and only Alexander's properties; for then there would be nothing to distinguish him from Alexander (the possibility of his being distinguished by accidental properties, remember, has been ruled out).[55] In short, if an individual is to be distinct from Alexander, there must be some essential difference (some difference in kind) between them. And what is true in this case is true of any two substances. Each individual substance is of a different kind (is its own '*species*'); and, conversely, if *X* and *Y* are of the same kind, they must be one and the same individual (this corresponds to the celebrated Leibnizian principle of the 'identity of indiscernibles').[56]

The view that each substance must be unique does not of itself explain Leibniz's pluralistic theory of substance. Spinoza, as we have seen, also considered that there could not be two substances of the same nature; but the direction in which this leads him is towards the idea of a single, all-embracing substance. To account fully for Leibniz's pluralism, then, we need to look further afield. A major clue lies in some fundamental intuitions which Leibniz had about the way the world is divided up (intuitions, moreover, which are not peculiar to Leibniz, but which most people would probably regard as 'common sense'). Some of the things around us seem to be simply arbitrary collections of items—mere 'heaps' or 'piles'—but others appear to have a genuine intrinsic unity. Thus a living human body, Leibniz suggested to Antoine Arnauld in 1686, is more than a 'mere phenomenon' (like a rainbow) or an 'accidental unity' (like a heap of stones) (GP II. 58; P 62).[57] Suppose, to pursue Leibniz's remark, one finds a heap of pebbles on the beach and asks what makes them constitute a single entity. The right answer, surely, is that there is nothing more to it than that they happen to be piled up by the wind or the waves, or as part of a child's game; there is no internal principle as it were holding them together. But if, on the other hand, we find a lobster on the beach, we would certainly regard it as more than a mere 'heap' of ingredients. Ultimately, as Leibniz was later to put it, there must be something there which possesses a 'true' or 'substantial' unity (GP IV. 494; P 126).

Reflections on the problem of individual unity had led Leibniz to suggest in his *Discourse on Metaphysics* that there must be in all bodies that are true unities something 'analogous to a soul', 'something which is commonly called a "substantial form"' (GP IV. 436; P 22). According to the scholastic theory, which still had considerable support when Leibniz was writing, something is what it is (a stone, an oak tree) in virtue of its 'substantial form'; further, it is the substantial form which remains constant through the various accidental changes (getting colder, growing older) which things undergo. Leibniz's readers would also have been aware of the standard scholastic definition of the soul as the 'substantial form' of the body.[58] Now to invoke substantial forms—at any rate with respect to the explanation of natural phenomena—was regarded as highly suspect by the progressive philosophers of the seventeenth century (see above, p. 102; compare Descartes, A T V I I I. 322; C S M I. 285 and Spinoza, G I V. 64; C 208), and Leibniz was well aware that his 'rehabilitation' of a term of ancient philosophy that had 'practically been banished' might provoke adverse criticism (G P I V. 435; P 21). In fact Leibniz was fairly sensitive to the criticism of Descartes and others, that substantial forms (together with their 'real qualities') were often used in a way which was vacuous from an explanatory point of view. If one wants to know how a clock tells the time, Leibniz readily admitted, it is no use invoking a 'horological quality' which comes from the 'substantial form' of clockhood (*Discourse on Metaphysics*, ch. 10). But the fact that substantial forms had fallen into disrepute did not alter the need, as Leibniz saw it, for some notion that would provide a 'principle of true unity'.

The puzzled comments which Antoine Arnauld sent to Leibniz in 1686 give a good sense of the difficulties Leibniz faced in conveying how he wished to adapt the traditional notion of substantial forms in order to give an account of individual unity. 'Is it the substantial form of a block of marble which gives it unity?' asked Arnauld. 'If so, what becomes of the substantial form when the block of marble is split into two?' (G P I I 66). Leibniz's reply is instructive:

> I hold that a block of marble is no more a genuine single substance than . . . a flock of sheep, even supposing the sheep are tied together so that they can only walk in step, and you cannot touch one of them without making all the others bleat . . . Substantial unity implies a being that is utterly indivisible and naturally indestructible, since its notion comprises everything that must happen to it . . . We cannot find such

unity in shape or movement . . . but only in a soul or substantial form analogous to that which is labelled the 'I' (GP II. 76; M 94).

Later on Leibniz made less frequent use of the term 'substantial form' partly, no doubt, because of the opprobium the notion aroused in progressive philosophical circles. He toyed with various other labels, including 'substantial unity', 'atom of substance', and 'metaphysical point' (GP IV. 482–3; P 120–1); in many of his papers he employs a term with Aristotelian connotations, 'entelechy' or 'primitive entelechy'.[59] But the term which he eventually came to favour, and which has become a trademark of the Leibnizian theory of substance, is, of course, 'monad'. Though the word was not coined by Leibniz himself,[60] its etymology makes it highly appropriate for what Leibniz had in mind. The Greek adjective *monas* means 'solitary', and the word is also used as a noun, meaning 'a unit'. The latter notion has an obvious relevance to Leibniz's purpose of characterizing 'true unities' of nature (cf. GP VI. 598; P 195); the former, as will appear in a moment, has exactly the right connotations in view of the Leibnizian thesis that monads are 'windowless'—not subject to any external influence whatsoever.

The monads: activity and self-containedness

The most important characteristic of Leibniz's units of substance is that they are *active*: 'we may give the name *entelechies* to . . . monads. For they have within them a certain perfection (*echousi to enteles*);[61] there is a self-sufficiency . . . in them which makes them the sources of their internal actions' (*Monadology*, para. 18). Now the Cartesians maintained that minds were active substances, but their definition of matter as mere extended stuff meant that the physical world was essentially inert. Though he was impressed with many aspects of the Cartesian system,[62] Leibniz came to believe that, as he put it in his *New System* of 1695, 'extended mass is not of itself enough, and use must also be made of the notion of *force*, which is fully intelligible although it falls within the sphere of metaphysics' (GP IV. 478; P 116—we shall return to the Leibnizian notion of force in the next chapter).

In rejecting a passive conception of matter, Leibniz was rejecting not only the Cartesian system, but also its chief rival, the atomistic theory of Gassendi. Explaining his dissatisfaction both with Cartesian 'extended mass' and with Gassendian 'atoms in the void', Leibniz wrote:

> I perceived that it is impossible to find the principles of true unity in matter alone, or what is merely passive . . . To find real unities, I was constrained to have recourse to what might be called an animated point or atom of substance which must embrace some element of form or activity in order to make a complete being (ibid).

There is a link between Leibniz's insistence on the active nature of substances and his *Inesse* principle. Since all the predicates of a given subject are for Leibniz contained within the concept of that subject, each substance will carry inside itself, so to speak, the 'foundation and reason for all the predicates that can truly be asserted of it' (see above, p. 69). This includes not just every state that is now attributable to it, but every state it has ever been in, and every state it ever will be in. 'The present', says Leibniz's famous dictum, 'is big with the future and laden with the past' (RB 55; P 156). According to Leibniz, then, any changes or developments in a monad are not due to the impinging of external causes but rather to the unfolding of its own internal nature. 'The natural changes of monads come from an internal principle, since an external cause would be unable to influence their inner being' (*Monadology*, para. 11). Monads are thus completely self-contained—they have 'no windows by which anything could come in or go out' (para. 7); the fact that things appear to interact causally is therefore, on the Leibnizian view, a kind of illusion.

Now this 'solitariness' of monads—the lack of any transfer of information or interaction of forces between them—might seem to suggest a chaotic universe of separate individuals all 'going their own way'. But the Leibnizian universe is in fact one of perfect rational order; there is 'no chaos, no confusion in the universe save in appearance' (para. 69). The order in the universe, since it cannot be due to causal interactions between monads, must come from none other than God: 'The influence of one monad over another is *ideal* only; it can have its effect only through the intervention of God. . . . since it is impossible for a created monad to have a physical influence on the inner nature of another . . .' (para. 51). Despite the word 'intervention', Leibniz is emphatically not following the suggestion of Malebranche that God continuously and miraculously intervenes to change X when Y changes. Rather God, in creating the universe, has made a selection from all possible monads, and brought into existence just those which will express the greatest degree of mutual harmony. Thus each monad, despite its isolated and self-enclosed nature, acts in a way which is in perfect harmony with the way in which all the others act. This is the famous doctrine of 'pre-established harmony':

> Now this connexion or adaptation of all the created things with each other, and of each with all the rest, means that each simple substance has relations which express all the others, and that consequently it is a perpetual living mirror of the universe. And just as the same town, when looked at from different sides, appears quite different, and is as it were multiplied *in perspective*, so also it happens that because of the infinite number of simple substances, it is as if there were as many different universes, which are, however, but different perspectives of a single universe, in accordance with the different points of view of each monad (paras. 56 and 57).

In a curious and fascinating transformation, Spinoza's single, infinite, all-embracing universe is fragmented into not just many, but infinitely many substances, each of which is none the less a complete and all-inclusive model of the single whole.

Causality, connection, and the role of God

The doctrine of pre-established harmony may seem nowadays to be no more than a baroque piece of metaphysical speculation; but it should be clear from what has already been said that, far from being something 'tacked on' to the rest of his system, the doctrine flows from certain central assumptions which Leibniz makes about the nature of predication and the uniqueness of each substance. Moreover, the moves which Leibniz makes in arriving at the doctrine are but one set of variations on an enduring theme of seventeenth and eighteenth-century philosophy: the problem of how to analyse the notion of causality. The rationalism of Descartes and Spinoza required, as we have seen, that there be some intelligible 'connection' between cause and effect—a connection which would make it possible, in principle, to demonstrate that a certain effect must of necessity follow from a certain cause. Nicolas Malebranche gave precise expression to this view in his *Recherche de la vérité*, when he wrote that 'a true cause is one such that the mind perceives a necessary connection between it and its effect'.[63]

On its strongest interpretation, this thesis (which we may call the 'Connection Thesis') leads to the conclusion that only God can count as a true cause, since only the effects produced by an omnipotent being are strictly and absolutely necessary (it being a contradiction to suppose that what God decides to bring about does not occur). This is exactly the line taken by Malebranche. Modern readers may be sceptical about such 'absolute' necessity, but may be inclined to allow that effects are necessitated in the weaker 'hypothetical' sense that they are deducible from explanatory laws or principles (as the conclusions of a valid argument are deducible from the premises). But this weak notion of deducibility could be satisfied by an argument of the form 'Whenever C then E; C; therefore E', where the first premiss has the status of a mere contingent generalization. The rationalists wanted something stronger: ideally, they wanted the effects to be directly deducible from the causes alone (see above, pp. 55–9). The explanatory premises or principles invoked were themselves required to be as transparent to the intellect as the principles of mathematics. This seems to be part of the rationale behind the 'causal similarity' requirement—that a cause must be of the same kind as its effect: we can, it is supposed, 'see' how like gives rise to like (how motion produces further motion, or a thought generates further thoughts), but we cannot understand how two utterly heterogeneous substances could be causally related.

Against this background, it is easy enough to see, given that Leibnizian substances are all different in kind (each being its own '*infima species*'), that there is no room for any causal interaction of a kind which would satisfy the rationalist insistence on a transparent connection between cause and effect. Hence for

Leibniz, there simply cannot be causal transactions, but only a pre-programmed harmony. The only alternatives, as Leibniz saw it, were either to posit some kind of mysterious 'influx'—an occult transaction between cause and effect, which was repugnant to his rationalist principles—or else to adopt the Malebranchian solution of giving God all the work to do. The former notion, that of an inflow or influx between cause and effect (an *influxus physicus*), had been proposed by the scholastic philosopher Francisco Suarez in his *Metaphysical Disputations* (1597); Leibniz dismissed it as a 'barbarous notion . . . metaphorical and more obscure than what it defines' (GP IV. 150; L 126).[64] The second, Malebranchian alternative Leibniz rejected as an *ad hoc* expedient, the invoking of a '*deus ex machina*' (CO 521; P 90).

But although Leibniz's solution does not have God perpetually springing on to the stage (every time, for example, that a body is caused to move), it does none the less give God a central (if rather less busy) role to play. For without appeal to the divine purpose of producing maximum harmony, there would be no explanation for the remarkable 'concomitance' (to use a term Leibniz at one point employs: CO 521; P 91) between event *A* (what we normally call a cause) and event *B* (what we normally call an effect). It is perhaps natural to wonder at this point whether it might not be better to abandon the Connection Thesis altogether. Why not propose, as David Hume was to suggest not long afterwards, that despite our strong psychological propensity to believe in some necessary link between cause and effect, all that actually occurs in nature is a mere regular concomitance or conjunction of events.[65] Leibniz's answer is contained in a remarkable passage in the *Monadology*, which in many ways anticipates the Humean line on causation:

When dogs are shown a stick they remember the pain it has caused them in the past and howl or run away . . . Often a vivid impression has in a moment the effect of long *habit*, or of many perceptions long repeated. Men act like brutes in so far as the sequences of their perceptions arise through the principle of memory only, like those empirical physicians who have mere practice without theory. We are all merely empiricists as regards three-fourths of our actions. For example, when we expect it to be day tomorrow, we are behaving as empiricists, because until now it

has always happened thus. The astronomer, however, knows by reason
. . . It is the knowledge of necessary and eternal truths which distinguishes
us from the animals, and gives us reason and the sciences (paras. 26–9).

There could be no clearer statement of Leibniz's faith in the
rational foundation of science and his rejection of what was to
become the Humean line, that it is *habit* not reason that is the
basis of our expectations and predictions about the world. This is
no place for an 'adjudication' between these two philosophical
positions—especially since the sense in which science can be said
to be rational is a matter on which philosophers today have
reached no clear consensus.[66] What is clear, as far as Leibniz is
concerned, is that his commitment to the rational intelligibility of
the universe is firmly grounded in his belief in the existence of the
chief monad, or 'supreme substance', God. It is the creative
selection God makes in accordance with the 'principle of fitness
or the choice of the best' (para. 46) that guarantees the ordered
harmony of things.

Although God has a central place in the Leibnizian system,
there are some aspects of Leibniz's theory of substance which
initially tend to suggest an independent and self-sufficient universe. Since monads are active substances (containing their
principle of action within themselves), they do not, like Cartesian
matter, require a God in order to have their initial motions
imparted to them (contrast Descartes, *Principles* II, 36). Furthermore, they are like the ultimate units of the ancient Greek
atomists in being indivisible and having no parts, and Leibniz
takes it (following a traditional line of argument) that this implies
that they are incorruptible: they 'cannot begin or end naturally'
and consequently they last as long as the universe (GP VI. 598;
P 195). Handled differently, these ingredients might have formed
the material for a materialistic and atheistic philosophy of the
kind developed by the Greek atomist Democritus and popular-
ized by Lucretius.[67] But in the Leibnizian universe, things are
radically different, for two main reasons.

First, unlike the inanimate and sterile particles of the atomists,
Leibniz's monads are described as being *alive*: 'There is nothing
sterile, nothing dead in the universe'; 'in the least part of matter

there is a world of . . . living things, animals, entelechies and souls' (*Monadology*, paras. 69 and 66). The implications of this 'pan-psychism', as it is often (somewhat misleadingly) called, will be examined when we come to discuss Leibniz's views on mind and matter in the next chapter. Suffice it to say here that despite Leibniz's frequent insistence that monads are to be compared to 'souls', he is certainly not committed to the extreme view that every substance has consciousness. Most monads are described as having 'perceptions' only in the attenuated sense that their structure mirrors that of the entire universe; only as we go up the hierarchy to those 'dominant monads' that are entitled to be called 'minds' do we reach true consciousness (GP VI. 599–601; P 196–8).

The second reason why Leibniz regarded his substances as fundamentally different from the eternal and self-sufficient particles on which the materialists based their universe concerns the question of existence. Although monads contain within themselves everything that is true of them, there is one exception: they do not contain the reason for their own existence. They are *contingent* beings, and, as Leibniz says in an early paper, 'a reason must be given why contingent beings should exist rather than not exist'. He goes on: 'but there would be no such reason unless there were a being which is *in itself*, that is, a being the reason for whose existence is contained in its own essence' (GP VII. 310; P 77). This reasoning, Leibniz explained in a paper entitled 'Of the Ultimate Origin of Things' (1697), is not affected by the supposition that the universe is eternal:

> Even if you suppose the world eternal, you will still be supposing nothing but a succession of states, and will not in any of them find a sufficient reason; so it is evident that the reason must be sought elsewhere . . . From this it is evident that . . . we cannot escape the ultimate extra-mundane reason of things, or God (GP VII. 302; P 137).

This argument (the 'argument from contingency', as it is called) was not invented by Leibniz,[68] though it is perhaps fair to say that by linking it to one of the fundamental principles of his philosophy, the principle of sufficient reason, he made it distinctively his own. What is striking, however, as we come to the end of this review of the notion of substance in Descartes, Spinoza, and Leibniz, is that all three philosophers, though taking different routes, end up by placing at the heart of their systems the notion of a necessary being, a being who contains within himself the reason for his existence (though Spinoza of course rejected the notion that this being must be something outside the world or 'extra-mundane'). The affirmation of an ultimate substance in the primary sense of 'a thing that exists in such a way as to depend on nothing else for its existence' (Descartes, *Principles* I, 51) forms common ground for all three philosophers. It is perhaps this fact above all others which marks a gulf between the thinking of the great seventeenth-century rationalists and our own world view, notwithstanding all the 'modern' aspects of their thought, and the role they played in the philosophical and scientific revolution which laid the foundations for much of our modern outlook on the world. For it seems inconceivable that a philosophical system founded on the notion of a necessarily existing substance could find acceptance today (and indeed the very idea of a complete philosophical system embracing all aspects of explanation—metaphysical, ethical, and scientific—has itself ceased to be a viable possibility nowadays). However that may be, the metaphysical core which is common to the thinking of Descartes, Spinoza, and Leibniz did not prevent their taking widely divergent positions regarding the nature and explanation both of the physical world and of its relation to the phenomena of human consciousness. It is to these areas that we must now turn.

4
Matter and Mind

The matter existing in the entire universe is one and the same, and it is always recognised as matter simply in virtue of its being extended (Descartes, *Principia philosophiae*, 1644).

Being neither material or extended, the mind of man is undoubtedly a simple, indivisible substance, without composition of parts (Malebranche, *De la recherche de la vérité*, 1674).

I found no way to explain how the body causes anything to take place in the soul, or vice versa . . . So far as we can tell from his writings, Descartes gave up the struggle at this point. But . . . his disciples concluded that . . . God causes thoughts to arise in the soul on the occasion of material movements, and that when our soul wishes to move the body, God moves the body for it (Leibniz, *Système nouveau*, 1695).[1]

The history of seventeenth-century philosophy is largely the history of a battle between traditional modes of thought and the 'modern' systems—most importantly that of Descartes—which aimed to take their place. Although Descartes's work was quickly condemned as new-fangled and dangerous, Descartes himself claimed that it was based on simple and straightforward principles that were far from 'new', since they were readily available to any human being who was prepared to direct his thoughts aright (AT VII. 580; CSM II. 392). In place of the elaborate intricacies of scholastic philosophy, the aim above all was clarity and simplicity: the world around us was to be understood solely in terms of the clearly and distinctly perceived properties that were the subject-matter of pure mathematics, while our own essential nature was to be understood solely in terms of the attribute of thought, of which each of us was taken to have an immediate and transparent awareness. Yet Spinoza and Leibniz, though they strongly supported the Cartesian goal of providing a clear and all-embracing account of the physical universe and of human nature, came to develop theories, both of the physical universe and of human nature, that were radically opposed to those of Descartes. In particular, as will appear, Spinoza took fundamental issue with the immaterialism that is at the core of Descartes's theory of the mind, while Leibniz equally emphatically rejected the Cartesian theory of matter as definable in terms of pure extension.

Descartes's immaterialist theory of the mind

Although Descartes's view of the mind as something essentially non-physical still commands a surprising degree of acceptance among the population at large, and even among some philosophers and scientists, it is certainly out of tune with the prevailing scientific and philosophical orthodoxy of our time.[2] But it would be a mistake to suppose that resistance to the Cartesian view is a twentieth-century phenomenon; even among Descartes's contemporaries, there were serious doubts about the validity of his arguments. 'The onus is on you to prove that you are unextended and incorporeal,' wrote Pierre Gassendi to Descartes, objecting that this was something that had been 'asserted without proof' (AT VII. 338 and 342; CSM II. 235–7). And an anonymous group of 'philosophers and geometers' observed acidly that 'after reading the *Meditations* seven times' they were still quite unable to see any valid basis for Descartes's claim that the soul was 'wholly distinct from any kind of body' (AT VII. 421; CSM II. 283).

Descartes initially seems to present his reasons for maintaining the distinctness of mind and body as flowing from the technique of wholesale doubt with which his metaphysical reflections begin. As he wrote in the *Discourse on the Method*,

> In examining my nature I saw that while I could pretend that I had no body, and that there was no world and no place for me to be in, I could not for all that pretend that I did not exist . . . From this I knew that I was a substance whose whole essence or nature is simply to think, and which

does not require any place, or depend on any material thing in order to exist. Accordingly, this 'I'—that is, the soul by which I am what I am—is entirely distinct from the body . . . (AT VI. 33; CSM I. 127).

But as several of Descartes's critics, notably Antoine Arnauld, pointed out, this reasoning is quite invalid. I may be able to doubt that I have a body, I may think I can imagine myself still existing without a body, but I cannot validly infer from this that having a body is no part of my essential nature. For my ability to doubt that X has Y does not entail that Y is not an essential part of X (for example, my ability to doubt that a triangle has some property does not entail that this property is really not essential to the triangle).[3]

Descartes seems to have acknowledged the justice of this objection, and he later wrote that he merely intended in this passage to point out that he could form a conception of himself that was independent of anything corporeal; it still remained to be proved that his exclusion of body from his essence corresponded to the 'actual truth of the matter' (cf. Preface to the *Meditations*: AT VII. 8; CSM II. 7). Where Descartes does explicitly claim to offer such a proof is in the Sixth Meditation, which contains two separate arguments for the distinctness of mind and body. One of these stresses the fact that the mind, unlike the body, cannot be divided into parts, and therefore must be different in nature:

There is a very great difference between mind and body inasmuch as the body is by its very nature always divisible, while the mind is utterly indivisible. For when I consider the mind, or myself in so far as I am merely a thinking thing, I am unable to distinguish any parts within myself; I understand myself to be something quite simple and complete (AT VII. 86; CSM II. 59).

The denial that there are parts to the mind may seem curious in the light of the traditional division of the mind into distinct faculties (the will, the understanding, the sensory faculty, and so on); but Descartes observes that this does not represent a genuine division into parts: 'the faculties cannot be termed "parts" of the mind, since it is one and the same mind that wills, understands and has sensory perceptions' (ibid.). The underlying idea here seems to be that whatever mental activity I engage in, it is always the same, single 'I' that is the indivisible, conscious subject of that activity. Although this notion of the simplicity and unity of individual consciousness has a certain intuitive plausibility (and many, including, for example, Leibniz, have regarded it as unquestionably true[4]), recent work in empirical psychology and physiology has suggested that our thought processes may in fact be the result of complex interactions of several distinct subsystems; and some have argued as a result that the very idea of a single, indivisible 'ego' to which all mental experience is referred may be, quite literally, an illusion.[5] But however that may be— and even if one accepts the Cartesian thesis of the unity and indivisibility of consciousness—that thesis still seems insufficient to establish the desired result that the nature of the mind is wholly independent from that of the body. For consciousness might indeed be simple and unitary—an 'all or nothing' business—but none the less be an activity that stems from, and inheres in, a purely physical system. Consciousness, that is to say, might be an indivisible *property* of an extended physical thing (for example, the brain).[6]

It is not clear that Descartes ever seriously considered this last possibility. But he does offer one piece of evidence which could count against it: 'if a foot or arm or any other part of the body is cut off' he observes, 'nothing has thereby been taken away from the mind' (AT VII. 86; CSM II. 59). Thought is immune to damage to any part of the physical body; hence it cannot be a property of that body. Unfortunately, the premiss here (for which Descartes offers no support) seems to be just false. It may look plausible if the physical part one selects is the hand or foot; but nowadays no one could possibly accept the claim that if one cut out, say, the cerebral cortex, 'nothing is thereby taken away from the mind'. Descartes himself, indeed, since he gave a crucial role to the pineal gland as the 'seat' of the soul (see below, p. 125), would have to admit that consciousness would be radically *different* if the brain, or certain parts of it, were excised. Activities such as sensation and imagination, for example, would not be possible, on Descartes's view, without a brain (AT V. 162; CB 27).[7] But Descartes nevertheless maintained that individual consciousness—the pure thought that is the defining attribute of the immaterial, unextended mind—could continue without any physical organs at all. This is a claim which those who subscribe to the Christian doctrine of an afterlife would presumably want to support.[8]

The other argument for the immateriality of the mind in the Sixth Meditation is generally known as the 'argument from clear and distinct perception'. In fact it comes before the indivisibility argument in the development of the Sixth Meditation, and is presented by Descartes as the principal argument designed to establish the claim, announced in the title of the final Meditation, that there is a 'real distinction between mind and body'. The proposition that there is a 'real' (Latin *realis*) distinction between X and Y means that X and Y are genuine independent *things* (Latin *res*); in other words (as Descartes explains in the *Principles*), they are substances, capable of existing on their own (so that X could exist without Y and vice versa) (AT VII. 28; CSM I. 213). That body and mind are distinct in this sense can be seen, argues Descartes in the Sixth Meditation, from the fact that it is possible to have a clear and distinct understanding of mind apart from body and vice versa:

> The fact that I can clearly and distinctly understand one thing apart from another is enough to make me certain that the two things are distinct since they are capable of being separated, at least by God . . . Thus simply by knowing that I exist and seeing at the same time that absolutely nothing else belongs to my nature or essence except that I am a thinking thing, I can infer correctly that my essence consists solely in the fact that I am a thinking thing . . . (AT VII. 78; CSM II. 54).

The reference to God may be puzzling; but at this stage in the *Meditations*, Descartes takes himself to have established the existence of a perfect God, who created him and who would not have bestowed on him an intellectual faculty that was inherently faulty and unreliable: 'I have perceived that God exists, and that everything else depends on him, and that he is no deceiver; and I have drawn the conclusion that everything which I clearly and distinctly perceive is of necessity true' (AT VII. 70; CSM II. 48). So if I can clearly and distinctly perceive X apart from Y, then X

must be 'really distinct' from *Y*. More specifically, I can clearly
and distinctly think of myself as existing as a pure 'thinking
thing', without any other attributes at all; and therefore these
other attributes (most importantly, the possession of a body)
cannot be part of my essential nature.

It is important not to misunderstand Descartes here. He is not
denying that in our ordinary everyday existence we live as
creatures of flesh and blood; we are, as he puts it elsewhere,
'intimately conjoined and intermingled with the body' (AT VII.
81; CSM II. 56). But for all that, we can (it is claimed) form a clear
conception of ourselves as pure thinking things, independent of
the body; and that is enough to make mind and body really
distinct. It is rather as if all the triangles we encountered were
inscribed in circles; in such a situation we could none the less
clearly and distinctly conceive of a triangle apart from a circle,
and hence we could know that the two were really distinct. Thus
we can be sure that God, at least, could separate mind and body,
so that they continued to exist independently. It does not matter,
says Descartes, if God has in fact 'conjoined some corporeal
substance to the thinking substance so closely that they are
compounded into a unity'; none the less if he *could* separate
them, 'they remain really distinct' (AT VIII. 29; CSM I. 213).
This invoking of the *conceivability* of a disembodied mind may
strike a chord for those familiar with some modern defences of
mind–body dualism; indeed, even opponents of dualism are
sometimes inclined to concede that it is at least a *logical*
possibility that we might exist as pure disembodied spirits.[9] The
implication of Descartes's argument is, in effect, that if such a
thing is even a logical possibility, then mind–body dualism is
true. For if *X* and *Y* could conceivably exist apart, then they must
be really or essentially distinct: if *X* can exist without *Y* then *Y*
cannot be a part of the essential nature of *X* or vice versa.

Although this reasoning may initially seem persuasive, it is
vulnerable to an important objection that has force against many
commonly accepted techniques of philosophical argument. The
crux of the objection is that before we blandly accept some
hypothesis or scenario as 'at least conceivable' or 'a logical
possibility' we need to pause; for why should conceivability, or

logical possibility, be straightforwardly self-manifesting?[10] It may perhaps be obvious enough in the case of extremely simple and elementary objects and properties; but where we are dealing with something as complex as the nature of a mind, what is conceivable may be a difficult question that cannot be settled merely by the speaker's summary judgement that such and such a scenario seems possible. The logician Antoine Arnauld, author of the Fourth Set of Objections published with the *Meditations* in 1641, neatly highlighted this difficulty by taking an example from geometry. Is it conceivable that there should be a right-angled triangle lacking the property of having the square on its hypotenuse equal to the squares on the other two sides? Well, someone fairly ignorant of geometry could easily suppose that such a thing was possible; he might even (if misled by some faulty line of thought) suppose that one could actually construct such a triangle. So he might think it quite conceivable, or logically possible, that the triangle should exist without the property in question. But in fact *he would be wrong*: the property is an essential part of the triangle's essence:

Although the man in the example clearly and distinctly knows that the triangle is right-angled, he is wrong in thinking that the aforesaid relationship between the squares on the sides does not belong to the nature of the triangle. Similarly, although I clearly and distinctly know my nature to be something that thinks, may I too not perhaps be wrong in thinking that nothing else belongs to my nature apart from the fact that I am a thinking thing? Perhaps the fact that I am an extended thing may also belong to my nature (AT VII. 203; CSM II. 142).

To repeat: what is essential to something's nature may well require complex and difficult investigation; it cannot simply be settled by someone's bald assertion that he can conceive of X without Y (myself without a body, the triangle without the relevant property).

If Arnauld's criticism is correct (and it seems unanswerable), Descartes's central argument for the immateriality of the mind must fail; and since his other argument (the indivisibility argument) has also been found wanting, the upshot is that the 'real' distinction between mind and body has not been established.

Descartes has, however, one further string to his bow, which is never made explicit in the *Meditations*, but which is hinted at in a comment he makes in reply to Arnauld's objections: 'when I examine the nature of the body,' he tells Arnauld, 'I find nothing at all in it which savours of thought' (AT VII. 227; CSM II. 160). What this suggests is that in addition to the arguments in the *Meditations*, all of which proceed from the subject 'outwards', starting from the meditator's awareness of himself as a thinking thing, there may be another argument for the mind–body distinction which operates the other way round, and starts from our conception of the nature of *matter*. Interestingly enough, this was precisely the approach taken by Nicolas Malebranche later in the century. According to Malebranche, we are correct in ascribing conscious states to a wholly non-corporeal mind or soul. But such a conclusion, says Malebranche in his *Méditations chrétiennes et métaphysiques* of 1683, rests *solely* on our idea of a *body*:

> You conclude that pleasure, sadness and all the rest belong not to corporeal substance, but to another which you call soul, spirit . . . But all of these conclusions rest *only* on the clear idea you have of body . . . since you see clearly in the idea of extension that what you feel in yourself cannot belong to matter.[11]

In Descartes's *Meditations*, matter is defined as *res extensa*—extended stuff. But it was not until he came to write the *Principles of Philosophy* that Descartes provided a full exposition of exactly what this implied. Matter, or corporeal substance, it emerges, is really no more than what we might call 'dimensionality' or 'spreadoutness'. It is, in other words, simply that which occupies space. Indeed, Descartes goes so far as to say that the concepts of 'space' and 'corporeal substance' are not really distinct at all:

> Suppose we attend to the idea we have of some body, for example a stone, and leave out everything we know to be non-essential to the nature of the body: we will first of all exclude hardness, since if the stone is melted or pulverised it will lose its hardness without thereby ceasing to be a body; next we will exclude colour, since we have often seen stones so transparent as to lack colour; next we will exclude heaviness, since although fire is extremely light it is still thought of as being corporeal;

and finally we will exclude cold and heat and all other such qualities, either because they are not thought of as being in the stone or because if they change the stone, it is not on that account reckoned to have lost its bodily nature. After all this, we will see that *nothing remains in the idea of the stone except that it is something extended in length, breadth and depth. Yet this is just what is comprised in the idea of a space* . . . (AT VIII. 46; CSM I. 227, italics supplied).

On this extraordinarily austere conception of materiality, to say 'there is matter here' is no more than saying there is geometrical space or volume of such and such dimensions. If matter is thought of in this way, then the possibility that it could have complex properties like *consciousness* seems to be ruled out from the start. Indeed, it becomes hard to see how matter, so conceived, can *do* anything at all (except lie around, and perhaps be shoved about so as to bump into other bits of matter—though there are problems even here[12]). As long as the Cartesian notion of matter held sway, the complete inertness of material substance was guaranteed. Hence George Berkeley (who in any case denied the existence of material substance) was able to argue that even if one granted the existence of matter, it could not possibly affect our senses in any way, since we are 'not one wit nearer explaining how body could *act* on spirit'.[13]

Given his conception of matter as purely geometrical and wholly inert, it is thus easy to see how Descartes was able to take it as axiomatic that matter, *qua* pure extension, was distinct, indeed wholly alien, from any kind of thinking substance. Later in the century, it is true, John Locke (who selectively attacked the Cartesian framework regarding thought and extension[14]) was to raise the possibility that God might 'superadd to Matter a Faculty of Thinking';[15] but such 'superadding' could only be, as it were, by arbitrary divine fiat, by a kind of miraculous *ad hoc* decree.[16] And even were this to happen, thought would still, in Cartesian terms, be really distinct from anything material, since there would be no connection between extension and thought, no property of extended stuff which enabled it, *qua* extended stuff, to think. (Compare Descartes's own comment: 'no matter how closely God may have united [mind and body], the power which he previously had of separating them, of keeping one in being

without the other, is something he could not lay aside; and things that God has the power to separate, or to keep in being separately, are really distinct' (AT VIII. 29; CSM I. 213).) The Cartesian challenge to the materialist, then, is to show how consciousness could possibly be something arising from a modification of 'mere matter'. And to the extent that present-day materialists have begun to see how to take up the challenge, this is at least partly because the very concept of matter has now progressed so far beyond the Cartesian model of inert, extended stuff characterizable in purely geometrical terms. This is not the place to discuss the tenability of modern materialist views of the mind. But in all events the proposition that thought may be a property of a dynamic electro-chemical system comprising over ten billion neural connections no longer seems a 'tall order' in anything like the same ways as it seemed, for Descartes, a tall— indeed impossible—order to suppose that mere extension could give rise to thought.[17]

The problem of interaction

The thesis of the immateriality of the mind presented Descartes with a nest of problems that were to become notorious stumbling blocks for Cartesian philosophy. To begin with, however much reason may tell me, according to Descartes, that I am a substance that is entirely independent of the body and 'does not require any place or depend on any material thing', my everyday experience (seeing with my eyes, feeling with my hands, hearing with my ears, feeling hungry, having toothache) none the less unmistakably testifies to the fact that I am very much an embodied being. Yet what is it for an immaterial spirit to be embodied? Descartes sometimes seemed to toy with the idea that the mind is somehow 'diffused' throughout the body (AT VII. 442; CSM II. 298), but this risked attributing to the mind some kind of extension or 'spreadoutness'—the very feature his official theory of the mind denies. In general he insisted that the soul 'must be of such a nature that it has no relation to extension, or to the dimensions or other properties of the matter of which the body is composed: it

is related solely to the whole assemblage of the body's organs' (*Passions of the Soul*: AT XI. 351; CSM I. 339).

But how does an immaterial mind achieve such a unified relationship to the entire body? Descartes's physiological reflections led him to believe that the soul exercised its functions in one particular portion of the brain: the *conarion* or pineal gland. In his primitive 'pneumatic' theory of the nervous system, the muscles of the body are activated by a kind of fine gas known as the 'animal spirits', which flows back and forth via the nerves between the brain and the relevant organs. The pineal gland, Descartes observed, 'is situated in the middle of the brain's substance and suspended above the passage through which the spirits in the brain's anterior cavities communicate with those in its posterior cavities'. It is thus ideally suited to initiate, and respond to, movements of the 'animal spirits': 'the slightest movement on the part of this gland may alter greatly the course of these spirits, and conversely any change, however slight, in the flow of the spirits may do much to change the movements of the gland' (*Passions* I, 31).[18]

Although the details of this story may sound quaint now, Descartes's general approach to the physiology of human behaviour has turned out to be in broad outline correct: there *is* a transmission of impulses between brain and bodily organs via the nerves (though to replace the crude mechanics of Descartes's pneumatic account we are now in a position to provide a more complex electro-chemical description). But however much the details are refined, there remains a philosophical puzzle at the heart of the Cartesian theory, namely that we are asked to accept the notion of a two-way causal flow between immaterial spirit and extended matter. We know from everyday experience that a mental change (for example, a decision to vote) can result in bodily movements (the raising of one's hand); and equally we know that bodily events can cause modifications in our consciousness (for example, when stubbing one's toe produces a distinctive sensation of discomfort). Descartes has sketched out some intermediate mechanisms: the soul does not directly interact with the hand or foot, but with the pineal gland, which in turn generates or responds to movements in the nerves connected to the hand or foot. But at some point—in the pineal gland, or whatever part of the brain is chosen as the 'seat of the soul'—there has to be a raw interaction between the two wholly alien substances, mind and matter. This is the central difficulty for Descartes's account of the mind.

When questioned as to how the soul can be affected by the body and vice versa, given that their natures are so completely different, Descartes is reported to have admitted that this was 'very difficult to explain' (AT V. 163; CB 28). Unfortunately an explanation, in Cartesian terms, seems not just difficult but impossible. For the Cartesian model of explanation requires that if X and Y are causally related, then there must be some intelligible link between X and Y: the cause must be 'like' the effect, or the features found in the effect must be present in some form in the cause (see above, pp. 81–2). Yet Descartes has to admit that there is no intelligible relationship *at all* between a certain type of movement in the brain (or pineal gland) and a certain type of sensation. It just so happens that movement-pattern number 3,094, let us say, gives rise to a distinctive type of sensation (for example, a feeling of pain), but things might well have been different: 'God could have made the nature of man such that this particular motion in the brain indicated something else to the mind' (AT VII. 88; CSM II. 60). God simply ordains that movement M should give rise to sensation S, but S and M remain utterly heterogeneous and unconnected modifications of two wholly alien substances.[19]

This purely contingent or 'arbitrary' character of the relation between brain events and mental events was something which was underlined by Leibniz as a major defect of Descartes system. As he aptly observed in his *New Essays on Human Understanding*, 'the Cartesians . . . regard it as arbitrary what perceptions we have of [sensible] qualities, as if God had given them to the soul according to his good pleasure, without concern for any essential relation between perceptions and their objects' (RB 56).[20] Descartes's position is in fact not far from to the 'occasionalism' of his disciple Malebranche, according to which God miraculously intervenes to ensure that our volitions are followed by those movements in the body designed to carry them out, and, conversely, that certain patterns of bodily movement give rise to appropriate emotions and sensations in the soul:

> It is the continuous and efficacious action of the will of God on us that binds us so closely to one part of matter, and if this action of His will should cease but for one moment, we would immediately be freed from our dependence upon the body and all the changes it undergoes. For I cannot understand how certain people imagine that there is an absolutely necessary relation between the movement of the [animal] spirits or blood and the emotions of the soul. A few tiny particles of bile are violently stirred up in the brain—therefore the soul must be excited by some passion—and this must be anger rather than love. What relation can be conceived between a passion . . . on the one hand, and the corporeal movement of the blood's parts striking against certain parts of the brain? How can people convince themselves that the one depends on the other, and that *the union or connection of two things as remote and incompatible as mind and matter* could be caused and maintaned in any way other than by the continuous and all powerful will of the author of nature?[21]

So far from being some fanciful and baroque elaboration of the Cartesian system, as is sometimes suggested by commentators, Malebranchian occasionalism is directly reminiscent of Descartes's own invoking of God's decrees to explain why such and such sensations follow on such and such brain events. Only a divine ordinance can bridge the gap between two things as 'remote and incompatible' as mind and matter.[22]

The Spinozan response

Spinoza was fascinated by Descartes's philosophy, and in much of what he says about mind and matter he shows himself to be deeply imbued with Cartesian ideas. Spinoza broadly accepted Descartes's account of the physical world as extended stuff; and just as Descartes argued that the apparent diversity and variety of physical phenomena around us was to be explained simply as a set of modifications or 'modes' of extension ('such as all shapes, the positions of the parts and motions of the parts': AT VIII. 32; CSM I. 216), so Spinoza argues that all the various bodies we see around us are 'distinguished from one another simply by reason of motion and rest, speed and slowness' (G II. 97; C 458). Remarkably, however, Spinoza rejects the fundamental Cartesian thesis that corporeal substance is divisible. For Descartes, extension automatically implies divisibility: to be extended is to have dimensions, and this in turn implies that we are dealing with such and such a quantity of matter; and where there is a quantity, there is always the possibility of division. Thus in Descartes's physics the notions of 'corporeal substance', 'extension', 'quantity', and 'space' are virtually interchangeable (*Principles* II, 8–11); and it is explicitly stated that whatever possesses a determinate extension can always be divided into two or more smaller parts (II, 20). Spinoza, however, insists that there can be but one single, all-embracing, and infinite substance (see above, p. 92); and from this he argues that 'it is impossible to form a true conception of any attribute of substance which entails that a substance can be divided (*Ethics* I, prop. 12).[23] Corporeal substance then, even though it is extended, is not divisible.

If we consider the physical world around us, Spinoza's thesis seems strongly counter-intuitive, since we can clearly conceive of a quantity of extended stuff being divided into parts (for example, a quart of water being divided into two pints). Spinoza replies, perhaps somewhat obscurely, that this sort of conception is based on our ordinary (inadequate) sensory perception or visual imagination: 'if we attend to quantity as it is in the imagination, it will be found to be finite, divisible and composed of parts; but if we attend to it as it is in the intellect, and conceive of it *qua* substance, then it will be found to be infinite unique and indivisible' (G II. 59; C 424).[24] Spinoza accepts, then, that we can think of water as separable into parts, but insists that this is true of it *qua* water, not *qua* corporeal substance.[25] *Qua* substance it is inseparable, indivisible, and, Spinoza adds, eternal—incapable of being destroyed or brought into being.

One important result flows from Spinoza's denial that extended substance *qua* substance is divisible, namely that thinking substance and extended substance are no longer characterized in incompatible terms. For Descartes, as we have seen, thinking stuff is by nature indivisible and extended stuff by nature divisible, so that the two are not merely different, but have utterly alien and incompatible natures. For Spinoza, by contrast, there is no necessary contradiction between the propositions '*X* is thinking' and '*X* is extended'; there is therefore no bar, as there would be for a Cartesian, to the supposition that the attributes of extension and thought characterize the same being.[26]

Spinoza's single substance is officially characterized as having an 'infinite' number of attributes; but Spinoza does not satisfactorily explain exactly what this implies, and often the assertion seems to boil down to little more than an expression of the supreme all-embracing reality and infinitude of 'God or Nature'. For practical purposes, the attributes which attract all the analysis and discussion in the *Ethics* are the two attributes of extension and thought.[27] 'Thought' (*cogitatio*) is an attribute of God, says Spinoza (*Ethics* II, prop. 1): God is *res cogitans*, a thinking thing, since we can conceive an infinite being 'by attending to thought alone'. But, by similar reasoning, extension is an attribute of God: God is a *res extensa* (prop. 2). The celebrated Cartesian duality is thus in a sense retained—not, however, as a duality of substances but as a duality of attributes.[28] Thought and extension characterize distinct aspects of one and the same being:

> Everything that can be perceived by an infinite intellect as constituting the essence of a substance belongs to the essence of the one unique substance; and consequently thinking substance and extended substance are one and the same substance which is comprehended now under the former attribute and now under the latter (*Ethics* II, prop. 7, schol.).

Applied to the universe in its entirety, the assertion that there is but one unique substance that is both conscious and extended is perhaps difficult to grasp; but Spinoza makes it clear that the attributive duality extends right down what are ordinarily thought of as individual items. Thus 'a circle existing in nature and the idea of the existing circle, which is in God, are one and the same thing which is explained through different attributes' (ibid.). For every divine idea there is a corresponding *ideatum*, or object; but for each idea–object pair, what is involved is not two separate items but just one, which may be conceived of either as a modification of the attribute of thought or as a modification of

the attribute of extension. 'A mode of extension and the idea of
that mode are one and the same thing, but expressed in two ways'
(ibid.). Thus we may think of a tree, for example, as a certain
characteristic modification of extension or extended substance
(with this Descartes would have agreed: AT VIII. 52; CSM I. 232);
but we may also think of the idea of the tree in the divine
consciousness, and then we are conceiving of it as a certain
modification of thought. But since there is but one substance,
God-or-Nature, the object and the idea are in reality identical:
'the order and connection of ideas is the same as the order and
connection of things' (*Ethics* II, prop. 7).

Despite the identity of the order of ideas and the order of
things, it is important for Spinoza that these two aspects of reality
are *distinct*. Each of the attributes involved is 'conceived through
itself' (*Ethics* I, prop. 10). The unfolding of each set of causes is,
as it were, self-contained, and proceeds without any reference to
the items in the other set:

> So long as things are considered as modes of thinking, we must explain
> the whole order of nature, or the connection of causes, through the
> attribute of thought alone. And so long as they are considered as modes
> of extension, the order of the whole of nature must be conceived through
> the attribute of extension alone (*Ethics* II, prop. 7, schol.).

Despite the perfect match between any given mode of extension
and any given mode of thought, each set of modes can be fully
and adequately understood without reference to the other. In one
sense this is in accordance with Cartesian orthodoxy: thought and
extension are quite distinct and self-contained notions. But by
rejecting Descartes's thesis that they are *incompatible* notions,
Spinoza is able to go on to construct a radically unCartesian
picture of reality. The picture which finally emerges is a strange,
almost mystical, fusion of idealism and materialism. If Spinoza
were right, there would be room for a Berkeleyan conception of
the world as a set of ideas in the divine mind; but there would also
be room for a Hobbesian conception of the world as essentially
material. But instead of being at loggerheads, the two accounts
would be thought of as representing distinct aspects of a single
underlying reality.[29]

Mind and body in Spinoza

It is probably fair to say that Spinoza's general account of reality
would have remained a metaphysical curiosity in the history of
philosophy, were it not for its application to the more specific
problem of the *human* mind and its relation to the body. In
accordance with the general theory, the individual human mind is
regarded as 'part of the infinite intellect of God'; it is an 'idea'—a
certain modification of the divine consciousness. But for every
idea there is a corresponding object, and in the case of the human
mind, the object, says Spinoza, is the body (that is, a certain
modification of the attribute of extension: *Ethics* II, prop. 13).
This leads Spinoza to a conception of the mind–body relation
that is radically different from that of Descartes. Many of the key
terms in Descartes's account reappear, but their significance is
fundamentally altered.

Take first the notion of the *union* of mind and body. Descartes,
though insisting that mind and body are distinct, frequently
stresses the unavoidable fact of their interaction: they are 'so
closely conjoined and intermingled as to form a unit', he wrote in
the *Meditations* (AT VII. 81; CSM II. 56); and in the correspondence with Princess Elizabeth of Bohemia, he spoke of the
idea of the union of mind and body as one of the fundamental
notions 'on which all our other knowledge is patterned' (AT III.
665; K 138). Spinoza acknowledges that 'man consists of a mind
and a body', and that 'the human mind is united to the body' (G
II. 96; C 457). But what he means by this 'union' is very different
from what Descartes meant. In the Preface to Part V of the *Ethics*
he pours scorn on the notion of any sort of 'interaction' between
mind and brain, of the sort which Descartes envisaged in his
account of the role of the pineal gland:

What, I ask, does [Descartes] understand by the union of Mind and
Body? What clear and distinct concept does he have of a thought so
closely united to some little portion of quantity . . . ? I should very much
like to know how many degrees of motion the mind can give to that
pineal gland, and how great a force is required to hold it in suspense. For
I do not know whether this gland is driven about more slowly by the
Mind than by the animal spirits, or more quickly; nor do I know whether

the motions of the passions which we have joined closely to firm judgements can be separated from them again by bodily causes (G II. 280; C 596).

For Spinoza, no coherent account can be given of the idea of an immaterial spirit generating movements in the pineal gland and vice versa. Such interactions between 'ghost' and 'machine' are not rationally intelligible.[30] When Spinoza himself speaks of the mind and body as being 'united', or of their 'union', he emphatically rejects the Cartesian idea of union as an intermingling or joining together; what is meant, rather, is that mind and body are *unum et idem*, one and the same: 'We have shown that the Mind is united to the Body from the fact that the Body is the object of the mind . . .'; 'The mind and the body are one and the same individual which is conceived now under the attribute of thought, now under the attribute of extension' (G II. 109; C 467).

As for the Cartesian doctrine of the *distinctness* of mind and body, Spinoza of course denies that body and mind are distinct substances. But in rejecting the separate substance view of the mind, he must not be thought of as proposing a reductionist account of the kind suggested, for example, in some modern materialist accounts of the mind. In saying that mind and body are one and the same, he is *not* saying that mental states can be read off from, or are a straightforward function of, brain states. In is quite wrong, Spinoza asserts, to suggest that the activities of the mind are causally determined by physical events (for example, in the brain). What determines the mind is a mode of thinking, and not of extension (that is, not anything bodily). Similarly, what determines the body cannot be anything mental (*Ethics* III, prop. 2).

It is this last feature—what we may call the 'nomological self-containedness' of the attributes of thought and extension—that makes Spinoza's theory of the mind so hard to assess. Although on the one hand it is wrong to interpret Spinoza as a straightforward reductionist, on the other hand, since thought and extension are attributes of one and the *same* substance, he clearly cannot be maintaining that mental and physical events are separate, unconnected events that just happen to run in parallel (for this reason the label 'parallelism', which is often applied to Spinoza's theory of the mind, is not helpful). But if reductionism and parallelism are ruled out, what is left? We have already spoken of thought and extension as representing for Spinoza two distinct *aspects* of the same reality; and Spinoza's theory is indeed frequently referred to as a 'double aspect' or 'dual aspect' theory of mind–body relations. The label, however, is not entirely satisfactory: it has a certain vagueness which has allowed it to be used to cover a variety of rather different views on the relation between mind and body.[31] Spinoza himself is not particularly helpful in explaining exactly what his view of that relation is. One example he gives of how 'one and the same thing can be designated by two labels' concerns the Third Patriarch in the Old Testament: 'By "Israel" I understand the Third Patriarch, . . . but I also understand the same by the name Jacob, since the name Jacob was given to him because he had seized his brother's heel' (G. IV. 46; C 196).[32] But the application of two distinct designations to the same person, though of course it establishes that one individual can be referred to in distinct ways, hardly provides us with more than a weak analogy for the relation between thought and extension; we are not much nearer to grasping what Spinoza's claim about mind and body really amounts to. Slightly more suggestive, perhaps, is a passage in the *Ethics* where Spinoza talks of a mode of thought and a mode of extension as one and the same thing, but 'expressed in two ways' (*duobus modis expressa*: G II. 90; C 451). This has suggested to one commentator that what Spinoza has in mind is something like the relation between a proposition and its linguistic expression.[33] Clearly the same thought (for example, 'Spinoza was a philosopher') can be expressed in two different ways—for example, as an English sentence and a French sentence; there is also a sense in which the two languages are distinct and 'nomologically self-contained'— following their own separate rules of grammar, spelling, and so on. So the notion of genuinely distinct ways of 'expressing' the same thing is one which we can at least make sense of. Again (reverting to Spinoza's own example of the circle), if I take a pair of compasses and draw a circle, there is some sense in saying that what is expressed in my mind as an idea is expressed on paper as a circle.[34] But if we try to cash out these analogies (the language analogy, the diagram analogy) and apply them to the particular case of minds and bodies (John's mind and John's body), it is still far from clear what Spinoza meant by saying that bodily modes are *expressions* of thinking modes and vice versa.

The modern theory of the mind that perhaps best exemplifies a 'dual aspect' approach is the theory, or group of theories, known as functionalism. The central idea here is that mental states are logical, organizational, or functional states of the brain (or central nervous system). This approach does not aim to describe the structure of the mind in neurophysiological terms; rather, it characterizes it as a kind of complex information-processing system, providing specifications both of all the relevant inputs and outputs, and of the sets of rules whereby outputs appropriate to the various inputs are generated. The most important feature of this functionalist model is that the descriptions it comes up with are purely abstract descriptions of inputs, outputs, rules of procedure, and logical connections; they are, that is to say, 'software' descriptions, which are quite neutral as to the kind of hardware (copper, silicon, protoplasm, grey matter, or whatever) of which the being that instantiates these functional states is actually composed.[35]

Can such an approach be called 'Spinozistic'—at least in general terms? There are some suggestive parallels. For one thing, in the modern theory the chain of explanations at the functional level operates quite independently of the chain of explanations at the neurophysiological level. Any given functional state is described in purely functional language, and explained purely by reference to other sets of functional states. The descriptions which the functionalist gives are, in this sense, quite distinct from, and independent of, the 'hardware' descriptions which the neurophysiologist provides. This seems to correspond quite well with Spinoza's concept of the distinctness and independence of mental modes from physical modes. Notice, moreover, that the functionalist, though he operates independently of the neurophysiologist, is very far from being obliged to support Cartesian dualism. He does not need to see himself as describing some immaterial substance called 'the mind'; on the contrary, most functionalists take it as axiomatic that the functional states they describe must, in order to operate, be realized by, or instantiated in, some organized physical system. This gives us a second close parallel with Spinoza: we have two types of attribute but a monistic ontology—only one underlying reality.

It is impossible to say what Spinoza would have made of these parallels, and they probably should not be pushed too far. One particular disparity lies in the fact that Spinoza's picture of reality requires a neat, one-one correspondence between mental modes and physical modes, whereas there is an asymmetry between functional states and physical states: although it may turn out that for any given physical state there is a unique corresponding functional state, the converse is certainly not true. The brain may be able to perform a given function in a variety of different ways; more generally, a given functional state could be instantiated or realized in a variety of different physical configurations or systems (just as the function of a clock, for example, could be realized by a variety of mechanisms: calibrated candles, sets of hourglasses, rotating cogs and wheels, or modern electronic devices). Further reflection on this point suggests another difference between Spinoza's account of the mind and modern functionalist theories, namely that the functionalist is able to offer a more precise account of the *relation* between the mental and the physical than anything to be found in Spinoza. For the functionalist, we have on the one hand an organizational (or 'software') description and on the other hand a physical (or 'hardware') description: the relation between the two lies precisely in the fact that the physical configuration (the circuitry, the arrays of neurons) must be such as to enable the relevant functions to be performed effectively. A major problem with Spinoza's theory, by contrast, is that the relation between the two 'distinct' attributes of thought and extension remains, in the end, unclear. The spirit of Spinoza's rationalism requires that there should be something more than a mere arbitrary coincidence or parallelism between them; yet Spinoza does not succeed in giving a satisfying account of what it means to say that they are two expressions of the same reality. Nevertheless, Spinoza's writings on the mind remain of considerable philosophical importance, both for the acute critique they offer of Cartesian interactionism, and for the suggestion they offer, however abstract and schematic, that a recognition of the distinctness of thought and extension need not force us into the incoherencies of substantial dualism.

Leibniz's critique of Cartesian matter

Descartes's great claim for his physics was that it employed only clear and distinct notions; corporeal nature was defined simply as 'extended stuff' and hence was wholly transparent and accessible to rational understanding in so far as it was 'comprised in the subject-matter of pure mathematics'. Some of Descartes's critics were worried by the abstractness of this conception of matter: 'the whole of Cartesian physics', wrote a group of supporters of Pierre Gassendi in 1644, 'must be imaginary and as fictitious as pure mathematics, whereas real physics requires the kind of matter that is real, solid and not imaginary' (AT IX. 212; CSM II. 275).[36] Later, the Cambridge Platonist Henry More wrote to Descartes objecting that he had not shown *tangibility* or *impenetrability* to be properties of extended substance. Descartes replied somewhat curtly (in a letter of 15 April 1649) that 'it is impossible to think of one part of extended substance penetrating another part without *eo ipso* thinking that half the total extension is taken away or annihilated; but what is annihilated does not penetrate anything else' (AT V. 342; K 249).

Another worry for Cartesians concerned the explanation of *movement* in the universe: could the principles of motion be derived from the Cartesian account of matter? Descartes had baldly asserted (in a letter to Princess Elizabeth of 21 May 1643) that 'extension entails the notions of shape and motion' (AT III. 665; K 138). But whereas being extended in space necessarily implies having a shape, there seems no necessary connection between extension and motion. Pierre Bayle put it as follows in his *Dictionary* (first published 1697), summing up what had become a standard criticism of Cartesian physics:

Motion is not essential to extension. It is not contained in the idea of it, and many bodies are at rest from time to time. Motion is thus an *accident* [a non-essential property]. But is it distinct from matter? If it be distinct, from what will it be produced?[37]

Difficulties about solidity and motion apart, there was a problem about the infinite divisibility of Cartesian matter. Leibniz described this problem, known as the problem of the 'composition of the continuum', as one of the 'two great labyrinths of the human mind' (the other being the problem of free will: P 107); he maintained that unless it could be solved, the notion of extension could not be regarded as 'so clear as is commonly supposed' (GP VII. 314; P 81). The problem, in a nutshell, is that matter is defined as extended and hence divisible into parts; but then the resulting portions of matter must themselves be divisible . . . and so on *ad infinitum*. (Descartes insisted that one could not reach atoms, or smaller, indivisible units, since, being material, they would by definition have to be divisible.) Descartes was driven to admit that this actual divisibility of matter *ad infinitum*, although 'following necessarily from what we know most evidently of the nature of matter', was something that 'belongs to the class of things that are beyond the grasp of our finite minds' (*Principles* II, 35).

Spinoza, while making extension a defining attribute of his unique, all-embracing substance, nonetheless insisted, as we have seen, that substance *qua* substance is not divisible. But since being extended in three dimensions seems clearly to imply the possibility of division, the Spinozan doctrine appears to offer not so much a solution to the problem about the divisibility of matter, as a further piece of mystification. Leibniz's view was that 'we will never be free of the difficulties concerning the composition of the continuum so long as extension is regarded as constituting the substance of bodies' (GP II. 98; P 68). One possible solution to the problem that was canvassed in the late seventeenth century was to conceive of extension as being composed of mathematical points which themselves had no extension. But this seemed to deprive matter of its *substantiality*: since mathematical points are only abstractions, not real entities, it could never be shown how 'several nonentities could make up real extension'.[38] Leibniz's proposed answer was twofold. First, he borrowed from the mathematical approach the idea of a point having no parts and no extension; but he then insisted that the ultimate elements of matter were *real* points—not mathematical abstractions, but

what he called 'metaphysical points' (GP IV. 482; P 121). Just as
there are infinitely many mathematical points in an extended
space, so 'no portion of matter is so small that there is not in it a
world of created things, infinite in number' (*Monadology*, para.
66). The second strand in Leibniz's solution was to move away
from Cartesian extension altogether, and make the essence of
matter consist instead of *activity* (see Chapter 3, p. 107). Leibniz's
units of substance have been described by one modern commentator as 'point particles of energy'—a conception pointing the
way to the foundations of modern physics and the notion that
mass and energy are interchangeable.[39] But Leibniz's anticipation, if such it can be called, was too general and speculative
to have been capable of constituting a scientific advance at the
time. Cartesians, moreover, could have objected with some
justification that the notion of an *infinity* of active creatures
within each portion of matter was hardly more intelligible than
the notion of infinitely divisible extension.

In his later writings Leibniz's characteristic addiction to reconciliation leads him to propose a kind of compromise between the
mechanism of the Cartesians and the 'vitalism' suggested by his
own theory of monads:

in the case of bodies, everything occurs mechanically, that is, through the
intelligible qualities of bodies, namely magnitude, shape and motion; in
the case of souls everything is to be explained in vital terms, that is
through the intelligible qualities of the soul, namely perceptions and
appetites (*Metaphysical Consequences of the Principle of Reason*: CO 12;
P 173).

This suggests that Leibniz is quite prepared to allow that Cartesian explanations in terms of 'size, shape and motion' have a
perfectly proper role to play in natural science. But there is a sense
in which the concession is misleading. For at a deeper level
Leibniz believed that the ultimate properties of matter could not
be explained in Cartesian terms. 'In the final analysis of the
principles of physics and mechanics', he wrote to Arnauld in
1686, 'it is found that these principles are not explicable purely by
the modifications of extension, and the nature of *force* requires
something else' (GP II. 78; M 96). Leibniz was thus convinced of

the explanatory inadequacy of the Cartesian programme for reducing all the properties of the physical universe to mere modes of 'extended substance'; and from our modern perspective there is no doubt that his conviction has been fully vindicated.[40]

Leibniz had a further objection to the Cartesian notion of matter, namely that it failed to explain the 'genuine unity of real things' (GP II. 97–9; M 120–4). What he seems to have had in mind here is that since physical objects on the Cartesian view are merely determinate quantities of extended stuff—mere modifications of dimensionality—they must lack the status of genuine individual objects (see Chapter 3, p. 84). But it is far from clear that Leibniz's own theory of matter solves this problem, since although his monads are certainly units, ordinary objects seem to come out as mere collections—collections of infinite sets of monads. It seems likely that, despite his earlier concern about the 'genuine unity of things', Leibniz eventually came to see ordinary material things as merely 'well founded phenomena'—items that do not possess any substantial individuality of their own, but which are simply the result of, or a function of, underlying realities (monads) that do have substantial unity. 'Matter is a phenomenon like a rainbow, not substantial but the result of substances.'[41] Only in the case of minds did Leibniz continue to maintain unequivocally that our ordinary intuitions about what counts as a genuine individual truly reflect the nature of underlying reality (GP IV. 482; P 120).

Leibniz's theory of the mind

Explaining his rejection of the Cartesian conception of matter, Leibniz wrote in 1695 in his *New System*: 'it is only atoms of substance, that is to say unities that are real and absolutely without parts, which can be the sources of *actions* and the absolute first principles of the composition of things' (GP IV. 482; L 456). In place of inert homogeneous extended stuff, Leibniz has an infinity of active substances, each unfolding its nature with 'a perfect spontaneity' and yet—in virtue of the principle of pre-established harmony—'in perfect conformity with the things outside it' (GP IV. 484; L 457). It might be thought that this active and harmonious conception of matter would put Leibniz in an ideal position to provide a radical solution to the mind–body problem that bedevilled post-Cartesian philosophy. Instead of an immaterial soul mysteriously interacting with inert matter, why not say that mental states (thought, perception, consciousness) arise from the 'dance of activity', as it were, of the countless monads composing the brain or nervous system of man—all acting together spontaneously yet in perfect harmony. This would be reductionism of a kind—the reducing of mental states to physiological states—yet given Leibniz's revision of the Cartesian conception of matter, it would be a reduction of a kind that would not be vulnerable to the objection that thought could not possibly be a property of mere extended stuff. As Leibniz himself pointed out, if matter is understood to mean 'that which includes only passive and indifferent concepts such as extension and impenetrability', then one would indeed need something further, to give it 'determinate form or activity' (GP VI. 506; L 551). But a richer, more active conception of matter might seem to avoid the need for attributing consciousness to a separate non-material substance.

In fact, however, Leibniz shrank from this kind of reductionist approach to mental properties, and ended up with a position that was uncomfortably close to the problem-ridden theory of Descartes, in its acceptance of the thesis that mental properties must be properties of an immaterial spirit. '*L'âme est une substance incorporelle*', wrote Leibniz in a letter to Ernst von Hessen Rheinfels in January 1691; and in the Preface to the *New Essays* it is explicitly stated that the soul is an immortal and immaterial substance in which the faculty of thought naturally inheres (RB 67–8). 'I am above all', Leibniz wrote of his purpose in the *New Essays*, 'concerned to vindicate the immateriality of the soul which M. Locke leaves doubtful.' (GP III. 473).[42] To see why Leibniz insisted on the existence of an immaterial soul in man, it is instructive to examine his reactions to the Cartesian treatment of human and animal physiology. The Cartesian programme here was strongly reductionistic: everything going on inside our bodies (digestion, nutrition, respiration, and the like) was to be explained purely mechanistically, in terms of configurations of particles of a certain shape and motion. In a letter of 1678 Leibniz expresses his strong support for the new mechanistic philosophy—the doctrine, as he puts it, 'that everything happens in nature according to certain mechanical laws prescribed by God'. He goes on to echo Descartes, saying that he recognizes 'nothing in bodies in so far as they are separated from mind, except magnitude, figure, situation and changes in these, either partial or total'; and he further argues that this approach may profitably be applied to the mechanisms for discriminating sensible qualities such as colours, sounds, odours, and tastes:

What is more probable than that all sensible qualities are merely tactual qualities varying according to the variety of sense organs? But touch recognises only magnitude, motion, situation or figure and various degrees of resistance in bodies . . . How can we expect to understand the causes of such things except by mechanical laws . . . (GP I. 197; L 189).

Descartes had made it abundantly clear that his mechanistic approach could be extended to the automatic sensory responses associated with vision, hearing, smell, and the like in animals:

This will not seem strange to those who know how many kinds of automatons or moving machines the skill of man can construct with the use of very few parts, in comparison with the great multitude of bones, muscles, nerves, arteries, veins and all the other parts that are in the body of an animal. For they will regard this body as a machine which, having been made by the hand of God, is incomparably better ordered than any machine that can be devised by man . . . (AT VI. 55; CSM I. 139).

Leibniz continued to be strongly attracted by this approach, as far as physiology was concerned, and there are many passages even in his later writings where we find echoes of the Cartesian conception of the body as a machine: 'each organic body of a living thing is a kind of divine machine or natural automaton which infinitely surpasses all artificial automata' (*Monadology*, para. 64). But he came to dissociate himself from the Cartesian programme in two respects. First, as already discussed (above, p. 107), he developed a conception of matter itself that was less 'mechanical' and more 'vitalistic' than anything Descartes had envisaged. Though the body of an animal might be a machine, it was a machine whose smallest elements were not merely inert, extended matter but active, self-moving 'entelechies' or monads.[43] Second, as regards the status of animals, Leibniz was disinclined to believe that their behaviour was as mechanistic as the Cartesians maintained:

> In Holland they are now disputing loudly and soundly whether beasts are machines, and people are ridiculing the Cartesians for believing that a dog when it is clubbed cries in the same way as a bagpipe when pressed. As for me, I grant the Cartesians that all external actions of the beast can be explained mechanically; but I nonetheless believe that beasts have some knowledge, and there is something in them . . . which can be called a soul . . . (Letter to Von Tschirnhaus of 1684: L 275).

Many of Descartes's critics had pointed out that animals seem to have knowledge; Gassendi, for example, had cited against Descartes examples of highly intelligent behaviour in dogs (A T VII. 270; CSM II. 189). But those who believed animals were genuinely intelligent had two choices: either they could accept the Cartesian idea of an immaterial soul and maintain, *contra* Descartes, that even non-human animals were endowed with souls; or they could accept the Cartesian programme of mechanistic reduction, and extend it upwards to man himself. For if the Cartesians had gone as far as explaining the human *body* as a machine, why should not the whole human being—thoughts, knowledge, and all—be a machine, albeit a machine of an extraordinarily sophisticated kind?[44] Leibniz was unable to accept the second alternative; part of the reason for this emerges in the *Monadology*, where there is a vivid thought-experiment designed to show that the phenomena of conscious thought cannot be explained in purely mechanical terms. Imagine, says Leibniz in effect, that the brain were enlarged, but with all the relative proportions of its parts preserved, so that we could walk inside it as one might enter a factory or a mill (French, *moulin*): 'On going inside we should only see the parts impinging on one another; we should not see anything which would explain a perception. The explanation of perception must therefore be sought in a simple substance and not in a compound or in a machine' (para. 17).

The argument has its modern adherents: if we open up the

brain, it is said, all we find is blood, gristle, grey matter, and white matter; if we use a microscope, then we find clusters of nerve cells, axons, dendrites, and so on; but at no point, it is argued, do we discover anything corresponding to *consciousness*.[45] But the argument is a bad one. Suppose one were to argue that if we dissect a watch all we find are cogs and wheels, nothing corresponding to the watch's 'time-keeping function', and hence that there must be an immaterial soul in the watch that keeps time. The inference would of course be faulty: the reason why the 'time-keeping function' of the watch is not to be straightforwardly inspected at the microscopic level is that it is what one might call a 'high level' (or perhaps 'holistic') property which depends on the totality of the parts all working together. Yet the reductionist can still quite properly maintain that everything that the watch does is ultimately explicable in physical terms.[46] Similarly, nothing that Leibniz has said about the impossibility of straightforwardly 'observing' perceptions at the microscopic level is sufficient in itself to rule out the possibility of a reductionistic explanation of consciousness in physical terms.

Leibniz has, however, another argument to support his insistence that mental activity cannot be a function of mere physiology—an argument which hinges on a claim about the unity of consciousness. 'There is', wrote Leibniz in his *New System*, 'a true entity which corresponds to what is called the "I" in us, which could not occur in artificial machines, nor in the simple mass of matter, however organised it may be' (GP IV. 482 L 456). But how can we be sure of such a 'true unity'? Leibniz is implicitly relying here on a direct appeal to our own inner experience—a point which comes out explicitly in a paper written in 1702:

> So far as the details of the phenomena are concerned, everything takes place in the body as if . . . man himself were only an automaton . . . But *internal experience*, the consciousness within us of this Ego which perceives the things occurring in the body . . . makes us recognise an indivisible substance in ourselves (GP IV. 560; L 577–8).

Although Leibniz was distinctly scathing about Descartes's arguments for the immateriality of the mind,[47] it seems that he is

moving on to ground which is as shaky as that occupied by
Descartes in his discussions of the 'indivisibility' of the mind. For
even if one accepts (and one does not have to[48]) the phenomeno-
logical point that we have internal awareness of a single 'I' or
'ego', it is not at all clear that we are entitled to 'read off' from
this any ontological conclusions about an indivisible immaterial
substance that is the subject of consciousness. Indeed, since
Leibniz himself came to acknowledge that the appearance of
unity in ordinary physical items like trees and mountains might
be deceptive, and not such as to correspond one-to-one with
an underlying substantial unity, it is curious that he never seriously considered the possibility that the same might be true of
the mind.[49]

Admittedly, if we reflect on 'what it is like' to have a mental life,
it is the subjective dimension that seems crucial; when we
introspect, each of us is aware of a series of subjectively accessible
thoughts and feelings rather than a complex set of objectively
observable physiological events. Nevertheless the 'Spinozistic'
interpretation remains possible, and has certainly not been
refuted by Leibniz: that what we experience 'from the inside' is
simply the self-same set of events that is constituted by neurophysiological happenings in the brain.[50]

Although Leibniz sides with Descartes against Spinoza by
insisting on the immateriality of the mind, there are passages in
his writings that are reminiscent of Spinoza's notion of two chains
of causes—the mental and the physical—operating, as it were,
side by side. Picking up the Aristotelian distinction between on
the one hand *efficient* causes (that is, the ordinary mechanisms for
bringing about some physical change), and on the other hand
final causes (the ends or goals for the sake of which something is
done), Leibniz writes of two 'kingdoms' of causes in harmony:
'Souls act according to the laws of final causes by appetitions,
ends and means. Bodies act according to the laws of efficient
causes by motions. And the two kingdoms of efficient and final
causes are in harmony with one another' (*Monadology*, para. 79).
It is tempting, from a modern perspective, to see this as an
anticipation of the illuminating notion of different *levels of
description*: if *A* passes some gold coins to *B*, for example, we can

describe the transaction in teleological (or 'final causality') terms ('it was done in order to pay off a debt'); but we can also speak in mechanical (or 'efficient-causality') terms and refer to the contractions of muscles and the transfer of so many grams of metal from one vicinity to the other. This is fine as far as it goes. But notice that given Leibniz's insistence on the immateriality of the mind, he cannot allow for any 'crossing' between the realms: there can be no meeting point between the language of consciousness and the language of mechanics. Thus we are not allowed to say something like '*A*'s resolve to pay the money caused him to stretch out his hand and offer the gold to *B*'. Minds are non-physical substances, and cannot transmit force to bodily matter; they cannot initiate motion in matter, nor even alter the *direction* of motion, as the Cartesians had proposed. Leibniz is quite firm on this point: the laws of physics require the conservation of momentum, that is mass times velocity—the latter being a measure not just of speed but of speed in a given direction (cf. para. 80).[51] Once the immateriality of the mind is acknowledged, then there cannot (*pace* Descartes) be any interaction whatever with matter.

To explain the fact that mind and body certainly *appear* to interact, Leibniz propounds his theory of pre-established harmony. As we have already seen (Chapter 3, p. 109), this theory is required not just to explain the apparent transactions between mind and body, but also to account for the apparently interactive behaviour of *all* monads. Since monads are self-contained and windowless, they cannot strictly speaking interact at all; they merely spontaneously express their unique natures, but all in perfect harmony, so as to give the appearance of causal intercommunication. Replying to the reservations of Antoine Arnauld about the intelligibility of this notion, Leibniz distinguished between three possible ways of producing 'agreement' between substances:

Imagine two clocks or watches which are in perfect agreement. This agreement can come about in three ways. The first consists of a natural *influence*... The second method [the way of *assistance*] would be to have the clocks continually supervised by a skilful craftsman who constantly sets them right. The third method is to construct the two clocks so skilfully and accurately at the outset that one could be certain of their subsequent agreement (*Explanation of the New System*: GP IV. 499; P 131).

The first way—that of direct causal influence—Leibniz rejects for rationalistic reasons which many of Descartes's supporters (such as Malebranche) readily acknowledged: 'it is impossible to conceive of either material particulars or immaterial qualities as capable of passing from one of these substances to the other' (ibid.).[52] The second way, the way of assistance, corresponds to Malebranche's occasionalism, where God acts to produce movements in the body corresponding to the volitions in the mind; but Leibniz rejects this as an elaborate *ad hoc* artifice—the 'bringing in of a *deus ex machina* for a natural and ordinary thing'. And the third is of course Leibniz's own solution of pre-established harmony, whereby a 'divine anticipatory artifice' guarantees, in creating mind and body, that 'merely as a result of mind and body each following its own laws' everything comes about just *as if* each were mutually influencing the other.

Although Leibniz went in for elaborate self-congratulation concerning his solution to the mind–body problem,[53] it is in many respects unsatisfying. First, the slur with which Leibniz reproaches Malebranche, of introducing *ad hoc* theological solutions, seems equally applicable to the Leibnizian system, albeit perhaps in a less blatant form (see Chapter 3, p. 111). Second, and more important, the consequence of Leibniz's view—that the transmission of causal influence is only an illusion—seems at first to be strongly counter-intuitive. 'What is the point of this complex organization [of pre-established harmony] between substances?' wrote Leibniz's critic Simon Foucher in an article published in 1695. 'It seems that the only thing it achieves is to make us firmly believe that substances interact with each other, despite the fact that [on your view] this is precisely what does *not* occur!'[54] From our own modern perspective, Leibniz's theory may also seem implausible on empirical grounds. Physiology clearly suggests that there is a transmission of impulses from one nerve cell to another (when, for instance, there is damage to the foot), and that this step-by-step causal flow generates changes in the spinal cord, and then later in the brain; what appears to be involved here, at least as far as the nervous system is concerned, is a set of actual chemical and electrical *transfers*.

Leibniz's response here would undoubtedly be to challenge the objector to explain exactly what is the cash value of our commonly used metaphors such as that of *transfer*, when applied to causal processes. Scientists frequently talk of transfers of energy or of momentum (indeed Descartes, in formulating his laws of motion in 1644, had spoken of one body transferring or imparting motion to another: *Principles* II, 40);[55] but can this mean any more than that there is a lawlike correlation between a decrease in momentum in some kinds of bodies and an increase in momentum in others?[56] One great merit of Leibniz's writings on causation is that they force us to consider what work metaphorical notions such as 'transfer,' 'transmit', and 'influence' are really doing.

To put this matter in historical perspective, it is worth noting that some models of causation that were widely supported in the seventeenth century appeared to require a quite literal 'flow' of items between cause and effect. The standard scholastic theory of sense-perception held that when we perceive any object, what the intellect apprehends is the 'sensible form' (Latin, *species*) of that object; on some seventeenth-century versions of the theory, this was supposed to involve the actual transmission of some kind of 'image' or 'semblance' from object to observer.[57] Descartes rejected this latter notion for reasons based largely on empirical physiology: observation failed to confirm the existence of any such 'little images flitting through the air', as he scathingly termed them (AT VI. 85; CSM I. 154); it could be shown that nothing reached the sense-organs except for local motions of matter (AT VIII. 322; CSM I. 285). Leibniz's objections to 'sensible forms' were of a more theoretical and purely logical kind: to talk of a transfer between object and observer seemed to imply that a modification of one substance could be passed on to another. Yet 'accidents cannot become detached, or wander round about outside substances, as the *sensible species* of the scholastics were supposed to do' (*Monadology*, para. 7).

As far as ordinary parlance was concerned, Leibniz was quite

ready to allow that the language of causal interaction was
permissible up to a point:

> I should have no objection even to saying that the soul moves the
> body, in the same way as a Copernican rightly speaks of the rising of the
> sun . . . I believe that it is very true to say that substances act upon one
> another, provided it is understood that the one is the cause of changes in
> the other in consequence of the law of [pre-established] harmony (GP IV.
> 495; P 128).

So to describe causal phenomena in terms of one thing's acting on
another is perfectly allowable; Leibniz simply maintains that a
proper analysis of what is going on is possible only if we move
beyond the vague and misleading metaphors of interaction and
transmission.

Leibniz can thus be cleared of the charge that his theory is
'counter-intuitive' or that it involves an 'unscientific' denial of the
existence of causal phenomena. What is at issue is not what we
observe, but what is the most scientifically and philosophically
satisfying analysis of what we observe; and it is by no means clear,
for example, that the laws of the conservation of motion or
energy are most perspicuously explicated in terms of the transmission metaphors which Leibniz rejected. Nevertheless, when we
move from the world of physics to the relation between mind and
body, there remains a sense in which it seems fair to call the
Leibnizian theory of pre-established harmony distinctly unsatisfying. In the case of sense-perception, for example, when there is a
mental change consequent on the stimulation of the sense-organs,
what Leibniz is asking us to accept, in addition to whatever may
be happening in the body and in the brain, is a further, wholly
non-physical, event—a modification of an immaterial soul arising quite spontaneously but (through divine creative foresight) at
precisely the right time, and in precisely the right manner to
constitute an appropriate response to what is happening in the
body. (And vice versa: 'the animal spirits and the blood take on,
at exactly the right moment, the motions required to correspond
to the passions and the perceptions of the soul'—*New System*: GP
IV. 484; L 458.) Little further can be added to explain or elucidate
the mind–body relations that, as Leibniz himself has to admit, are

a 'natural and ordinary' part of our everyday experience (GP IV. 499; P 131).

Souls, consciousness, and transparency

Although Leibniz accepted, on the whole, the Cartesian thesis of the immateriality of the mind, it would be quite wrong to represent him as a prisoner of the Cartesian framework in his views of mind and body. In many respects, he strove to close the mysterious gap between mind and matter that had plagued Descartes and Malebranche. Perhaps the most striking difference between the Cartesian approach and that of Leibniz lies in the fact that for Descartes consciousness is an 'all or nothing' property. Either something is *res cogitans*—a self-aware, thinking being with conceptual and linguistic abilities[58]—or else it is a mere modification of 'extended stuff', simply a piece of machinery. Leibniz, by contrast, was, as we have seen, prepared to admit that animals have consciousness of a kind; more radically, he regarded the whole universe as, in a sense, animated or 'ensouled'. Monads, those soul-like atoms of substance that are the ultimate constituents of reality, are all described by Leibniz as having *perceptions* (*Monadology*, paras. 14 and 19).

The term might almost seem to be chosen on purpose to irritate the Cartesians. Descartes and his followers had reserved the term *percipere* for the purely intellectual acts characteristic of a *res cogitans*. For Leibniz, however, to say that a monad 'perceives' is to say that it has an inner state whereby it 'represents' external things (GP VI. 600; P 197). Such representation is characteristic of every monad, however humble; each monad is a 'perpetual living mirror' of the whole universe. And as the universe is eternal and indestructible, so is each monad (*Monadology*, para. 77).

All this is as different as could be from the Cartesian plenum of inert, extended substance (indeed matter, for Descartes, so far from being indestructible, needs the perpetual active concurrence of God to keep it from slipping out of existence: AT VII. 49; CSM II. 33). But when it comes to *thought* in the full-blooded sense of self-conscious, reflective activity, Leibniz makes it clear that this is restricted to that special class of monads which he terms

'rational souls' or minds. 'It is well', he says, 'to distinguish between *perception*, which is the inner state of the monad representing external things, and *apperception*, which is consciousness,
the reflective knowledge of this inner state which is not given
to all souls, nor at all times to the same soul . . .' (GP VI. 600;
P 197). Leibniz is thus radically unCartesian in his inclination
to espouse the 'panpsychistic' view that all things are active
and 'ensouled'—the bearers of some kind of informational or
representational content.[59] But he goes along with the Cartesians
in regarding thought in the narrow sense as a special kind of
activity attributable to a special kind of substance (compare the
Preface to the *New Essays*, where it is taken as axiomatic that a
'substance with a faculty of thinking inherent in it' is an
immaterial substance: RB 67; P 170). 'Souls in general', writes
Leibniz in the *Monadology*, 'are living mirrors of the universe . . .;
but Minds are also images of the Divinity himself, or the Author
of nature, capable of knowing the system of the universe . . .'
(para. 83).

Leibniz's comment, in the passage quoted above, that conscious thought or apperception is 'not given at all times to the
same soul', contrasts interestingly with a celebrated and much debated thesis of Descartes, that the mind 'always thinks'. This had
struck many of Descartes's contemporary critics as absurd: could
it really be supposed that a young infant, for example, perpetually indulges in cogitative activity? 'During early life,' Gassendi
objected, 'thought is meagre, obscure and virtually non-existent'
(AT VII. 264; CSM II. 184). Even if we construe *cogitatio* in the
widest sense, to include any conscious activity, common sense
suggests that both in children and adults (during deep sleep)
consciousness can be suspended entirely. In confronting these
objections Descartes refused to abandon his thesis, and insisted
that thought occurs even in the deepest sleep, and begins right
from the moment when the soul is implanted in the body—that is,
even before birth. He conjectured, however, that during these
early years the mind's activities are subject to a good deal of
interference from bodily stimuli—thus explaining why we have
no coherent recollection of what we thought as infants (AT V.

150; CB 8). Later in the century John Locke was to pour scorn on these claims as fruitless: 'We know certainly by Experience that we sometimes think, and then draw this infallible Consequence, That there is something in us that has a Power to think: but whether that Substance perpetually thinks, or no, we can be no farther assured than Experience informs us.'[60] Although Descartes was frequently drawn into discussing how his 'perpetual thought' thesis stood up to the supposedly negative evidence of what happens when we are very young, or asleep, his main reasons for maintaining the thesis were purely a priori. Given the premiss that each of us is 'a substance whose whole essence or nature is simply to think' (AT VI. 33; CSM I. 127), it follows that we *must* continue to think so long as we exist. For a thing's essence is, by definition, that which it cannot lack; in scholastic terms, the *accidental* properties of X can be present or absent, depending on circumstances, but the *essential* properties of X must always be present (or else one would not be talking about X at all but about something else).

When commenting on the dispute between Locke and the Cartesians on this issue, Leibniz appears at first to range himself with the Cartesians: 'There are at all times an infinite number of perceptions in us'; 'we never sleep so soundly but that we have some feeble and confused sensation' (RB 53, 54; P 155, 156). But it soon becomes clear that Leibniz is not so much following Descartes's theory of mind as proposing a radically different theory of his own. The Cartesians had argued that mental substance cannot be without its defining characteristic of thought; Leibniz matches this by insisting that a monad cannot be without the defining characteristic of a substance, perceptual activity. But he goes on:

There are at all times an infinite number of perceptions in us, though without apperception [consciousness] and without reflection; that is, changes in soul which we do not apperceive because their impressions either are too small and too numerous, or too unified, so that they have nothing sufficiently distinctive in themselves—though in combination with others they do not fail to have their effect and to make themselves felt, at least confusedly, in the mass (RB 53; P 155).

'The mind always thinks' thus meant something very different for Leibniz than it did for Descartes. For Descartes it meant that the conscious cogitative activity that constitutes the very essence of a mind is perpetual and uninterrupted. For Leibniz, fully conscious thought may often be suspended; what continues is a host of subconscious or even unconscious events—what are later on called *petites perceptions*. These 'minute perceptions' are 'mental' only in the attenuated sense that their effects may be felt at the threshold of consciousness (RB 54).

Some of Leibniz's arguments for the hypothesis of *petites perceptions* are distinctly weak. We could not hear the roar of the waves, Leibniz maintains, unless we had some unconscious perception of the noise made by each wave: 'to hear the noise as we do, we must surely hear the parts of which the noise is made up' (RB 55; P 155). On the face of it, this seems as dubious as arguing from the fact that we feel the weight of a stone that we must have an unconscious perception of the weight of each of the molecules that make it up. A more general consideration that Leibniz offers in support of *petites perceptions* is that their existence is required by what he calls his 'most important and best verified maxim'—the *lex continui* or 'law of continuity', the principle that 'nature never makes leaps' (RB 56; P 158). Leibniz's invoking of the principle in this particular context seems to tie in with his attempt to close the Cartesian gap between the material and spiritual realms: instead of a universe where there are on the one hand physical events, and on the other hand utterly unconnected conscious events, Leibniz proposes a universe in which perception is a matter of degree, something which is present in rudimentary form in all things, even though it only takes the form of full awareness in minds. ('Noticeable perceptions come by degrees from those which are too small to be noticed': P 158). This may at least partly explain why Leibniz saw his system of pre-established harmony as such a clear advance on Malebranchian occasionalism. The latter, as applied to mind and body, requires divine action to bring into harmony two utterly distinct and alien substances. But in Leibniz's system, the postulated harmony is a harmony of monads which have at least something in common. In general it may be said that the traditional barriers between the organic and inorganic, the sensitive and non-sensitive, and finally the conscious and non-conscious realms, are all played down in Leibniz's system of infinitely many organic, perceiving substances which 'all conspire' so that even the lowliest carries information from which one could in theory 'read off' the entire structure of reality.[61]

In allowing the possibility of degrees of awareness, and of perceptions at or below the threshold of consciousness, Leibniz breaks with another important Cartesian thesis, the so-called doctrine of the 'perfect transparency of the mind'. The mind, for Descartes, is simply *res cogitans*—a thinking thing; and thought, its defining attribute, is explicated by Descartes in terms of *awareness* (Latin, *conscientia*): 'I use the term "thought" to include everything that is within us in such a way that we are immediately aware (*conscius*) of it' (Second set of Replies: AT VII. 160; CSM II. 113). Clearly there is no room here for 'unconscious' percep-tions. But things are not quite as simple as this definition of thought suggests, for in talking of the 'contents' of the mind, or what we have 'within us', Descartes also uses the terminology of *ideas*—a term fraught with ambiguities and philosophical pit-falls.[62] In his official definition of the term 'idea', Descartes says, somewhat obscurely, that it is the 'form of any given thought, immediate perception of which makes me aware of that thought' (ibid). But although the ideas are 'in' the mind, Descartes cannot mean that we are actually aware of all of them at any moment: clearly the mind can only be aware of a limited number of things at a given time, and since 'ideas' seem to be the concepts or notions with which the mind is stocked, it would be a manifest absurdity to suggest that anyone could have simultaneous im-mediate awareness of all the concepts which he possesses.[63] It seems clear that any remotely adequate theory of the mind will need two notions: first, that of immediate awareness, and second something like the notion of the 'storage' of information which the mind has the ability to 'access' (to use modern computer jargon), but which need not always be present to consciousness. Descartes himself uses the metaphor of 'store-house' or 'treasure-house' (*thesaurus*) in this connection. It is possible, he allows, for someone never to think about God at all—he may never 'light on any thought of God'; but whenever he does choose to 'bring forth the idea of God from the treasure-house of the mind', he will necessarily be aware of certain properties which are applicable to the divine nature (AT VII. 67; CSM II. 46).

The metaphor of the store-house to some extent clouds the transparency doctrine. It is not claimed that the mind is actually aware of all its contents; what is claimed is that when suitably directed it can become aware of any of its contents. But reflection suggests that this is not at all a simple process like turning to a certain page in a book. Sometimes great effort is needed to formulate a principle that is within us (as Leibniz points out: RB 50). Sometimes, as when we suddenly see the solution to a problem in mathematics, no doubt making use of information that is in some way stored within us, we are far from being aware of the exact sequence of 'ideas' that led to the solution. Furthermore, as Descartes's unorthodox disciple Nicolas Malebranche objected, to say that mental representation involves pulling ideas out of a store-house simply raises the further question of how the mind is able to identify and select the relevant ideas in the first place.[64] The notion of ideas 'contained' or 'stored' within the mind, waiting to be revealed when our awareness is directed towards them, like a searchlight, thus begins on reflection to look distinctly unhelpful. All this lends some support to Leibniz's rejection of the Cartesian thesis that consciousness is a simple all-or-nothing process that is straightforwardly revealed in introspection.[65]

Descartes's claim that we have transparent awareness of our own mental processes and contents is closely connected with a thesis that is central to the development of his metaphysics: the mind, Descartes frequently asserts, has a perfect understanding of its own essential nature. As he puts it in the *Meditations*, 'I can achieve an easier and more evident perception of my own mind than of anything else' (AT VII. 34; CSM II. 23). This doctrine provides one of the most striking issues on which Malebranche finds himself unable to follow in Descartes's footsteps:

> It is true that we know well enough through our consciousness, or the inner sensation we have of ourselves, that our soul is something of importance. But what we know of it might be almost nothing compared

with what it is in itself . . . To know the soul perfectly, it is not enough to know only what we know through inner sensation, since the consciousness we have of ourselves perhaps shows us only the least part of our being.[66]

Even when we are having a vivid sensation such as that of a particular colour or sound, Malebranche goes on to say, the experience does not introspectively reveal itself as a 'modification of the soul'. Malebranche concludes that although Descartes is right in saying that the mind knows its own *existence* better than the existence of anything else, none the less our knowledge of the soul's *nature* is 'not as perfect as our knowledge of the nature of bodies' (ibid.). In his *Christian Metaphysical Meditations* of 1683, Malebranche goes so far as to say that introspection gives us no information at all from which we may infer the nature of the mind or soul. 'Je ne suis que ténèbres à moi-même', asserts Malebranche: 'to myself I am but darkness, and my own substance seems something which is beyond my understanding'.[67]

Malebranche's pointed questions about the mind's alleged ability to grasp its own nature by simple introspection are not only threatening to the Cartesian conception; they seem to bear with equal force on Leibniz's claim that internal experience enables us to recognize a simple, indivisible substance within ourselves (GP IV. 560; L 578). At the end of the day, despite his more sophisticated conception of consciousness as a matter of degree, Leibniz is not very much closer than Descartes to achieving a genuine understanding of the nature of mental phenomena. The language that runs through seventeenth- and eighteenth-century discussions of the mind—the language of 'ideas', 'perceptions', and 'impressions'—often seems little more than a jargon masking fundamental ignorance of the mind's nature and workings. It can hardly be a fair criticism of Descartes, Spinoza, and Leibniz that they did not succeed in providing a viable explanatory framework for phenomena that modern cognitive science, with vastly enriched theoretical and empirical resources, is only just beginning to get to grips with. If one can level a criticism against seventeenth-century theories of the mind, it is that they manage to conceal just how complex and problematic those phenomena are.

5

Freedom and Morality

Human power is very limited and infinitely surpassed by
the power of external causes . . . Nevertheless we shall
bear calmly what happens to us against our advantage if
we are conscious first that we have done our duty, second
that the power we have could not have stretched to the
point where we could have avoided those ills, and third
that we are a part of the whole of nature, whose order we
follow (Spinoza, *Ethica, c.*1665).

Such joy we can always create for ourselves when our
minds are well ordered . . . when we feel a strong
inclination and towards the good and the true . . . and
we discover the chief source, the course and purpose of
everything, the Supreme and All-encompassing Nature
. . . Then it is as if we . . . were looking down from the
stars and could see all earthly things under our feet
(Leibniz, *von Weisheit, c.*1695).

That an infinitely good, infinitely holy, infinitely free
God, being able to make creatures good and happy,
should have preferred that they should be eternally
criminal and miserable, is something that troubles reason
. . . (Pierre Bayle, *Dictionnaire historique et critique,*
1697).[1]

The modern sharp separation between the philosophy of
knowledge and the philosophy of practice is largely alien to
seventeenth-century modes of thought.[2] In establishing new and
reliable foundations for knowledge, Descartes hoped to facilitate
the development of a complete philosophical system that would
include not only an account of the physical universe, but also a
recipe for human welfare. In the celebrated metaphor used by
Descartes and others, medicine and morals take their places
alongside mechanics as branches of the tree of knowledge of

which the roots are metaphysics and the trunk physics (AT IXB. 14; CSM I. 186). For Spinoza, too, metaphysics is not an abstract academic inquiry divorced from practical concerns; on the contrary, the attainment of a worthwhile life is presented as a direct consequence of the kind of rational understanding of the universe and our human nature that is the goal of metaphysics. Spinoza's greatest work is appropriately called the *Ethics*, since its object is to unfold the knowledge whereby we may make the transition from 'human servitude' to 'human freedom' (G II. 277; C 594). And in Leibniz the ethical dimension is perhaps most striking of all. Leibniz depicts a 'living universe' which is perfectly regulated by the 'supreme wisdom and goodness of its creator'; the beauty of creation can be 'learnt in each soul'; and the minds of men may 'enter by virtue of reason into a kind of society with God' so as to become 'members of the city of God' (GP VI. 604; P 201, 202). Thus, when we turn to the views of the great seventeenth-century rationalists on the human predicament and the way to lead a worthwhile life, we are certainly not leaving behind the themes of earlier chapters and addressing a wholly separate set of doctrines. The goal of attaining happiness may perhaps not have been the initial motivation for Descartes, Spinoza, or Leibniz, nor did it define the starting point of their philosophical inquiries; but none the less they would surely all have accepted such a goal as integral to their very conception of what the philosophical enterprise was about.[3]

Divine goodness and Cartesian freedom

Most modern philosophy students, if asked to list the major themes of Descartes's metaphysical masterpiece, the *Meditations*, would probably mention philosophical doubt, the nature of knowledge, the Cogito argument, and the relation between mind and body. But the dominant leitmotif of the work, the theme to which the meditator most frequently returns in his reflections, could be described as a theological-cum-ethical one: how to reconcile the benevolence of God with the existence of human error. There is an important sense in which the *Meditations* can be seen as a work of theodicy, an attempt to provide a vindication of the goodness and justice of God.

Even in the morass of doubt of the First Meditation, it is readily granted that 'God is supremely good and the source of truth' (AT VII. 22; CSM II. 15).[4] Later, in the Third Meditation, God is described as 'the possessor of all the perfections which I cannot grasp but can somehow reach in my thought—subject to no defect whatsoever' (AT VII. 52; CSM II. 35). The theme recurs in the Fourth Meditation: he is 'supremely perfect and cannot be a deceiver on pain of contradiction' (AT VII. 62; CSM II. 43), and again at the end of the Sixth Meditation: there is 'absolutely nothing in my sensations that does not bear witness to his goodness and power' (AT VII. 88; CSM II. 60). But the undoubted fact that human beings do frequently fall into error poses a problem for the Cartesian meditator that is closely parallel to the traditional theological puzzle of the existence of evil. Just as, if God is good and the omnipotent creator of all, it seems odd that there should be evil in the world, similarly if God is good and the source of all truth, it seems odd that there should be error. More specifically, if God created me and gave me a mind which is in principle a reliable instrument for the perception of truth ('a reliable mind was God's gift to me': AT V. 148; CB 5), how does it come about that I often go astray in my judgements?

One of the standard theological responses to the problem of evil was to lay the blame on man's exercise of his free will, and Descartes's response to the problem of intellectual error is closely similar. In order to make a judgement, he explains, both the intellect and the will are required: the intellect perceives the content of a given proposition, but then the will is required in order for assent or denial to be given (AT VIII. 18; CSM I. 204). Now the intellect is indeed a reliable instrument: whatever it does clearly and distinctly perceive is, of necessity, true (AT VII. 70; CSM II. 48). But though reliable, the intellect is limited: there are many things that it does not clearly perceive. The will, by contrast, extends much further than the intellect; indeed its scope is indefinitely great (AT VII. 57; CSM II. 40). The cause of error is thus quite straightforward: in cases where we do not clearly perceive something, we should suspend judgement; but often we rashly give free rein to our will, jumping in and giving our assent. In such circumstances, Descartes insists, there is nothing that casts doubt on the benevolence of God. I cannot complain that my intellect is limited, since it is in the nature of a finite being to be limited in some respects—a point which Leibniz was to take up in his own *Theodicy* (I, 20). Nor can God be blamed for bestowing on me an unlimited will. For the power of the will to assent or not to assent does not at all mean that I *have* to fall into error. On the contrary, there is a simple and infallible recipe for the avoidance of error: 'provided I restrain my will so that it extends to what the intellect clearly and distinctly reveals and no further, then it is quite impossible for me to go wrong' (AT VII. 43; CSM II. 62).[5] In the exercise of our free will lies both the source of our error and the means for its avoidance.

Both Spinoza and Leibniz were committed to providing a convincing analysis of the concept of freedom, and for this reason they took a close interest in the theory of the will that is presupposed in Descartes's account of the problem of error. Spinoza offers, to begin with, a technical objection to Descartes's account, namely that it falsely supposes that the will and the intellect are two distinct faculties. In reality, Spinoza argues, the will and the intellect are 'one and the same'. One cannot conceive of a particular idea without an affirmation, nor of an affirmation without an idea. So far from being distinct from the intellect, then, the will is 'something universal which is predicated of all ideas' (G II. 135; C 489). Part of what Spinoza is getting at here is that 'suspending judgement' is not a separate act which we decide to perform at will in relation to a given proposition. In the case where something is perceived 'adequately' (for example, when we perceive that some property necessarily belongs to a triangle), then it is not a case of first perceiving and then affirming; rather, the affirmation is involved in the very perception. Similarly, the suspension of judgement is not a decision we take as a result of recognizing the inadequacy of our perceptions; rather it is the very recognition of that inadequacy: 'when we say that someone suspends judgement, we are saying merely that he sees that he does not perceive the thing adequately' (G II. 134; C 488).[6]

In criticizing Descartes, Spinoza does not merely complain that he gives a distorting account of the nature of belief and judgement.

He has a more general complaint, namely that Descartes has an untenable conception of what human freedom consists in. 'There is no absolute freedom [of the kind Descartes supposed],' asserts Spinoza in the *Ethics* (II, prop. 48). Descartes insisted that 'we have inner awareness of our freedom' (AT V. 159; CB 21. Cf. *Principles* I, 41), to which Spinoza replied that 'men think themselves free because they are conscious of their volitions and their appetites, yet never give a thought to the causes which dispose them to desire or to exercise the will as they do, since they are wholly unaware of them' (G II. 78; C 440). Leibniz put forward a very similar criticism: 'Monsieur Descartes', he wrote, 'requires a freedom for which there is no need, when he insists that the actions of the will of man are altogether undetermined— a thing which never happens' (*Theodicy*: GP VI. 89).

Both Leibniz and Spinoza take a strictly determinist view of the universe. 'If men clearly understood the whole of nature,' claims Spinoza, 'they would find everything just as necessary as the things treated of in mathematics' (G I. 266; C 332); this entails that for any given event X, there can be no possibility that it could have been otherwise.[7] For Leibniz, there is the celebrated 'principle of sufficient reason' which asserts that 'no fact can be real and no proposition can be true unless there is a sufficient reason why it should be thus and not otherwise' (*Monadology*, para. 32); and it follows from this that whatever in fact occurs in the universe is 'certain and determined beforehand' (*Theodicy* I, 52). Those who espouse such determinist views, but also wish to find a place for human freedom, have two choices. Either they can attempt to exempt human beings from the laws of nature, and maintain that we have some absolute or 'contra-causal' power of choice whereby we are able, as it were, to stand outside the framework of determining conditions; or else (the so-called 'reconciliationist' or 'compatibilist' line[8]) they can propose a concept of freedom which allows someone to be acting freely even though, given all the circumstances that in fact obtained, he could not have done otherwise. Both Spinoza and Leibniz favoured the second of these alternatives; and, as the passages quoted above make clear, they took Descartes to be committed to the first.

Certainly there are many passages in Descartes which seem to support the 'absolutist' view of freedom which Spinoza and Leibniz attributed to him. Particularly striking is the honorific language used in the Fourth Meditation to describe the human power of choice. 'My freedom of choice', Descartes observes, 'is so perfect that the idea of any greater faculty is beyond my grasp; so much so that it is above all in virtue of the will that I understand myself to bear the image and likeness of God' (AT VII. 57; CSM II. 40). The comparison with God's will does indeed suggest a sovereign, contra-causal power of choice. But when Descartes comes to be more specific about the relation between the will and the intellect, a rather different picture emerges. Although in the *Principles* freedom is defined as 'the power to assent or not assent at will' (I, 39), Descartes goes on to make it clear that such a power is limited to cases where the intellect does not enjoy clear and distinct perceptions. When such clear perception *is* present, then, says Descartes, 'we spontaneously give our assent and are quite unable to doubt the truth' (I, 43).

There are two important points here. The first is that the will loses all independence when the deliverances of the intellect are sufficiently clear. 'From a great light in the intellect, there follows a great propensity of the will,' says Descartes in the Fourth Meditation (AT VII. 59; CSM II. 41). Secondly, and remarkably, Descartes insists that in such a situation, when the will is determined, and our assent necessitated by our intellectual perception, we are none the less acting freely. 'The more I incline in one direction either because I clearly understand that reasons of goodness and truth point that way, or because of a divinely produced disposition of my inmost thought, the freer is my choice' (AT VII. 58; CSM II. 40). The conception of freedom which Descartes is proposing here seems much closer to the 'compatibilist' approach favoured by Spinoza and Leibniz. Freedom ceases to be presented as a contra-causal power; rather it is 'freedom of enlightenment'[9]—a movement of the will that is fully determined, but is none the less the expression of a spontaneous internal inclination on recognizing the truth. 'Neither divine grace, nor natural knowledge ever diminishes freedom; on the contrary they increase and strengthen it . . .' (ibid.). Freedom increases in direct proportion to the degree of internal spontan-

eity, and is in inverse proportion to the degree of 'indifference'—
that state of mind where each of two alternatives seems open
(AT VII. 59; CSM II. 41). For Descartes, the highest grade of
human freedom is not 'freedom of indifference' but 'freedom of
spontaneity'.[10]

Leibniz on liberty

The spontaneity conception of freedom is the central plank in
Leibniz's account of human freedom (though in criticizing the
Cartesian account of freedom he failed to recognize the emphasis
it laid on precisely this notion). In his *Theodicy*, Leibniz argues
that the dependence of our voluntary actions on a chain of causes
does not exclude a 'marvellous spontaneity which in a certain
sense makes the soul in its resolves independent of the physical
influence of all other creatures' (I, 59). The absence of external
constraint is an important element in our ordinary use of the term
'free'. I am normally said to be acting freely and voluntarily when
I act from my own inner desires and inclinations, when my
actions flow from my own decisions, unconstrained by external
pressures and forces. And in Leibniz's case, this conception is
reinforced by the theory of monads as individual, self-contained
substances that are 'windowless'—sealed in from external influences and behaving as they do simply in virtue of an unfolding
of their own inner nature.

   From one point of view, Leibniz's account of freedom is
attractive: what more could I want than the ability to express my
own inner nature, spontaneously, without being subject to external constraints? Nevertheless, if 'all is certain and determined
beforehand, in man, as everywhere else', it seems to follow that in
any given situation, the notion we have that a variety of possible
options are open to us is an illusion. We may do *X* because we will
it, but our willing is itself causally determined. We may often be
unaware of the causes that determine us to will *X* rather than *Y*
but, as Leibniz himself admits, this proves nothing about the
causal independence of our actions: 'It is as though the magnetic
needle took pleasure in turning towards the north; for it would

think that it was turning independently of any other cause, not being aware of the imperceptible movements of the magnetic matter' (I, 50). So are we humans ultimately any better off, in respect of freedom, than the magnetic needle? Leibniz's initial reply is not particularly satisfying:

Although the whole future is doubtless determined, since we know not what it is, nor what is foreseen or resolved, we must do our duty according to the reason that God has given us ... and thereafter we must have a quiet mind and leave to God himself the care of the outcome (I, 58).

This might suggest a kind of quiescent fatalism; but Leibniz is adamant in rejecting the 'lazy sophism' according to which if all is determined there is no point in taking any decisions whatever. Since 'effects come about by virtue of a proportionate cause', our careful actions now are part of the chain of events that determine the future; so there is nothing to be said for a superstitious belief in a *Fatum Mahometanum* of the kind which 'causes the Turks not to shun places ravaged by the plague' (I, 57).

But if Leibniz effectively disposes of the fatalistic view of determinism, he is less convincing on the apparent threat to our freedom posed by the possibility that all human behaviour is causally necessitated. In his earlier *Discourse on Metaphysics*, Leibniz had observed that 'one must distinguish between what is certain and what is necessitated' (GP IV. 437; P 23): a future event may be determined with certainty, but that does not detract from its status as a contingent event. As Leibniz puts it elsewhere, '*determination*, which could be called certainty if it were known, is not incompatible with contingency' (*Theodicy* I, 36). Nevertheless, Leibniz's doctrine that 'the predicate is in the subject' (see Chapter 2, p. 68) does at any rate *appear* (as he himself acknowledges) to threaten contingency. For 'we maintain that every thing that is to happen to some person is already contained implicitly in his nature or notion, just as the properties of a circle are contained in its definition' (GP IV. 437; P 23). From this it seems to follow that, for example, Julius Caesar's decision to cross the Rubicon rather than remain in Gaul was quite inevitable, since it was necessarily true of him from eternity, just as the properties of a triangle are eternally and necessarily true of the figure in question.

Leibniz's reply to this is to distinguish between what is 'absolutely' and what is only 'hypothetically' necessary. Caesar's decision is not absolutely necessary, or 'necessary in itself' (as is the case with the truths of arithmetic or geometry). The decision is indeed necessary *given* the total set of antecedent conditions involved, but 'if someone were to do the opposite, he would do nothing that is impossible in itself' (p 24). The background to this is Leibniz's thesis that there is an infinity of possible universes: from among the infinite set of possible substances, God selected, and brought into existence, just those that would make up the best and most perfect universe (cf. GP VI. 616; P 187 and see above, p. 109). There is a possible world, then, in which Caesar's crossing the Rubicon did not occur. Hence Caesar's decision, or the predicate in virtue of which this decision is true of him, 'is not as absolute as the predicates of arithmetic and geometry but presupposes the sequence of things that God has chosen freely, which is based on the primary free decree of God, namely always to do that which is the most perfect . . .' (GP IV. 438; P 25).

This appeal to the metaphysics of possible worlds does not entirely get Leibniz off the hook. For it is still true of the particular Caesar who belongs to this actual universe that all that is predicated of him (including the decision to cross the Rubicon) is necessarily part of him—'contained in the notion' of this particular subject for all time. So the possibility of an alternative universe, with a 'twin Caesar' who did not cross the Rubicon, hardly seems enough to remove the necessity from this actual Caesar's decision. Leibniz would have to agree that our Caesar, the actual Julius Caesar that is part of our universe, could not possibly have done otherwise. This emerges with some force in a passage from the correspondence between Leibniz and Antoine Arnauld in the 1680s: God created a particular Adam, determinate with respect to all his predicates, from among an infinity of possible Adams. Hence, says Leibniz, if we suppose a universe in which Adam did not take the apple, then we are not talking about this particular Adam, but some other: 'he would not have been our Adam, but some other, if different things had happened to him' (GP II. 42 P 55–6).

These sometimes tortuous manoeuvrings over the 'necessity' of human decisions have important consequences for ethics. Our conception of ourselves as human beings requires us to be able to say in what sense it is true that we act freely and are responsible for our actions. Now Leibniz's account of the way in which our actions can be seen as a spontaneous and unimpeded expression of our own inner nature certainly provides a clear and consistent model of human freedom. But on the question of responsibility his position is less happy. For to hold someone responsible or 'answerable' for their actions, to regard them as fit subjects for praise and blame (and possibly punishment), seems to presuppose that they have a genuine two-way power, to X or not to X. Judgements like 'You are to blame for Xing' seem appropriate only where not Xing was in the circumstances a genuine option for you. It is here that Leibniz's failure to provide a convincing sense in which Caesar (our Caesar) could have done otherwise than cross the Rubicon seems damaging to the traditional concept of responsibility.[11] Sometimes Leibniz attempts to solve this problem by producing the slogan that motives 'incline without necessitating'. 'Motives do not act on the mind like weights on a balance', Leibniz wrote to Samuel Clarke in 1716; 'rather it is the mind which acts by virtue of the motives' (GP VII. 392; P 222). This is a telling point as far as it goes: when I decide to X because my disposition and desires lead me to see X as the best course, I am not being constrained to do X by some outside force: it is *my* decision.[12] Yet this still does not remove the problem of necessity—the question of whether I could, in the circumstances, have done otherwise than I did.

In the light of this, it is interesting to see that when Leibniz comes to discuss the justification for rewards and punishments he offers an account which aims to bypass the question of necessity, by showing that even if no human decision could in fact have gone otherwise than it did, there is still a sense in which the bestowing of rewards and punishments is quite rational. Leibniz points out, first, that dangerous and anti-social conduct needs to be suppressed, irrespective of the question of moral fault; second, that it is a fact of experience that 'the fear of punishments and the hope of rewards serves to make people abstain from evil and strive to do good' (*Theodicy* I, 68–71). Deterrence thus takes its place as a causally efficacious mechanism whose justification is not at all undermined by the possibility of determinism. Leibniz does, however, acknowledge 'a different kind of justice and a certain sort of reward and punishment' which do not seem compatible with the possibility that human beings cannot act otherwise than they do; this he calls 'avenging' or 'punitive' justice, and what he has in mind is the approach to punishment that is nowadays labelled 'retributivist'. Leibniz's characteristic philosophical stance—that of the reconciler—leads him to offer a defence of retributive punishment, but it is a defence that is richer in rhetoric than in argument. Retribution has a 'foundation in the fitness of things'; it 'gives satisfaction to cultivated minds even as a beautiful piece of music or a good piece of architecture' (I, 73).[13] Leibniz should be judged, however, not for his unsuccessful excursion into retributive theory, but for his defence of a 'spontaneity' conception of freedom and his advocacy of a purely instrumental account of punishment; for it is here that he succeeds in mapping out the territory that must be occupied by those who wish to construct an ethical system that is compatible with universal determinism.[14]

Spinozan freedom: endeavour and rationality

Spinoza and Leibniz were both committed to strict determinism, so it is no accident that there are a number of parallels between Leibniz's account of freedom and that of Spinoza. It is, as we have seen, central to Leibniz's theory of freedom that monads— and most importantly the monad that constitutes the rational soul of man—are determined to act not from the outside but from the inside: 'there is a self sufficiency which makes them the source of their internal actions' (*Monadology*, para. 18). In equating freedom with internal determination, or self-determination, Leibniz is in accord with Spinoza, who asserts in the *Ethics* that 'a thing is called free if it is determined to act by itself alone' (I, def. 7). But Spinoza draws an important contrast between God and finite beings: God 'exists from the necessity of his nature alone' (ibid.), whereas singular finite things 'are determined by the necessity of the divine nature . . . to exist in a certain way and to produce effects in a certain way' (I, prop. 29). Given Spinoza's definition of 'free' as 'determined to act by itself alone', it might seem to follow that there is no possibility of any genuine freedom for finite human beings. It is important to remember, however, that the determination of finite things by God does not, in Spinoza's system, carry quite the implications that would be present if we were dealing with a conventional account of God as a 'transcendent' creator separate from the universe. Singular finite things are, for Spinoza, ultimately 'modes' of God—'modes whereby the attributes of God are expressed in a certain and determinate way' (III, prop. 6). Because of this, Spinoza is able to attribute to singular things a certain active inner power or force not altogether unlike that which Leibniz (though for very different reasons) attributed to his monads. In Part II of the *Ethics* Spinoza talks of 'a force (*vis*) by which each thing perseveres in its existence'—a force which is derived 'from the eternal necessity of God' (prop. 45, schol.). And in Part III he introduces a special technical term for this force— *conatus* ('striving' or 'endeavour'): 'each thing in so far as it is in itself[15] strives to persevere in its being' (prop. 6).

Conatus is not restricted to conscious, or even living things. Indeed, Spinoza's statement of his *conatus* principle is partly reminiscent of Descartes's statement of the principle of inertia— that other things being equal a moving thing will continue in motion, and what is at rest will continue at rest, and in general 'each thing will always remain in the same state, as far as it can, and never change except as a result of external causes' (*Principles* II, 37).[16] As applied to human beings, however, Spinoza's *conatus* is far more than a tendency to continue in the same state. When related to the mind, *conatus* is a conscious striving, and when related to mind and body together it is identified with appetite. 'This appetite', says Spinoza, 'is nothing but the very essence of man, from whose nature there necessarily follow those things that promote his preservation' (G II. 147; C 500). This might seem to pave the way for a purely Leibnizian conception of freedom—the view that we are free in so far as the principle of our actions is within ourselves, and our behaviour expresses our own nature, free from external constraints. But in Part IV of the *Ethics*, *De servitute humana* ('On Human Servitude' or 'On Human Bondage'), Spinoza makes it clear that the force of *conatus* within each of us is 'limited and infinitely surpassed by the power of external causes' (prop. 3). There is no escaping these causes, for man is necessarily a part of God-or-Nature; the notion that he can be a wholly self-determining being is, quite simply, a fantasy. 'Man necessarily . . . follows and obeys the common order of Nature and accommodates himself to it as much as the nature of things requires' (corollary to prop. 4).

In so far as we can be free (and Spinoza is adamant that we have no 'absolute' or contra-causal freedom: *Ethics* V, Preface), our freedom lies in the exercise of our reason. This much the title of Part V of the *Ethics* makes clear; the 'power of the intellect' is the key to human liberty.[17] The groundwork for this has been prepared earlier. In Part III of the *Ethics* Spinoza points out that our mind both acts and is acted upon: in so far as it has adequate ideas it is acting (*agit*), but in so far as it has inadequate ideas it is acted upon (*patitur*) (prop. 1). Now the Latin noun which corresponds to the verb *patior* (to be acted upon) is *passio* (generally translated 'passion'); and much of Part III of the *Ethics* is devoted to an analysis and classification of the 'passions' (such emotions as despair, remorse, hate, anger, envy, longing, timidity, lust, and many more).[18] The labelling of these emotions as passions suggests that when we are in such states, we are not fully 'in charge', but are acted upon (compare the phrase 'to be *in the grip* of the emotions'). The role of reason is to help us escape from this servile and passive condition; Spinoza's thesis is that a passion ceases to be a passion as soon as we form a clear and distinct idea of it (V, prop. 3). 'Each of us has the power to understand himself and his emotions, and consequently to bring it about that he is less acted on by them' (prop. 4, schol.).

Adequate understanding of a phenomenon, for Spinoza, involves a complete understanding of its causes, and this in turn involves a dissolving of the illusion of contingency and a recognition of the necessity of its being thus and not otherwise (see Chapter 2, p. 58). It is certainly true that much of our human emotional life is tied up with the belief that things might be otherwise. We desperately hope that X rather than Y will come about; we feel bitter remorse that X rather than Y occurred; we torment ourselves with the thought 'if only things had gone differently'; we have obsessive fears of the form 'what if such and such should occur'. Such emotions can be seriously destructive of our peace of mind; and Spinoza's recipe for the conquest of the passions through understanding holds out the promise of a more serene and less anguished mental life. A typical example is given in Part V of the *Ethics*: 'sadness over some good which has perished is lessened as soon as the man who has lost it realizes that this good could not, in any way, have been kept' (prop. 6, schol.). As many commentators have objected, however, the Spinozan recipe does not seem infallible. Knowledge of the causes of a distressing event does not cause the distress to go away; understanding of the causes of a feared event does not necessarily diminish the fear.[19] Spinoza at one point admits that clear and distinct knowledge may not 'absolutely remove' the passions; but he claims that at least 'it will bring it about that they constitute the smallest part of the mind' (prop. 20, schol.).

Although Spinoza's picture of the good life can often seem cold, detached, and austerely intellectual,[20] he does not represent the life of the *homo liber*, the free man, as entirely devoid of emotion. The overcoming of the passions—emotions whereby we are 'acted upon', or which we 'undergo'—still leaves room for active emotions whereby our strivings are directed and controlled by reason; such positive 'affects' include sobriety, courage, moderation, courtesy, and mercy' (G II. 188; C 529). In Spinoza's *Theologico-Political Treatise*, there is a comparison between the life of the slave and the life of the free subject, which to some extent illuminates the general Spinozan conception of freedom. The slave is one who is bound to obey the master's orders, irrespective of whether they are in his interests or not. The child is rather better off, for although he obeys the orders of another (the parent), these orders are given in his own interests. But the best situation is that of the free subject who, though obeying the orders of the sovereign, obeys them out of a rational recognition

that they are in the interests of all (including himself). 'He alone
is free who lives with free consent under the complete guidance of
reason' (Ch. 16: G III. 194).

Unlike Leibniz, Spinoza is no reconciler. His picture of the
human condition is a radical and revisionary one which would, if
we accepted it, call for many changes in our normal moral
outlook. Spinoza's account of the passions, in particular, has
considerable implications for our typical moral assessments and
appraisals of human action. For our moral responses to blame-
worthy acts often involve emotions such as resentment, indigna-
tion, remorse, and the like, which seem justified only on the
premiss that people could have behaved differently. Such a
premiss, on Spinoza's view, is just false, and it is only through
ignorance of the true causes of actions that we entertain it.
Remorse would not be appropriate for one who lived according
to the guidance of reason (G II. 246; C 573); repentance is
associated with a mistaken belief that an action was performed
'from a free decision of the mind' (G II. 197; C 537). And in
general the notions of 'praise, blame, sin and merit' have arisen,
Spinoza argues, from an ignorant conception of man as a self-
determining agent (G II. 81; C 444. Cf. G II. 138; C 492). The
assessment of Spinoza's position here is a complicated and
difficult matter. Even if one accepts his strictly deterministic
framework, it is not clear that it would be psychologically
possible for us to avoid all the moralistic and reactive attitudes
that are at present an integral part of the way in which we view
ourselves and the way in which we interact with others. And even
were it psychologically possible, it is not clear that living without
such attitudes would be better, in the sense of representing a
more worthwhile and fulfilled way for human beings to live.[21]
Although Spinoza does not have a worked out response to this
type of complaint, it seems likely that he would at least have
insisted that, irrespective of whether we could succeed in eliminat-
ing all 'reactive' passions such as resentment and anger, it still
remains the case that some forms of life are to be condemned,
quite objectively and dispassionately. Replying to a letter from
Henry Oldenburg in 1676 asking whether any of us could be
subject to blame for our actions in a Spinozan world in which

none can act otherwise than they do, Spinoza remarked that 'a horse can be excused for being a horse and not a man, yet for all that it must remain a mere horse'. It is one thing to withhold blame, in the traditional sense, for a given piece of conduct; but it is another to allow that everything about the conduct in question is as it should be. 'Men can be excusable, and nevertheless lack blessedness, and be tormented in many ways' (G IV. 327; W 358). On Spinoza's view, the writer on ethics has no business to bewail or censure the weakness of the human condition (*Ethics* III, Preface), but this does not prevent his advocating what he sees as a better way to live.

Human nature and the good life in Descartes and Spinoza

It is something of a paradox that Spinoza, who rejected Descartes's immaterialist theory of the mind, ended up with a conception of the good life that implies detachment from most bodily concerns and commitments. When the passions have been eliminated, or their power over us destroyed by rational understanding, we are free to concentrate on 'the things that pertain to the mind's duration without relation to the body' (*Ethics* V, prop. 20. schol.). The ignorant man is troubled by external causes and unable to possess true peace; the wise man, by contrast, is 'by a certain eternal necessity conscious of himself and of God' (prop. 42, schol.). Having achieved true understanding (see Chapter 2, pp. 58 ff.), the mind is able to attain to that state which Spinoza calls 'the intellectual love of God' (*amor intellectualis Dei*: prop. 33). In this state 'the mind cannot absolutely be destroyed with the body, but something remains of it which is eternal' (prop. 23).

This highly intellectual, almost spiritual, conception of our highest human destiny seems strangely close to the dualistic tradition of Plato and Descartes. But here a further paradox arises. For if we now compare Descartes's own conception of the good for man, we are immediately confronted with a much more robust and down-to-earth approach. Despite his official commitment to an immaterialist view of our essential nature, Descartes in his later writings becomes increasingly interested in man not as an intellectual spirit detached from bodily concerns, but as a

creature of flesh and blood, an embodied being. This interest was
stimulated in part by the acute questions posed by Princess
Elizabeth of Bohemia in her correspondence with the philosopher, which began in a letter of May 1643: how, she asked, could
the soul of man, being a purely thinking substance, produce the
physical changes in the body that are involved in voluntary
actions? In reply Descartes spoke of three 'primitive notions, or
models on which all our other knowledge is patterned'. In
addition to the notion of mind, and the notion of body, there is a
third primitive notion, that of the union of mind and body,
involving 'the soul's power to move the body and the body's
power to act on the soul and cause sensations and passions' (A T
III. 664; K 138). Descartes became increasingly concerned to give
a full account both of the mechanism of this union, and of its
implications for the question of how we should conduct our lives.

Descartes's attempts to describe the mechanism of the
body–mind union were far from successful; indeed the philosophical problems he faced here were intractable (see Chapter 4,
p. 124). But he was at any rate able to embark on a detailed
analysis of the 'sensations and passions' that, on his view, are the
principal manifestation of our embodied nature. The results of
Descartes's reflections on these matters are contained in his
Passions of the Soul, published in 1649, a work which defies
classification in terms of today's narrow academic specialisms,
ranging freely over metaphysics, physiology, psychology, and
ethics. Much of the ground covered overlaps with that of
Spinoza's *Ethics*: both works are concerned to provide a framework for a full and exhaustive classification of the passions, and
both frameworks are essentially reductionist. Descartes attempts
to show how all the various passions to which we are subject
result from combinations or modifications of six primary passions: wonder, love, hatred, desire, joy, and sadness ('all the
others are composed from some of these six, or are species of
them': *Passions* II, 69). In Spinoza the reduction is carried still
further, and just three primary passions—joy, sadness, and
desire—are invoked (G II. 149; C 501). Both philosophers,
moreover, saw it as their primary task to provide 'remedies' for
the passions. Descartes wrote to Elizabeth that the chief obstacle

to a happy life is that our passions 'represent to us the goods to whose pursuit they impel us as being much greater than they really are' (AT IV. 295; K 173).

Occasionally, Descartes was tempted by the thought that the best life would be one free from all passions, where the soul, detached from the traffic of the senses, would 'devote itself to the loving contemplation of the divine intelligence, of which it is a faint and imperfect emanation' (AT IV. 608; K 212)—a passage which has more than a little flavour of Spinoza's *amor intellectualis Dei*. But in general Descartes regards the passions as a quite proper and valuable part of our nature as embodied beings. 'The passions are all by their nature good, and we have nothing to avoid but their misuse or excess' (*Passions* III, 211). Despite the almost Aristotelian echoes of this passage, Descartes firmly retains his thoroughly non-Aristotelian belief in a separable soul.[22] The soul, he goes on to observe, can have pleasures of its own; but he is nevertheless at pains to stress that 'the pleasures common to it and the body depend entirely on the passions, so that persons whom the passions can move are capable of enjoying the sweetest pleasures of life' (AT XI. 488; CSM I. 404).

The crucial point about the passions, for Descartes, is that they are not under the direct control of the will. This is because they are not purely mental events, but irreducibly psycho-physical: they involve a certain kind of conscious awareness, but it is also part of the definition of a passion that it is 'caused, maintained and strengthened' by physiological events—in particular the 'animal spirits' that transmit movements throughout the brain, muscles, and nervous system (*Passions* I, 27). Because of this our power of control is limited, as Descartes explains in considerable detail:

There is one special reason why the soul cannot readily change or suspend its passions . . . namely that they are nearly all accompanied by some disturbance which takes place in the heart and consequently also throughout the blood and the animal spirits. Until this disturbance ceases they remain present to our mind in the same way as the objects of the senses are present to it while they are acting upon our sense organs. The soul can prevent itself hearing a slight noise or feeling a slight pain by attending vry closely to some other thing, but it cannot in the same way prevent itself hearing thunder or feeling a fire that burns the hand. Likewise, it can overcome the lesser passions, but not the stronger and more violent ones, except after the disturbance of the blood and the spirits has died down (*Passions* I, 46).

But although one cannot just *will* a passion to go away, there are, Descartes explains, certain techniques whereby the flow of the 'animal spirits' that give rise to the passions can be modified. For the correlations between a certain set of physiological events and a certain psychological response are not immutable; they can be affected by experience. Descartes deserves credit in this connection for pioneering the notion of the conditioned or associative response. 'When I was a child,' he wrote to Pierre Chanut in 1647, 'I was in love with a little girl my own age who had a slight squint. The impression made by sight in my brain when I looked at her cross eyes became so closely connected to the simultaneous impression arousing in me the passion of love that for a long time afterwards when I saw cross-eyed persons I felt a special inclination to love them, simply because they had that defect' (A T V. 57; K 224). Now if such an association can be set up involuntarily, it should also be feasible, Descartes reasoned, deliberately to bring about further associations whereby the passions can be brought under control. Even in animals, Descartes noted, it is possible by training to change familiar associations and set up new ones—as when a setter that would normally chase a partridge and bolt at the sound of a gun can be trained so as to freeze at the sight of the bird and retrieve it after the gun has fired (*Passions* I, 50). Through training and habit, then, the physiological and psychological responses which are, in the first instance, quite involuntary can be made to follow a desired pattern in a smooth and predictable way. Hence 'there is no soul so weak that it cannot, if well directed, acquire an absolute power over its passions' (ibid.).

Descartes's account of the control of the passions comes under heavy criticism from Spinoza, for two main reasons. First, Spinoza takes issue with the dualistic framework in terms of which Descartes formulates his story: the description of the soul acting on and being affected by the pineal gland in the brain.[23]

Second, Descartes's talk of the 'absolute mastery' of the passions reinforced Spinoza's view that Descartes was committed to an untenable conception of the will, wholly free and unconstrained by determining causes. Spinoza's dissatisfaction with the picture of the soul as a strange kind of homunculus dwelling within the brain is certainly justified; but on the question of the will's mastery of the passions he does not seem fully to have appreciated the subtlety of Descartes's position.[24] Descartes is certainly not saying that the will has a sovereign power to control the passions simply as it chooses. Indeed, one of his chief messages is that to live as we should it does not suffice to decide, intellectually, how we should behave. What is also required is that we train ourselves in advance, so that we set up the right kinds of associations and habits. If a dog or a horse can be trained to be steady in the vicinity of gunfire, so can a human. And this is not a case of 'mind over matter'; rather it is a case of using our ingenuity to devise a training programme that will ensure that the body itself—the physiological events comprising the pulse level, the flow of blood, the activity of the nervous system, and so on— will automatically perform in such a way that we become able to feel and act in the way we should. Descartes was not the first to recognize the importance of habit and training for the life of virtue; indeed, that is something that is central to Aristotle's account of ethical excellence.[25] Descartes's insight is the simple but none the less vitally important one that the ebb and flow of our emotions is not just a question of our 'mental' life, but is intimately and inextricably linked with patterns of physiological response. It is remarkable that the philosopher whose name is almost synonymous with a non-physical theory of the mind should have mapped out an ethical theory that lays so much stress on the need to understand our bodily nature.

Reason, faith, and the human lot

The seventeenth century is sometimes called the 'age of reason'— a phrase which has many different connotations, but which is perhaps chiefly suggestive of the emancipation of the human mind from an earlier age of faith. Indeed the term 'rationalist'

was used by some writers of the period as a virtual synonym of
'atheist'.[26] Given the central importance of God in the philosophies of Descartes, Spinoza, and Leibniz, it might seem strange
that any of them could be suspected of atheism. Nevertheless,
Descartes was bitterly attacked as a subverter of religion and
faith (cf. letter to Voetius of 1643: AT VIIIB. 26; ALQ II. 30);[27]
Spinoza withheld publication of his *Ethics* when rumours spread
that the work was an attack on the existence of God (G IV. 299;
W 334);[28] and even Leibniz, the great reconciler of the claims of
faith and reason, and a stalwart defender of Christian theism,
incurred suspicions of impiety through his failure to attend
church, and was nicknamed by his enemies '*Lövenix*' (Low
German for *Glaubenichts* or 'Believe-nothing')[29] During the
latter half of the seventeenth century it became a fairly common
accusation against the 'new' philosophy that it paved the way for
atheism. Pierre Bayle, writing at the turn of the century, summed
the matter up as follows:

> Generally speaking the Cartesians are suspected of irreligion; and their
> philosophy is believed to be very dangerous to Christendom, so that
> according to the view of a great many people, the same men who in our
> century have dispelled the shadows that the scholastics had spread
> throughout Europe have multiplied the number of free thinkers and
> opened the door to atheism or to Pyrrhonism.[30]

In the case of Descartes, although there is no good reason for
questioning the sincerity of his religious beliefs, there are some
aspects of his philosophy which, while not exactly subversive,
could plausibly have been seen by the church as posing a danger
to faith. First, Descartes drew a firm demarcation line between
the provinces of theology and of philosophy. He was sometimes
tempted to engage in discussion of how his philosophical views
affected doctrinal matters (the mystery of the Eucharist; the
interpretation of Genesis[31]), but his general response when
challenged about the possible clashes between his scientific
theories and the teachings of the church was 'we must leave that
for the theologians to explain' (AT V. 178; CB 50). Philosophy,
including physical science, becomes in Descartes a self-contained
discipline, guided by the light of reason; it has no need to be

supplemented by revelation, scripture, or ecclesiastic teaching. Thus, though Descartes piously acknowledges the truth of the doctrine that 'the world was created right from the start with all the perfections which it now has' (*Principles* III, 45), he none the less aims to offer an evolutionary account of how the universe must necessarily have reached its present state simply in accordance with the laws of matter and motion, even if the initial configuration of particles was quite chaotic (cf. *Le Monde*: AT XI. 34; CSM I. 91). And, despite a certain amount of judicious fudging over whether the earth 'really' moves,[32] Descartes was firmly committed to the new Copernican cosmology, whereby the Earth is dethroned from its central position. The Earth is simply a planet (*Principles* III, 30); it has the same status as Mars and Saturn—'bodies we do not make so much of' (AT V. 171; CB 40). What is more, the sun itself is only one star among innumerable others, each of which is the centre of its own celestial 'vortex' (*Principles* III, 46; cf. *Le Monde*: AT XI. 56).

Descartes saw all this as having important implications for human life. The universe, as conceived of in medieval and scholastic cosmology, was one which revealed, in all its details, the purposes of a benevolent creator. In the words of Paracelsus, writing some hundred years before Descartes, 'all things belonging to nature exist for the benefit of man'.[33] For Descartes, the vastly expanded size of the post-Copernican universe,[34] the possibility of innumerable other worlds, and the insignificance of our planet in comparison with the hugeness of the whole, made it impossible to continue to regard man as the 'dearest of God's creatures' (AT V. 168; CB 36). The belief that all things exist for our benefit alone, says Descartes at the start of Part III of the *Principles*, involves a presumptuous view of our status and a failure to recognize the unlimited vastness of God's creation (AT VIII. 80; CSM I. 248). Hence the attempt to explain physical phenomena purposively—in terms of 'final causes'—is brusquely condemned by Descartes as 'utterly ridiculous' (AT VIII. 81; CSM I. 249). 'The customary search for final causes is totally useless in physics' (AT VII. 55; CSM II. 39).

Descartes's fierce hostility to explanations in terms of final causes may nowadays strike us as excessive. Surely, we may feel, teleological explanations may contribute to our understanding by showing how a given item serves some purpose in terms of the functioning of the system as a whole (thus, to identify the kidneys as the organ whose function is to purify the blood may be essential for a correct understanding of their structure and workings). But our ability to take this favourable view of purposive explanations is partly due to the fact that in many cases we now have at our disposal a detailed account of the hidden mechanisms and microscopic structures which reveal *how* a given item is able to perform such and such a function. In the seventeenth century, such understanding was very largely lacking, so that the unfolding of purposes remained a self-contained and ultimately unproductive exercise. 'The search for final causes is sterile,' wrote Francis Bacon in 1623, 'and like a virgin consecrated to God brings forth no fruit.'[35] 'Abandon final causes and look for underlying structures' was a common slogan among progressive thinkers of the seventeenth century.[36]

   Quite apart from the issue of the progress of science, the rejection of final causes has an ethical dimension for Descartes. Final causes in scholastic philosophy were more than simply teleological explanations; typically what was invoked was a *divine* purpose—the idea that a given phenomenon could be explained in terms of the creator's special concern for the welfare of mankind. Descartes's conception of the universe, as we have seen, ruled out such special concern. To say that God's purpose in creating the sun was to give light to the earth is to take an absurdly anthropocentric view, he wrote in 1641 (letter to 'Hyperaspistes': AT III. 431; K 117). The general conception of the deity in Descartes is an austere and impersonal one. We may worship God and contemplate his unimaginable greatness (AT VII. 52; CSM II. 36), but his nature is largely beyond our grasp, and his purposes are utterly inscrutable to us (AT VII. 375; CSM II. 258). It is true, as noted earlier in this chapter (p. 157), that Descartes aims in the *Meditations* to establish the benevolence and perfection of God, notwithstanding the existence of human error. But the central point here is not that God has a special concern for the welfare of mankind; rather it is that since he is by definition wholly perfect, nothing that he creates can be inherently faulty (though it may be limited in various ways). As far as the conduct of human life is concerned, the way to happiness is to aim for internal contentment 'without external assistance', by regulating our passions in accordance with the dictates of reason (letter to Princess Elizabeth of 4 August 1645: AT IV. 263–5; K 165–6). The belief in 'particular providence' is an untenable superstition if it is taken to mean that the eternal and immutable decrees of God can be modified as a result of some special human relationship with the deity (6 October 1645; AT IV. 316; K 181).

Many of these Cartesian themes are echoed in Spinoza, who follows Descartes in the attempt to draw a firm demarcation line between theological and philosophical issues. 'Philosophy and revelation stand on totally different footings,' insists Spinoza in the Preface to his *Theologico-Political Treatise*; the autonomy of human reason must be respected—she must be liberated from her role as a 'mere handmaid of theology'. As for Spinoza's metaphysical system, this presents us with an even more austere and impersonal conception of the deity than that found in Descartes. Spinoza's God, the self-subsistent and self-creating substance that is identical with the natural universe, seems far removed from the personal God of traditional Judaeo-Christian belief, God, asserts Spinoza, is wholly without passions, and strictly speaking does not love anyone (*Ethics* V, prop. 17, cor.). He is, however, said to 'love himself'; but what is involved here is Spinoza's special notion of 'intellectual love', a kind of joyful self-knowledge whereby 'God enjoys infinite perfection accompanied by the idea of himself' (prop. 35). Human beings, in so far as they are part of the whole, can somehow mirror this state; for by understanding himself and his affects, and by clearly perceiving their causes, a man can be said to 'love God, and to do so the more, the more he understands himself and his affects' (prop. 15). Whatever we make of this strange conception, it is at least clear that Spinoza's metaphysics allows no room for the standard theological notions of personal providence and special benevolence. Spinoza is as adamant as Descartes in rejecting the search for final causes. Indeed, he goes further than Descartes; for

while Descartes is prepared to allow—for example, in the realm
of physiology—that the arrangement and working of our organs
is evidence of the benevolence of the creator,[37] Spinoza argues
that even here the inference to a good creator involves fallacious
and anthropomorphic reasoning:

> Finding many means that are helpful in seeking their advantage (e.g.
> eyes for seeing and teeth for chewing) . . . and knowing that they had not
> provided them for themselves . . . men had to infer that there was a ruler
> . . . endowed with human freedom, who had taken care of all things for
> them, and made all things for their use (G II. 78; C 440).

The belief that all is for our benefit rests, says Spinoza, on a crude
induction from limited instances. The fact is that 'amongst so
much that is beneficial there is so much that is harmful—storms,
earthquakes, diseases etc.'; and the *ad hoc* explanation that these
are sent as punishments for vice will not survive the unassailable
empirical observation that 'benefits and harms happen indiscrimi-
nately to the pious and the impious alike' (ibid.). The whole
notion of God as acting for a purpose or end is, Spinoza argues,
incoherent (for 'if he acts for the sake of an end, he necessarily
wants something which he lacks': G II. 80; C 442). To try to fit all
events into a providential scheme is a mark of 'foolish wonder',
and those who in their search for explanations take refuge in the
will of God are retreating to the 'sanctuary of ignorance' (G II.
81; C 443). To critics who raised the worry that this dismissal of
a providential conception of the universe might subvert religious
virtue, Spinoza replied that true religious virtue is promoted by
whatever is most in conformity with reason (G IV. 299; W 335);
the life of reason requires the elimination of superstition, which
Spinoza eloquently denounced as one of the greatest of human
evils, 'engendered, preserved and fostered by fear' (G III. 6).

Spinoza's uncompromising attack on superstition in the
Theologico-Political Treatise connects up with his vision of the
just and well-ordered state. Although Spinoza does not, as is
sometimes suggested, advocate a wholly secularized state, he does
insist that religious authority should be subordinate to the civil
power. Taking his cue from the ideas of Thomas Hobbes (whose

Leviathan had appeared some twenty years earlier),[38] Spinoza maintains that civil government gets its legitimacy from a contract; by this contract 'men with common consent agree to live according to the dictates of reason' (Ch. 19: G III. 230). Since 'everyone wishes to live as far as possible securely beyond the reach of fear', and since 'this would be quite impossible if everyone did everything he liked', it is rational for each person to enter into a covenant whereby everyone 'hands over the whole of his power to the body politic' (Ch. 16: G III. 193). The sovereign power, thus set up, has as its object not only the guaranteeing of security (as in Hobbes), but the preservation of a free and tolerant society in which 'men may employ their reason unshackled'. 'The true aim of government is liberty' (Ch. 20: G III. 241). Spinoza is scathing about the claims of 'revealed religion' to override the civil authority; indeed he argues that there is serious confusion in the anthropomorphic conception of God as a some kind of 'royal potentate' who gives laws to mankind (Ch. 6: G III. 81). A detailed analysis of the 'Hebrew theocracy' leads him to the conclusion that even the authority of Moses ultimately depended on a covenant whereby the Jews agreed to 'transfer their right of dominion' to him. 'Religion acquires the force of law only by means of the sovereign power'; hence 'after the destruction of the Hebrew dominion, revealed religion ceased to have the force of law' (Ch. 19: G III. 230).

For those who attempt to bolster the authority of revealed religion by appeal to miracles, Spinoza has nothing but contempt. It is of the essence of nature to preserve a 'fixed and immutable order' (G III. 82); the idea that God 'arranges the whole of nature for men's sole benefit' is 'so pleasing to humanity that men go on to this day imagining miracles so that they may believe themselves God's favourites, and the final cause for which he creates and directs all things' (ibid.). What is needed is a readiness to approach the scriptures and other reports of miracles in a rational and critical spirit. Spinoza adopts just such a stance in Chapter 6 of his *Theologico-Political Treatise*, reaching the conclusion that it is possible to explain the Bible stories as natural occurrences 'neither new nor contrary to nature, but in complete agreement with ordinary events' (ibid.). In short, Spinoza's conception of the good life is one in which each individual is guided solely by the 'light of reason' within him, and where civil government derives its authority simply from its role as a guarantor of the security and freedom of all.

If the overall effect of Spinoza's philosophy was to widen the gap between the life of reason and the life of faith, Leibniz's aim, by contrast, was to effect a reconciliation between the two. Such indeed was his declared purpose in writing the *Theodicy*.[39] Although Leibniz was aware of the challenge posed to religious orthodoxy by Spinoza's system, the immediate stimulus for the composition of his *Theodicy* was the publication in 1697 of Pierre Bayle's *Dictionnaire historique et critique*. In the dictionary Bayle had specifically attacked some of Leibniz's doctrines (for example, that of pre-established harmony, in the article 'Rorarius'); he had also argued that from the perspective of reason alone, unaided by faith or revelation, the existence of evil in the world must count as an insuperable obstacle to belief in a benevolent and omnipotent creator.

Leibniz's main claim in the *Theodicy* is the remarkable one that the universe we live in is, because it must be, the best of all possible worlds, since it is the creation of an infinitely perfect God:

> This supreme wisdom, united to a goodness that is no less infinite, cannot but have chosen the best; . . . there would be something to correct in the actions of God if it were possible to do better; . . . so it may be said that if this were not the best [*optimum*] among all possible worlds, God would not have created any (I, 8).

Although the phrase 'the best of all possible worlds' is apt to suggest a facile optimism, Leibniz is not here maintaining that the universe is perfect. His point, rather, is that only certain combinations of monads can logically exist together (are 'compossible') (GP VII. 304; P 138–9. Cf. GP III. 573; L 661), so that there are purely logical constraints on what even the most benevolent creator can achieve. We may suppose that such and such an evil could simply be eliminated or 'subtracted' from the universe, but 'the universe is all of a piece, like the ocean . . . so that if the smallest evil that comes to pass were missing in it, it would no longer be this world' (*Theodicy* I, 9). To the objection 'but why should there be any evil at all?', Leibniz replies that a certain amount of imperfection—what he calls 'metaphysical evil'—must exist if there is to be any created universe at all (since something that was completely and totally perfect would simply be identical with God).[40] As for other kinds of evil, which Leibniz classifies as 'physical and moral', the latter God does not will at all—it is a consequence of man's sin; while physical evil, or suffering, he 'does not will absolutely but often as a penalty owing to guilt and often also as a means to an end—to prevent greater evils or to obtain greater good' (I, 23). Thus every event, no matter how tragic, has its 'sufficient reason' in so far as it finds a place in the optimal design of the whole—a thesis which Leibniz is quite prepared to defend by reference to particular examples: 'The crime of Sextus Tarquinius serves for great things: it renders Rome free, and thence will arise a great empire which will show noble examples to mankind' (III, 416). Few of Leibniz's critics were satisfied with this strategy, which not only seems more than a little glib in its glossing over of the individual sufferings involved in such cases, but also appears quite inadequate to cope with events such as natural disasters, where the suffering involved seems isolated from any possible instrumental benefits. Voltaire's bitter satire *Candide* (published 1759) well illustrates how this critical reaction continued well into the middle of the eighteenth century. One of the book's central characters is the 'optimistic' philosopher 'Pangloss': when confronted with a horrendous earthquake in which thirty thousand men, women, and children are crushed to death, the good doctor blandly asks: 'What can be the "sufficient reason" for this phenomenon?'[41]

If Leibniz's account of the existence of particular evils is less than satisfactory, he is even less happy in his attempt to enlist the results of the new cosmology in order to vindicate the goodness of God. 'Since the proportion of that part of the universe which we know is almost nothing compared with that which is unknown,' Leibniz declares, 'it . . . may be that all evils are almost nothing in comparison with the good things that are in the universe' (*Theodicy* I, 19)—a line of argument which has been aptly compared with the kind of reasoning that infers from the fact that the top layer of a crate of oranges is rotten, that the ones underneath could well be sound. In a passage that strongly calls to mind Descartes's championing of the theory of an infinitely extended universe, Leibniz writes: 'The earth is only one planet, that is to say one of the principal satellites of our sun; and as all fixed stars are suns also, we see how small a thing our earth is in relation to visible things, since it is only an appendage of one amongst them' (ibid.). What is interesting about this passage is that Leibniz's earnest attempts to vindicate the benevolence of God lead him, paradoxically, to highlight that very aspect of the new world view which seems to put at risk the notion of a creator with a special and intimate concern for the welfare of mankind. Though it is no doubt conceivably true, as Leibniz suggests, that the universe as a whole may be full of blessedness and felicity, such felicity appears unimaginably remote from the concerns of our tiny planet.

In different ways, then, the writings of Descartes, Spinoza, and Leibniz on the place of man in the universe all represent attempts to retain the language of theism in the new and in many respects frighteningly vast post-Copernican universe—the universe that terrified Pascal with the 'eternal silence of its infinite spaces'.[42] For Descartes the solution lies in the abandonment of the search for purposive explanations in nature, and in the development of a conception of the universe that is, in its physical aspects at least, purely mechanical. The deity is retained, but as remote 'creator and preserver' who operates impersonally and in accordance with immutable laws. For Spinoza, the solution lies in rejecting the notion of any transcendent reality beyond the physical universe: the one all-embracing, self-sufficient, and self-sustaining substance of which the earth and all its inhabitants are 'modes' is all the reality that there is. For Leibniz, the solution lies in a continuing struggle to show that the claims of religious faith and rational philosophy are not after all in conflict. But with hindsight it is hard to avoid the impression that even as early as the seventeenth century, the 'melancholy long withdrawing roar' of the Sea of Faith had begun.[43] Strongly hinted at in Descartes, valiantly resisted in Leibniz, and most uncompromisingly proclaimed in Spinoza, there is the recognition that man has to live in an inconceivably vast and inscrutable universe which operates largely without reference to the concerns of mankind. It is the universe which we can recognize as our own.

Notes

1. *Dialogue on the two chief systems of the Universe, Ptolemaic and Copernican* (first day): Galileo VII. 129.
2. From *Cogitata et Visa* (1607): Bacon 225. Though Bacon is often supposed to be extolling the role of the ant, he in fact likens the 'true process of philosophy' to the activity of the bee, who first collects his material and then transforms it.
3. Bacon's 'rationalists' (*rationales*) were not of course Descartes, Spinoza, and Leibniz, who were unknown (the last two not even born) when he was writing; his target was the scholastics. See further R. Franks, 'The Case of Spinoza', in Holland 185 ff.
4. Cf. Kant, A51, B75 and A271, B327. Kant saw his own philosophy as a synthesis of insights that had been partially and distortedly achieved in the 'empiricism' of Locke and the 'rationalism' of Leibniz. Cf. Cottingham (1) 84 ff. The term *'empirique'* is used by Leibniz himself in the sense of one who relies on mere experience rather than reason; cf. *Monadology*, para. 28 (GP VI. 661).
5. Compare, for example, Spinoza's critique of Cartesian dualism, and Leibniz's critique of Descartes's theory of matter (see Chapter 4).
6. Cf. Chapter 4, note 14.
7. For the connection between Malebranche and Berkeley, compare Berkeley's account of the role of ideas in perception in the *Principles of Human Knowledge* (1710), paras. 1–23 (Berkeley 61 ff.), with Malebranche's account in his *Recherche de la vérité* (1674), bk. III., pt. 2 (Malebranche 217 ff.). For Malebranche's influence on Leibniz compare Malebranche's denial of causal interaction between objects (Malebranche 448) and Leibniz's comments at L 210. See also Brown (2), ch. 7.
8. The phrases *lumen naturale* ('natural light') and *lumen naturae* ('light of nature') are the phrases most commonly found in the *Meditations* and *Principles*. For the phrase *lux rationis* ('light of reason') see the *Regulae*: AT X. 368; CSM I. 14. The use of the metaphors of light and vision in connection with the powers of the intellect has a long history: see Plato, *Republic* 514–18 and Augustine, *De Trinitate*, XII, para. 4. The metaphors are also used by Spinoza (cf. Letter 21: G IV.

126; C 375) and Leibniz (letter to Queen Sophia Charlotte of 1702: L 549–50).

9. *Il Saggiatore* ('The Assayer'): Galileo VI. 232.

10. Compare Robert Boyle: 'If it be demanded how snow dazzles the eyes, they [the schoolmen] will answer that it is by the quality of whiteness . . .; and if you ask what whiteness is they will tell you that it is a real entity, which they term a quality' (*The Origins of Forms and Qualities* (1672): Boyle 16). See also Chapter 2, p. 32 for Descartes's comments on gravity.

11. For Aristotle, each subject had its own methods and its own level of precision or *akribeia*; cf. *Nicomachean Ethics*, I, 2. Compare the following remark by a seventeenth-century scholastic: 'All the sciences have their own principles and their own causes by means of which they demonstrate the special properties of their own object. It follows that we are not allowed to use the principles of one science to prove the properties of another' (*Considerazioni . . . da Accademico Incognito* (1612), printed in Galileo IV. 385). For the Platonic ideal of the unity of knowledge, cf. Plato, *Republic* 511.

12. Compare, for example, *Monadology*, paras. 31 ff. Stuart Brown, however, has argued that Leibniz's philosophical insights often have a piecemeal character which does not conform to the ideal of systematic unity. Cf. Brown (2) 204 ff. For a more standard 'systematic' interpretation, compare Rescher, ch. 1; and for a balanced overview see Ross 73–5.

13. Although, as noted above, the rationalists saw themselves as breaking with Aristotelian-scholastic orthodoxy in asserting the interconnectedness of all knowledge, there are many strands in Aristotle's own thinking that may fairly be called necessitarian. Compare his views on scientific understanding in the *Posterior Analytics* I, 4; cf. Cottingham (1) 28 ff.

14. See Hume (2), sect. VII, pt. 2. In an interesting paper entitled 'Harmony versus constant conjunction' Hide Ishiguro argues that instead of contrasting Hume's 'empiricist' view of causation with its 'rationalist' antithesis, it would be more fruitful to draw a contrast between 'the attitude of thinkers who believe that . . . the understanding of the global structure of things adds to our understanding of the processes . . . of things within it, and thinkers who want to stick to a case by case description of the concomitances . . . Descartes, Spinoza and Leibniz, as well as Locke, belonged to the former group whereas Hume and Berkeley belonged to the latter' (Kenny (2) 82–3).

15. But see further Chapter 2, p. 57 and note 43.

16. Locke IV. iii. 25.

17. For Locke's pessimistic view of our prospects for attaining demonstrative knowledge of the real essences of things cf. Locke III. vi. 9.

18. Kripke 138.

19. 'The type of property identity used in sciences seems to be associated with *necessity*, not with apriority or analyticity. For example the coextensiveness of the predicates "hotter" and "having higher mean kinetic energy" is necessary but not *apriori*' (ibid.). See further Cottingham (1) 115 ff.

20. The hostile view of rationalism has a long ancestry; compare Kant's famous strictures against the pretensions of 'pure reason': 'The light dove, cleaving the air in her free flight, might imagine that flight would be easier in empty space' (Kant A5, B8).

21. For rationalism as a cluster concept cf. Cottingham (1), ch. 1.

22. Formerly La Haye, the town was renamed La Haye-Descartes in 1802, and is now known simply as 'Descartes'. The house where Descartes was born still stands, and has been turned into a small museum.

23. In the *Discourse* Descartes describes La Flèche as 'one of the most famous schools in Europe'. His teachers included Père Dinet, later head of the Jesuit order in France, to whom Descartes later wrote an important open letter, published with the second edition of the *Meditations* (AT VII. 563 ff.; CSM II. 384 ff.).

24. Descartes implies in the *Discourse* that he was 'received into the ranks of the learned' (*au rang des doctes*: AT VI. 4; CSM I. 113). His doctoral dissertation has recently been discovered and is in process of being edited. See Marion vi.

25. The episode is recounted at length by Descartes's biographer Adrien Baillet (Baillet, bk. I, ch. 1). A translation of the relevant passage may be found in Cottingham (2) 161 ff.

26. Several letters suggest that although the *Geometry* was not published until 1638, Descartes's enthusiasm for the problems it deals with dates from many years earlier. Cf. letters to Mersenne of 15 April 1630 (AT I. 139) and 12 September 1638 (AT II. 361–2).

27. Cf. *Meterology*: AT VI. 239, quoted at CSM I. 187.

28. 'I desire to live in peace and continue the life I have begun under the motto *Bene vixit qui bene latuit*' (letter to Mersenne of April 1634: AT I. 285; K 25). The Latin tag (from Ovid) means literally 'he has lived well who has succeeded in escaping attention'.

29. The child was conceived while Descartes was living in Amsterdam;

born on 19 July 1635, she died on 7 September 1640.

30. Galileo was Descartes's senior by some thirty years, and was already famous throughout Europe by the 1630s. His discovery of the moons of Jupiter occurred in 1611, when Descartes was only fifteen; the event was celebrated at La Flèche by the recitation of a poem in his honour.

31. The first edition appeared in Paris; the second (including Bourdin's Objections) was published by Elzevir of Amsterdam. For further details of the composition and publication of the *Meditations* and *Objections and Replies* see CSM II. 1–2 and 63–5.

32. Descartes resided in Amsterdam from December 1633 to the spring of 1635. He lived in the Kalverstraat (a quarter where many of the city's butchers were to be found), and was thus able to further his interest in physiology by obtaining carcasses for dissection.

33. The doctrinal strictness of the Jewish community in Amsterdam is understandable in the light of the persecution in Spain from which many of its members had fled. Having been forced to betray their beliefs—even to the extent of undergoing compulsory 'conversion' to Christianity—it is hardly surprising that they felt the need to re-establish the integrity of their faith in an uncompromising way.

34. For more details of de Vries, Meyer, and Spinoza's other correspondents during this period, see the notes provided by Curley at C 159 ff.

35. The Dutch version, *Korte Verhandeling van God, de Mensch en des zelfs Welstand*, was known about as early as 1704, when it was inspected by Gottlieb Stolle. See further C 46.

36. Oldenburg wrote to Spinoza in July 1662: 'The group of philosophers I mentioned to you has now, by our King's favour, been converted into a Royal Society protected by Public Charter' (G IV. 37; C 189). Oldenburg himself became the Society's first secretary.

37. See the commentary at C 173–88 for more information as to the points on which Spinoza differed from Boyle. The most important of these was Spinoza's adamant rejection of anything that smacked of a teleological explanation (G IV. 32; C 185); cf. Chapter 5, p. 180. For more on Boyle see Alexander, pt. I, and M. A. Stewart's editorial introduction in Boyle ix ff.

38. Compare the 'moral code' which Descartes included in the *Discourse*—a code whose first maxim was 'to obey the laws and customs of my country, holding constantly to the religion in which by God's grace I had been instructed' (AT VI. 23; CSM I. 122). Descartes is reported to have observed later that he was 'compelled

to include these rules because of people like the Schoolmen who would otherwise have said that he intended to use his method to subvert religion and faith' (*Conversation with Burman* (1648): AT V. 178; CB 49).

39. According to Leibniz, Spinoza had prepared a placard inscribed *Ultimi barbarorum* ('utter barbarians') which he would have displayed to the mob, had not his landlord locked him in the house (source: a manuscript note of Leibniz, quoted in Friedmann 108).

40. The offer of the professorship came from the Elector Palatine, and was transmitted by Fabritius: see Letter 47 (G IV. 234; W 265).

41. The author of this letter is Dr Schuller, but he is reporting the description of Ehrenfried Walther von Tschirnhaus, an important correspondent of Spinoza whose letters contain some acute questions and criticisms relating to the *Ethics*.

42. See Letter 45 (dated 5 October 1671) and Letter 46 (Spinoza's reply) (W 261–5).

43. But Spinoza was characteristically cautious about allowing a stranger to see his work: 'As far as I could see from his letters, Leibniz seems to me a man of liberal mind and well versed in science. But still I consider it imprudent to entrust my writings to him so soon. I should like first to hear what he is doing in France and to hear the opinion of our friend Tschirnhaus; after all he knows his character more intimately' (Letter 72, 18 November 1675: G IV. 305; W 341).

44. *Tractatus Politicus*, ch. I, sect. 4. For Spinoza's views on the role of understanding in the conquest of the passions see Chapter 5, p. 168.

45. See Chapter 2, p. 64.

46. The editor of the *Acta Eruditorum* was Otto Menke, Professor of Moral and Political Philosophy at Leipzig; Leibniz had prior discussions with Menke about the setting up of the journal and contributed regularly to the early issues. See further Aiton 115 ff.

47. Leibniz was first president of the Berlin Society of Sciences, founded under the patronage of the Elector of Brandenburg in 1700 (see Aiton 251 ff.). Leibniz also worked (unsuccessfully) for the founding of similar societies at Dresden, Vienna, and St Petersburg.

48. Malebranche's mammoth volume *La Recherche de la vérité* ('The Search for Truth') was in process of composition while Leibniz was in Paris; it was first published in 1674–5 and subsequently underwent numerous modifications, the final edition appearing in 1712. Though the inspiration behind Malebranche's work was the philosophy of Descartes, the *Recherche* exerted a major influence

in its own right, particularly on questions relating to causality (see p. 110). For some important differences between Malebranche's views on the mind and those of Descartes, see p. 155.

49. Arnauld was the author of the Fourth Set of Objections to Descartes's *Meditations*, published in 1641; at the time of his meeting with Leibniz he was in his early sixties. For Arnauld's criticisms of Descartes, see p. 121; for his celebrated dispute with Malebranche, see p. 79.

50. Neither man published his results until the 1680s, but the Newtonians claimed that Leibniz had lifted the basic ideas from a letter he received from Oldenburg in 1675, which described Newton's results. But in fact Leibniz's terminology and method of procedure are entirely different from Newton's. For a detailed account of Leibniz's contacts with Oldenburg and Newton in the 1670s, see Aiton 54–65; for Leibniz's strenuous attempts to rebut the charge of plagiarism during the last years of his life, see Aiton 337 ff.

51. Leibniz's patron, the Baron of Boineburg, was by this time dead; the Elector of Mainz had also died (in 1673). See Aiton 59–60 for Leibniz's efforts to remain in Paris.

52. Russell (1), ch. 1, para. 1.

53. Leibniz's interest in machinery is illustrated by his complicated plan to drain the Harz mines, which involved the construction of a new type of windmill, and a virtually friction-free pump (cf. Aiton 87 ff.).

54. Queen Sophie Charlotte did not, however, see the publication of the *Theodicy*, for she died tragically in 1705. For an account of her discussions with Leibniz, see Aiton 255 ff.

55. Leibniz remarked soon after its publication that the *Ethics* contained a number of 'excellent thoughts' which agreed with his own but that it 'retained in word but denied in fact providence and immortality'. 'I therefore consider', he continued, 'that the book is dangerous for those who take the pains to master it; the rest will not make the effort necessary to understand it' (letter to Justel of February 1678: L 195).

56. From the *Principles of Nature and Grace* (1714). For Leibniz's attempts to reconcile his religious faith with the demands of the new cosmology, see chapter 5, p. 183.

Chapter 2

1. Quotations from Descartes: AT X. 217; ALQ I. 52; Meyer's Preface: G I. 128; C 225; Leibniz: letter to Thomasius: GP IV. 163; L 94.

2. Descartes's sense of mission dates from his famous day of meditation

followed by a night of dreaming in the 'stove-heated' room on the Danube in November 1619. See Chapter 1, note 25.

3. The Latin *principium* is the ordinary word for 'beginning' (for example it is the word used in the Vulgate version of Genesis 1: 1: 'In the beginning, God created the heaven and the earth'). The corresponding Greek term *arche* is also used to mean both a beginning and a 'first principle'. Cf. Plato, *Republic* 511.

4. Compare Galileo's criticism: 'to say that the wood of the fir tree does not sink because air predominates in it is to say no more than that it does not sink because it is less heavy than water' (*Discourse on Floating Bodies*, 1612: Galileo IV. 87).

5. Compare Descartes's scathing comments in *Le Monde* on the standard scholastic definition of motion (take over from Aristotle): *motus est actus entis in potentia, prout in potentia est.* Descartes observes: 'for me these words are so obscure that I am compelled to leave them in Latin because I cannot interpret them. And in fact the sentence "Motion is the actuality of a potential being in so far as it is potential" is no clearer for being translated' (AT XI. 39; CSM I. 94).

6. Bayle 364 (under 'Zeno of Elea').

7. Compare *Regulae* (AT X. 372; CSM I. 16) and *Search for Truth* (AT X. 485; CSM II. 400). For other occurrences of the metaphor of the 'light of reason' see Chapter 1, note 8. Compare also the biblical parallels quoted by Malebranche (Malebranche 231).

8. Cf. *Principles* IV, 196: AT VIII. 320; CSM I. 283. The phenomenon is well authenticated in modern medicine. In one sense, examples involving sensations are potentially misleading ones for Descartes to have chosen, since he maintains that even when all extraneous assumptions have been 'sliced off', there is still something inherently confused and obscure about our sensory experience. Compare *Principles* I, 68 and 69, and see later in this chapter, pp. 61–2.

9. Descartes makes the connection between *mathesis* and *disciplina* quite explicitly at AT X. 378; CSM I. 19. The notion of a 'universal discipline' has its roots in Greek philosophy, as Descartes acknowledges by his comment that it is a 'venerable term with a well established meaning'; the notion seems to have been particularly prominent in the doctrines of the Academy (founded by Plato's nephew Speusippus). Cf. ALQ I. 98.

10. *De Dignitate et Augmentiis Scientiarum* (1623), III, 1 (Bacon 453).

11. The famous Latin phrase does not occur in the *Meditations*, but may be found in the *Principles* (1,7), and in its French form ('je pense donc je suis') in part IV of the *Discourse* (AT VI. 32; CSM I. 127).

12. See the reference to Archimedes in the First Meditation: AT VII. 24; CSM II. 14. See also the Seventh set of Replies: 'when an architect wishes to build a house, he digs trenches and removes any loose sand . . . In the same way I threw out anything doubtful, and when I noticed that it is impossible to doubt that a doubting or thinking substance exists, I took this as the bedrock on which I could lay the foundations of my philosophy' (AT VII. 537; CSM II. 366).

13. For this phrase see AT VII. 70; line 17; CSM II. 48. Cf. *Search for Truth*: AT X. 513; CSM II. 408.

14. This point is connected with another feature of Cartesian *scientia*, which may be termed its *psychological stability*. Descartes maintains that once the meditator has established that the reliability of his perceptions is underwritten by awareness of the existence of a non-deceiving creator, there need be no fear that subsequent doubts could undermine his rational confidence in what he has clearly and distinctly perceived. Cf. Second Set of Replies: AT VII. 141; CSM II. 101. See further Kenny (1) 192 ff., and J. Tlumak, 'Certainty and Cartesian Method', in Hooker 56–61.

15. 'When someone says "I am thinking therefore I exist", he does not deduce existence from thought by means of a syllogism, but recognizes it as something self-evident, by a simple intuition of the mind' (AT VII. 140; CSM II. 100. See also *Conversation with Burman*: AT V. 147; CB 4).

16. From John Aubrey's brief life of Hobbes: Aubrey 230.

17. Pappus is referred to in the Dedicatory Letter to the *Meditations*: AT VII. 4; CSM II. 5.

18. 'In *analysis* we assume the result we are seeking as an established fact, and look for whatever gave rise to this fact, and then again for what was prior to *that*, and we trace our steps upwards in this way until we reach one of the propositions already known to us or having the status of an axiom. In *synthesis* by contrast, we assume as facts those very propositions which in analysis we reached last, and we set out as consequences of those propositions which in analysis had prior status, joining each proposition to the next one down until finally we reach a derivation of our desired result' (Pappus of Alexandria, *Collectiones*, 634–6, repr. in Engfer 79).

19. For this aspect of the *Meditations* see the commentary at CB 69 ff.; see also the introduction by Bernard Williams in Cottingham (3) viii–x.

20. For two of the clearer presentations among the many modern discussions of these themes, see Putnam chs. 3 and 5, and Churchland, ch. 7.

21. *Pensées*, no. 434 (Pascal II. 343). For the relation between Cartesianism and scepticism in the later seventeenth century, see Popkin, ch. 1.
22. The 'geometrical demonstration' was printed at the end of the Second Set of Replies to the *Meditations*. Cf. Axiom 4 at AT VII. 165; CSM II. 116. For discussion of the causal argument for God's existence see Chapter 3, pp. 78 ff.
23. For further discussion of Descartes's exchange with Burman on this issue, see CB xxvi ff.
24. See Cottingham (2) 66 ff. for further discussion of the problem of the Cartesian circle and possible solutions to it. Of the vast literature on this topic, some of the more illuminating discussions are A. Gewirth, 'Clearness and Distinctness in Descartes', *Philosophy*, 1943 (reprinted in Doney); Wilson 130 ff.; Williams 184 ff.
25. There are some scientific parallels: Newton's *Principia* (1687) employs an axiomatic presentation. But there is nothing to compare with the *Ethics* in the size and scope of its working out of the deductive model.
26. There are some variations: part III, for example, has 'postulates' but no axioms; part V has no definitions.
27. In fact only the first two parts of the *Principles* are expounded; the work breaks off soon after the start of the exposition of part III. An appendix known as the *Metaphysical Thoughts* contains interesting discussions of some of the areas where Spinoza's views differ from those of Descartes.
28. *Conversation with Burman*: AT V. 153; CB 12. Cf. Curley's comments at C 224, note.
29. See p. 44 for John Aubrey's famous story of how Hobbes fell 'in love with Geometry' after picking up a copy of Euclid (Aubrey 230).
30. The remainder are 'problems', that is, exercises in how to construct specified figures which are then proved to have the required properties.
31. Cf. Bennett 17.
32. Aquinas distinguishes between roughly these two senses of 'self-evident' (*per se notum*) in *Summa Theologiae* 2.I.ii. Compare the note by Curley at C 642–3.
33. 'Common notions' is the standard translation in philosophical Latin for the Greek term *koinai ennoiai*, used of Euclid's axioms. See further Descartes: AT VII. 164; CSM II. 116, and Spinoza: G IV. 13; C 171.
34. Bennett 19.
35. Euclid, *Elements* I, def. 26.

36. 'Eternal truths' was Descartes's term for logical maxims such as the law of non-contradiction or the principle that 'nothing comes from nothing'; such maxims, he says, are 'not regarded as existing things or modes' since they 'have no existence outside of our thoughts' (AT VIII. 22; CSM I. 208).

37. Spinoza, like Descartes, believed that the intellect, when directed aright and freed from misleading extraneous influences, was an inherently reliable instrument. For the difficulties in translating the Latin title see C 7 and 11.

38. For Descartes's metaphor of the 'seeds of knowledge', see AT X. 217; CSM I. 4. For the theory of innateness that is presupposed here, both by Descartes and Spinoza, see the concluding section of this chapter.

39. The Cartesian terms 'clear' and 'distinct' are used by Spinoza in the *Treatise on the Purification of the Intellect*: G II. 24; C 29. Like Descartes, Spinoza stresses the *simplicity* of the objects of the intellect as a prerequisite for such perception.

40. For a general discussion of Descartes's scientific methodology, see Cottingham (2), ch. 4; for an investigation of the role of experience in Cartesian science, see Clarke 21 ff.

41. See further R. Franks, 'Caricatures in the History of Philosophy: The Case of Spinoza', in Holland.

42. Compare Hume (2), sect. IV, pt. 2: The bread which I formerly ate nourished me, but it is 'nowise necessary' that it will nourish me tomorrow. See also sect. IV, pt. I.

43. The 'necessity' being affirmed here could be construed as an 'absolute' necessity, or alternatively as merely 'hypothetical'. To say that the weather pattern in a certain area is necessary in this latter sense is merely to say that it cannot be otherwise *given* certain antecedent conditions including the laws of meteorology; but the laws themselves, it might be said, are merely contingent generalizations which might be otherwise. Spinoza certainly maintained that singular truths are necessary in so far as they are entailed by causal laws; but he also regarded the laws themselves as necessary, since they 'follow from the essences or natures of things' (G III. 57–8). For a discussion of various kinds of necessity in Spinoza see Curley (1), ch. 3.

44. There are echoes of Descartes here; for Descartes maintains that if I make a judgement in the absence of a clear and distinct perception of the basis for its truth, then I am at fault *even if the judgement happens to be true*. Cf. *Principles* I, 44.

45. Not all *cognitio* counts as *scientia*; cf. the discussion of the atheist's awareness of the properties of a triangle in the Second Set of Replies: AT VII. 141; CSM II. 101 and note.

46. Cf. Descartes's discussion of the five *degrés de sagesse* in the preface to the French edition of the *Principles*: AT IXB. 5; CSM I. 181.

47. The point that language may mislead was a seventeenth-century commonplace. Bacon had coined the phrase *idola fori* ('idols of the market place') for forms of error traceable to the influence of language: *Novum Organum* I, 60 (Bacon 269). Cf. Descartes: 'One who aspires to knowledge above the level of the common herd should be ashamed to be guided by ordinary ways of talking' (AT VII. 32; CSM II. 21). Spinoza highlights the fact that the images evoked by a given word may vary from person to person, in a way which does not match the true and universal nature of the object in question (G II. 107; C 466).

48. Cf. Plato, *Republic* 479.

49. For Descartes's discussion of this problem see *Regulae*: AT X. 384; CSM I. 23.

50. Spinoza uses the term 'derive' or 'infer' (Lat. *concludere*) in discussing how we arrive at an answer by *scientia intuitiva*; and this has led some commentators to object that the distinction between reason and intuitive knowledge cannot straightforwardly correspond with the distinction between what is directly apprehended by the intellect and what has to be demonstrated via a chain of reasoning. But the Cartesian model of swiftly running over an inferential claim until the ensemble is grasped 'all in one go' shows how 'inferring' can merge gradually into directly apprehending. Another interpretative problem with Spinoza's account is that he says that intuitive knowledge is of singular things while the second kind of knowledge is universal *Ethics* V, prop. 36, schol.). The difficulty with this is that it seems to make reason and intuition relate to different objects; yet an earlier discussion had implied that the *same* correct answer could be arrived at either by reason (via a demonstration) or by direct intuition (II, prop. 40, schol. 2). For attempts to reconcile these passages, see Delahunty 78 ff. and Parkinson (4) 67. For a comprehensive discussion of Spinoza's views on knowledge, see Parkinson (1).

51. *Veritas sui norma* ('truth is its own standard'): G II. 124; C 479. *Est enim verum index sui et falsi* ('for the true is a sign of itself and of the false'): G IV. 320; W 352.

52. For the binary theory see the *Ars Magna* (c.1679): CO 430; P 2. Though Leibniz was not the first mathematician to use a binary

system, he seems to have discovered it independently (see W 240).

53. Though Leibniz knew of Descartes's discussion of this notion only by hearsay. Cf. L 84.

54. The date of this work is uncertain. Loemker puts it *c.*1679; Parkinson argues that it is more mature and dates from around 1683 (L 119; P 241).

55. Cf. *New Essays*, IV. ii. 1: 'All adequate definitions contain primitive truths of reason and consequently intuitive knowledge' (RB 367).

56. *Primary Truths*: L 267; P 87. In the *Metaphysics* and the *Posterior Analytics* Aristotle talks of propositions where what is predicated is contained in the definition of the subject; but there is no *general* claim in Aristotle that the predicate is 'in' the subject of any true proposition (indeed where an 'accident' is truly predicated of a subject, containedness would not apply).

57. This account is incomplete in one important respect: for Leibniz the *existence* of an individual is not contained in the concept of the subject, so that even an infinite analysis would not reveal that the universe must contain any given individual. The reason for the existence of things must be sought in God, who from among all possible things brings into existence just that set which will produce the best possible universe (*Theodicy* 1, 8). Cf. Chapter 5, p. 182.

58. Cf. S. Brown, 'Leibniz' break with Cartesian rationalism' (in Holland 195 ff.), where it is argued that there is a gradual retreat in Leibniz's philosophy from the 'rationalist' ideal of a priori deductivism. It seems, however, that throughout his career Leibniz upheld a priori demonstration as an ideal model of knowledge, while at the same time consistently maintaining that human beings often have to make do with hypotheses supported a posteriori. Cf. 'Of Universal Synthesis and Analysis' (*c.*1683): 'all things are understood by God *a priori*, as eternal truths . . . We on the other hand know scarcely anything adequately and only a few things *a priori*' (GP VII. 296; P 15). See also *New System* (1695), para. 16: 'It commonly suffices for a hypothesis to be proved *a posteriori* because it satisfies the phenomena; but when we have other reasons as well, and those *a priori*, so much the better' (GP IV. 496; P 128). In discussing the nature of the soul, Leibniz thus offers empirical support for his views, while at the same time deploying purely a priori arguments (correspondence with Arnauld: GP II. 123–4; L 345–6). For the term 'methodological rationalism' see Brown (2) 46.

59. See Plato, *Republic* 518; *Meno* 18.

60. Locke I. ii. 5.

61. Cf. Chapter 4, p. 153.
62. For the obstructive effect of the body and of sensations associated with our corporeal nature cf. *Conversation with Burman*: AT V. 150; CB 8. For preconceived opinions cf. *Principles* I, 1.
63. Cf. Plato, *Republic* 518; *Meno* 18.
64. See further Jolley 172 ff., where the distinction between 'virtual' and 'dispositional' knowledge is well brought out.
65. Cf. *Nicomachean Ethics* VII, 3 (1146b).
66. Locke I. ii. 5.
67. For implicit knowledge in Descartes, see *Conversation with Burman*: AT V. 147; CB 4. A dispositional account appears in Descartes, *Comments on a Certain Broadsheet*: AT VIIIB. 359; CSM I. 304; but this passage is particularly concerned with the way the mind is programmed to respond to external stimuli (in its apprehension of sensory qualities such as redness). See further Cottingham (2) 147 ff.
68. Cf. Plato, *Republic* 530; see further Cottingham (1) 17–19.
69. Compare Second Meditation (AT VII. 32; CSM II. 21), Fifth Meditation (AT VII. 71; CSM II. 49), *Search for Truth* (AT X. 495; CSM II. 400).

Chapter 3

1. Quotations from Descartes: AT III. 429; K 116; Bayle: Bayle 297 and 330 (under 'Spinoza'); Leibniz: GP IV. 439; P 26.
2. Hume (1) I. iv. 3 and I. iv. 4.
3. Cf. Plato *Republic* 479; Aristotle, *Posterior Analytics* 74b5. For Plato, the search for permanence led to the positing of a world of intelligibles lying *beyond* the observable world of change; see, however, Cottingham (1) 22 ff. for differing interpretations of exactly what the Platonic conception implies.
4. *Categories* 4a10: 'A substance, numerically one and the same, is able to receive contraries. For example, an individual man—one and the same—becomes pale at one time and dark at another.'
5. *Categories* 2a12. A substance in the primary sense is 'that which is neither said of a subject nor in a subject, e.g. the individual man or the individual horse'.
6. 'If the primary substances did not exist it would be impossible for any of the other things to exist': *Categories* 2a34. Predicates can exist only in so far as they 'belong to' (Gk. *hyparchein*) or, in the later scholastic terminology, 'inhere in' (Lat. *inhaerere*) a subject.

7. To this list should be added the notion of substance as '*substrate*'. Thus Locke in his *Essay concerning Human Understanding* (1689) observes: 'We have no ... clear Idea at all, and therefore signify nothing by the word *Substance*, but only an uncertain supposition of we know not what ... *Idea*, which we take to be the *substratum* or support of those *Ideas* we do know' (I. iv. 18). These remarks have given rise to what is sometimes called the 'empiricist critique of substance', viz. that there is no sense to the notion of an unobserved, and in principle unobservable, propertiless 'supporter' underlying what we observe. The Latin term *substratum* corresponds to the Greek *to hypokeimenon*, Aristotle's term for the subject (literally 'the underlying'); but it is far from clear that Aristotle meant by this a propertiless 'something we know not what'. Certainly in Descartes, Spinoza, and Leibniz there is no real separation between a substance and its defining attributes (the distinction between the two is merely a conceptual one, says Descartes at *Principles* I, 62); so the 'empiricist' criticism that they are committed to the notion of a mysterious, featureless property-bearer 'underneath' a thing's attributes is wide of the mark. Cf. Descartes, *Principles* I, 63: 'Thought and extension may be regarded as constituting the natures of intelligent substance and corporeal substance; they must then be considered as nothing else but intelligent substance itself and extended substance itself— that is, as mind and body.' See further *Conversation with Burman*: A T V. 155; CB 15, and the commentary at CB 79. See also Spinoza, *Metaphysical Thoughts*: G I. 258; C 323. For Leibniz's response to Locke's critique of the notion of substance, see *New Essays* (R B 218): 'If you distinguish two things in a substance—the attributes or predicates, and their common subject—it is no wonder that you cannot conceive anything special in this subject. This is inevitable because you have already set aside all the attributes through which details could be conceived. To require anything more of this "pure subject in general" beyond what is needed for the conception of "the same thing" (e.g. it is the same thing which understands and wills and reasons and imagines) is to demand the impossible.'

8. The scholastic term used by Descartes, *realitas objectiva* ('objective reality'), had a completely opposite connotation from our modern notion of objectivity. 'Objective reality' in Descartes is *not* a feature of the external world, but refers to the features that are depicted or represented by an idea in the mind. In the French translation of Descartes's Latin text (published in 1647) 'to exist objectively in the intellect' is glossed as 'to exist *representatively* in the intellect'.

9. *Recherche* III, ii, 6. It is not quite clear from the context whether Malebranche here has in mind a causal or an ontological approach to proving God's existence from the idea of God. He purports to defend the latter approach at *Recherche* IV, 11, but his discussion involves several appeals to causal considerations (cf. Malebranche 320).

10. Ibid. ch. 7: Malebranche 237.

11. Arnauld, *True and False Ideas*, ch. XXVI; for further details of the controversy see Church 61 ff. and Radnor 101 ff.

12. For a useful survey of these issues see H. M. Bracken's article on Arnauld in Edwards. The question of whether, in the Cartesian theory of ideas, representation is possible without resemblance became the focal point of the criticisms of Cartesianism mounted in the last two decades of the seventeenth century by the sceptic Simon Foucher (1644–96). For a detailed account of Foucher's work, and his exchange with Malebranche over the representative nature of ideas, see Watson, esp. ch. 5.

13. Berkeley, *Three Dialogues between Hylas and Philonous* (1713): Berkeley 198.

14. Whatever is in the effect must be present in the cause 'either formally or eminently'; that is, it may be present either literally, or in some higher form (AT VII. 41; CSM II. 28). In the Third Meditation, Descartes invokes the notion that items may be ranked according to the 'degree of reality' which they possess. Modes or modifications of a substance, for example, are of a lower order of reality than substances. Consider, for example, my ideas of physical things as extended and shaped and moving: could I be the cause of these ideas? Certainly I, *qua* a purely thinking thing, do not possess extension or shape or motion; so these features cannot be contained in me *formally*. But Descartes argues that 'since extension, shape and motion are merely modes, whereas I am a substance, it seems possible that they may be contained in me eminently' (AT VII. 45; CSM II. 31). The doctrine of degrees of reality invoked here is by no means easy for the modern reader to digest; it has been aptly described as 'part of the medieval intellectual order which more than any other succumbed to the seventeenth century movement of ideas to which Descartes himself powerfully contributed' (Williams 135). Compare the objections which Descartes had to face from Thomas Hobbes on this issue: AT VII. 185; CSM II. 30.

15. It has recently been argued by L. E. Loeb that 'Descartes does not impose the restriction that there must be a likeness in essence

between cause and effect' (Loeb 140). But when Descartes introduces his causal maxim in the Third Meditation, he does employ metaphors which strongly suggest that causal transactions must be a matter of the 'bestowing' or 'handing on' of features from cause to effect: 'where could the effect get its reality from if not from the cause; and how could the cause give it to the effect unless it possessed it?' (AT VII. 40; CSM II. 28). Admittedly, the reader of the *Meditations* might be forgiven for supposing that all this comes down to is that a cause must belong to an equal or higher order of reality than its effect (see above note 14). But when we come to Cartesian physics, it seems clear that Descartes wants something stronger. Suppose, for example, that someone were to suggest that a pond could spontaneously cause a part of itself to move, since a pond is a 'thing', and hence of a higher order of reality than motion, which is a mere 'mode'. It seems evident that Descartes would reject such a suggestion; for this would be a case of an increase in quantity of motion coming 'from nowhere' (cf. *Principles* II, 36). On Descartes's view, then, we must, it appears, be able to see where effects get their features from and this will typically require that the causes themselves possess the relevant features. Thus when Descartes formulates his principle of the conservation of motion, he conspicuously uses the same metaphor of causes 'imparting' or 'bestowing' features on effects that he had used in the *Meditations*. (Cf. *Principles* II, 40; compare Leibniz on the conservation of motion: see Chapter 4, note 51.)

It should be noted, however, that the idea of conservation, as employed in modern physics, does not require a straightforward qualitative similarity between cause and effect. (Compare explosions caused by atomic fusion: nature 'balances her books' in the sense that all the energy produced is accounted for; but the explosive effects may possess qualitative features not necessarily found in the cause). Descartes himself is in fact not always clear exactly what sort of 'qualitative similarity' his principle requires; sometimes, as in the case of divine creation, the 'resemblance' seems pretty vague and general (cf. *Conversation with Burman*: AT V. 156; CB 17. See further L. Frankel, 'Justifying Descartes' Causal Principle', *Journal of the History of Philosophy*, July 1986). Nevertheless, the causal adequacy principle and the various formulations (both seventeenth-century and modern) of the principles of conservation in physics all have in common an implicit rejection of the Humean notion that 'anything can cause anything'. It is regarded as unacceptable that causes and effects should be specified in utterly and irreducibly heterogeneous terms. If there is heterogeneity, then this is taken as a sign that there is still some further reductive work to be done. Compare Churchland, ch. 7.

16. See pp. 92 and 110, and Chapter 4, p. 126.

17. Cf. Fifth Meditation: AT VII. 63 and 71; CSM II. 44 and 49. Some forty years later, the sceptic Simon Foucher (1644–96) was to raise an apt question about the Cartesian route to establishing the existence of the external world via the idea of corporeal extension: 'how can ideas, which have neither shape or extension, be supposed to represent certain determinate extended shapes?' (*Apologie des academiciens*, 1687). For a detailed discussion of Foucher's critique of Cartesianism see Watson, ch. 3.

18. Cf. *Principles* I, 54: 'We can easily have two clear and distinct notions or ideas, one of created thinking substance, and the other of corporeal substance . . . We can also have a clear and distinct idea of uncreated and independent thinking substance, that is, of God' (AT VIII. 25–6; CSM I. 211).

19. The exception is the Third Meditation where the term 'substance' (together with many other scholastic terms) figures prominently. It is in this Meditation that the reader may find it hardest to accept that Descartes has succeeded in casting aside all preconceived opinion and starting again 'right from the foundations', guided only by the 'natural light'.

20. That continuous divine action is needed to preserve things in being is shown, according to Descartes, by the nature of time: 'The separate divisions of time do not depend on each other; hence the fact that [a] body is supposed to have existed up till now "from itself " . . . is not sufficient to make it exist in the future, unless there is some power in it that as it were recreates us continuously' (AT VII. 110; CSM II. 79). For a discussion of this argument see Sorell 60–1.

21. There is sometimes an imprecision about Descartes's language that may have been encouraged in part by the fact that Latin possesses neither a definite nor an indefinite article. Thus *substantia* could mean 'substance in general' (in the case of matter, corporeal stuff, or 'body-in-general'); but it could also mean 'a substance'. Thus in *Principles* I, 63 Descartes talks of extension as constituting the essence of corporeal substance; but in the following article he seems to slip into the conventional way of talking whereby substances are particulars: 'extension may be taken as a *modus substantiae* [mode of a substance] in so far as *one and the same body* may be extended in

many different ways' (AT VIII. 31; CSM I. 215).

22. Cf. Kenny (1) 58–60, following Bertrand Russell: 'The word "I" is grammatically convenient, but does not describe a datum' (Russell (2) 440).

23. See further the commentary on *Conversation with Burman*: CB 84–5.

24. Cf. Aristotle, *De Anima* II: since the soul is the 'form' of the body, it does not have a separate existence, any more than the form of any organized structure can exist apart from the material structure in question.

25. Cf. *De Anima* III, 5. The great Muslim philosopher and commentator on Aristotle, Averroes (1126–78), took it that human souls, after the death of the body, lost any individuality and were simply merged into a universal spirit. Aristotle's 'active intellect', on this interpretation, is identified with the eternal and universal spirit: there is no individual consciousness after death. Cf. Leibniz's attack on this doctrine in 'Reflections on the Doctrine of a Single Universal Spirit' (1702): GP VI. 529; L 554.

26. 'Per substantiam intelligo id quod in se est et per se concipitur: hoc est id cujus conceptus non indiget conceptu alterius rei a quo formari debeat' (*Ethics* I, def. 3). The gloss literally says 'that whose concept does not need the concept of another thing from which [concept] it must be formed'.

27. 'Quod intellectus de substantia percipit, tanquam ejusdem essentiam constituens.' Cf. Descartes: the 'principal property' of a substance 'constitutes its nature and essence' ('naturam essentiamque constituit') (*Principles* I, 53).

28. In the *Regulae* Descartes acknowledges, alongside material natures and thinking natures, 'common natures', such as existence, unity, and duration, which (as their name implies) are ascribed to both thinking things and corporeal things (AT X. 419; CSM I. 45). In the *Principles*, however, Descartes argues that such universal notions are not real attributes of things but simply 'modes of our thought' (cf. *Principles* I, 57 and 58). Cf. Spinoza's exegesis in *Metaphysical Thoughts*: G I. 244; C 310. In a critical paper on Spinoza, Leibniz attacks the 'no overlap' thesis, arguing that two substances A and B could have some attributes different and some in common, for example, A could have c and d, and B could have d and f ('On the Ethics of Benedict de Spinoza' (1678): GP I. 142; L 198).

29. The full argument here is rather more complex, and has puzzled commentators. If S_1 and S_2 are distinct, Spinoza argues that there must be a difference either in their attributes or in their 'affections' (that is, the modes or states they are in). The former kind of

difference is ruled out *ex hypothesi* (since we are considering two substances of the same nature). The latter (a difference simply in affections) can be 'set aside' says Spinoza, since 'a substance is prior in nature to its affections' (presumably this means that affections are irrelevant to something's identity as a substance). This leaves us with the supposition of two substances S_1 and S_2 such that the definition and concept of each is identical. But how, then, could there be any distinction between them? For criticism of this, and an 'analytic reconstruction' of the argument, see Bennett 66 ff.

30. Spinoza's actual example is of 'twenty human beings existing in nature'. The cause of this 'cannot be contained in human nature itself, since the true definition of man does not involve the number 20' (G II. 51; C 415). This is one of the two demonstrations which Spinoza provides of the proposition that there cannot be two substances of the same nature, the other being the one referred to above, note 29.

31. Cf. Bennett 30 ff.

32. But see above, note 15.

33. Noted, for example, in Scruton 20. It should be pointed out, however, that Spinoza was highly critical of many aspects of cabbalism; compare his comments on the 'lunacy' of the cabbalistic 'triflers' (G III. 135–6).

34. *Principles* I, 28. Significantly, the French version (published three years later) omits the reference to nature. Descartes's Latin phrase 'Deus aut natura' perhaps suggests a slightly sharper disjunction than Spinoza's 'Deus seu Natura' (that is, there is less suggestion of the interchangeability of the two terms); but there are several other places in Descartes where '*natura*' occurs in contexts which leave it in no doubt that what is meant is not (passive) creation but an (active) creator. Compare the talk of sensations as signs which are ordained by nature (*Treatise on Man*: AT XI. 4; CSM I. 81; cf. Sixth Meditation: AT VII. 87; CSM II. 60).

35. Malebranche 229. The thesis that 'we see all things in God' is explicitly stated and defended in the *Search for Truth*, III, ii, 6. Striking as it is, Malebranche's thesis is by no means revolutionary; as T. M. Lennon has aptly pointed out, it can be construed as a serious attempt to make philosophical sense of the Pauline conception of God as him 'in whom we live and move and have our being' (Acts 17: 28). Cf. Lennon's commentary at Malebranche 759.

36. Bayle 300.

37. *Summa Theologiae* I, qu. 2, art. 3: 'nec est possibile quod aliquid sit causa efficiens sui ipsius, quia sic esset prius se ipso, quod est

impossibile.' Cf. ALQ II. 527, note. The term 'efficient cause' comes from Aristotle's classification of causes: see note 39 below.

38. The first proof in the Third Meditation (discussed pp. 78 ff.) hinges on the objective reality (that is, representative content) of my idea of God. The second (much shorter) proof is introduced as follows: 'I should like to go further and inquire whether I myself, who have this idea, could exist if no such being existed' (AT VII. 48; CSM II. 33). For the relation between the two proofs in the Third Meditation see Cottingham (2), ch. 3.

39. *Causa* is the standard philosophical Latin rendering for the Greek *aitia*. Yet if we look at Aristotle's celebrated classification of *aitiai* into four kinds, it is clear that what he is discussing is much wider than causality in the modern sense. Rather he is discussing four kinds of 'reason why', or four kinds of place-filler for clauses beginning 'because . . .' These comprise specifications of *purpose* ('final causes'), of *material ingredients* ('material cause'), of *productive agency* or *source of change* ('efficient cause'), and of something's *nature* or *essence* ('formal cause'). See *Metaphysics* 1034a–b.

40. Though he does also offer what he calls an a posteriori proof: to be able to exist is to have power; so if finite beings possess the power to exist, while an infinite being lacks that power, finite beings would be more powerful than an infinite being, which is absurd (G II. 53, lines 30–5). But this argument is a posteriori only in the sense that one of the premisses refers to the existence of finite beings. It is the first premiss (that to exist is to have power—*posse existere est potentia*) that is the crucial one; it is supposed to be known a priori, and will (as Spinoza himself notes) enable a purely a priori version of the argument to be constructed (viz. that an infinite being must by definition possess the power of existing, and must therefore exist; G II. 54; lines 5–10). For Descartes's formulation of this version of the ontological argument based on the notion of the power to exist cf. AT VII. 119; CSM II. 85.

41. There is a dispute among commentators as to whether Descartes's a priori proof of God's existence is logically independent of his a posteriori proof. Some hold that the proof of God's existence in the Fifth Meditation only works once the general reliability of our clear and distinct perceptions is guaranteed, and that establishing *this* requires the earlier (Third Meditation) proof of a non-deceiving God. For more on this issue see Cottingham (2) 63–4. For the Third Meditation proof, see above pp. 78 ff.

42. Compare Gassendi's criticisms of Descartes in the Fifth Set of

Objections: 'existence is not a perfection either in God or anything else; it is that without which no perfections can be present' (AT VII. 323; CSM II. 224). Modern discussion of the ontological argument has tended to focus on the more general question of whether existence is a *predicate*. The extensive literature cannot be reviewed here; for a survey of some of the issues see Kenny (1) 168, Cottingham (2) 59 and 74–5, Curley (2) 153–4.

43. Though the notion of substance is explicitly linked to that of perfection at *Ethics* I, prop. 11, schol. (G II. 54, lines 20–35; C 419).

44. For *X* to exert a causal influence on *Y*, *X* must (in accordance with the causal similarity principle) have something in common with *Y*.

45. Bk. IV, ch. 11: Malebranche 317–18. But see note 9, above.

46. Descartes acknowledges that there can be 'fictitious' ideas, that is, concepts which do not correspond to true essences; but his attempts to show that we can straightforwardly distinguish such suspect concepts from those which do correspond to true essences are far from satisfactory (cf. AT V. 161; CB 23). Spinoza, in his discussion of fictitious ideas, says that their falsity is 'easily brought to light'; the 'easiness' begins to look rather questionable, however, when he goes on to say that the process requires careful attention and an unravelling of the implications of the relevant ideas (G II. 23; C 28). For more on Spinoza's views on truth and falsity see Chapter 2, pp. 63–4.

47. Thus Cartesian dualism is sometimes supported by the claim that disembodied existence is at least conceivable. Compare Arnauld's criticism of Descartes's argument for the distinctness of mind and body, discussed in Chapter 4, p. 121.

48. For discussion of this manoeuvre see Brown (2) 62.

49. 'I shall venture to affirm as a general proposition which admits of no exception that knowledge [of matters of fact] is not in any instance attained by reasonings *a priori* but arises entirely from experience': Hume (2), sect. IV, pt. 1.

50. Leibniz's description of having 'thrown off the yoke of Aristotle' comes in the *New System* (1695): GP IV. 478; P 116. In a much earlier letter written to Simon Foucher he remarks that Gassendi and Bacon were 'the first modern philosophers to fall into my hands' (G I. 370; L 152). Pierre Gassendi (1592–1655) had put forward an atomistic theory based on the system of the Greek philosopher Epicurus (341–270 BC); his major work, the *Syntagma Philosophicum*, was published posthumously in 1658. In Gassendi's physics, the behaviour of all material objects is explained in terms of combinations of

atoms in the void, the atoms being characterized solely in terms of the primary qualities of size, shape, and propensity to movement. But Gassendi drew back from full-blooded Epicurean materialism, and argued for the existence of an immortal rational soul. Francis Bacon (1561–1626) is now best known for the 'method of induction' set out in part II of his *Novum Organum* (1620). But his philosophy of science is not as straightforwardly 'empiricist' as is often suggested; he believed that the explanation of natural processes depended on the unobserved inner structure of bodies—what he called the *latens schematismus*. In a passage in the *Novum Organum* which may have influenced Leibniz he rejects the reductionism of the atomists, 'which presupposes the vacuum and unchanging matter, both of which are false', and suggests that the underlying structure of things depends on 'true particles, as they may be found to be' (*Novum Organum* II, 8: Bacon 307).

51. Cf. L 151. In Paris Leibniz also met the distinguished philosopher and theologian Antoine Arnauld, who had made a close study of Descartes's work (see Chapter 1, note 49). Arnauld was a member of the Jansenists (who took St Augustine as their model); his *La Logique ou l'art de penser* (which he wrote with Pierre Nicole) appeared in 1662, and is strongly influenced by Cartesian ideas. For Arnauld's dispute with Malebranche see pp. 79–80.

52. Despite his ontological reductionism, Spinoza insisted that the two attributes of exension and thought were distinct and incommensurable, thus retaining an *attributive* dualism. See Chapter 4, p. 129.

53. This was the 'Metaphysical Disputation on the Principle of Individuality' (1663); see Chapter 1, p. 23.

54. Traditional systems of definition by *genus* and *differentia* began with the 'highest classes of things' (*summa genera*) and then descended in a branching division until a set of *infima species*, or lowest natural kinds, was reached. This method was commonly known as the 'tree of Porphyry' (named after the third-century commentator on Aristotle). For Descartes's attitude to this method, see *Search for Truth*: AT X. 516; CSM II. 410.

55. Compare Spinoza's argument for the uniqueness of substance; see above, pp. 90 ff.

56. In his *Primary Truths* (c.1686) Leibniz formulates this principle as follows: 'In nature there cannot be two individual things which differ in number alone . . . two perfectly similar eggs, or leaves or blades of grass will never be found' (CO 519; P 88–9). For a discussion of the rationale (apart from the *Inesse* principle) behind Leibniz's assertion

of the identity of indiscernibles, see Brown (2) 182–3.

57. Leibniz frequently returns to this issue in his correspondence with Arnauld. In the text cited, as Stuart Brown has pointed out, Leibniz limits himself to the hypothetical claim that *if* bodies are true substances they must have a principle of unity (cf. Brown (2) 140). Compare 'A Specimen of Discoveries' (*c.*1686): '*either* there are no corporeal substances and bodies are merely phenomena . . . *or* there is [in them] something analogous to the soul' (GP VII. 134; P 81). Eventually, Leibniz came to believe that—certainly in the case of non-organic matter—bodies are mere 'well founded phenomena' (cf. his review of Berkeley's *Principles* (1710); quoted in Brown (1) 88). Cf. Chapter 4, p. 144.

58. Aristotle had defined the soul (*psyche*) as 'substance *qua* form of a natural body'; where by 'form' was understood, roughly, the organizational principle in virtue of which an organic body is able to perform its various functions (growth, nutrition, sensation, etc. Cf. Aristotle, *De Anima* 412a19). From this piece of terminology (soul as substance *qua* form) grew the elaborate scholastic doctrine of substantial forms: each thing is what it is in virtue of a substantial form—the prefix 'substantial' conveying, for some scholastic thinkers, the distinctly *un*Aristotelian thought that the form is capable in principle of existing 'in its own right', independently of the material structures and configurations involved. Hence, according to the doctrine of transubstantiation in the Eucharist, the matter of the bread and the wine remains unaltered, but the form is changed, so that after the consecration it becomes a different substance: the body and blood of Christ. For the role of the doctrine of substantial forms in connection with the dogma of transubstantiation, and the problems which Descartes encountered as a result of his denial of substantial forms, see R. A. Watson, 'Transubstantiation among the Cartesians', in Lennon 127 ff.

59. The Greek *entelecheia* (lit. 'activity' or 'actuality') is one of the terms used by Aristotle in his account of the soul in *De Anima* II. Cf. 'Leibniz' Reply to M. Bayle' (1702): 'the simple substances or active principles which I follow Aristotle in calling primitive entelechies' (GP IV. 556; L 576). In fact Aristotle himself distinguishes between 'first actuality' (or disposition) and 'second actuality' (or activity); the soul or psyche is defined as the 'first actuality of a living body'. The cognate Greek adjective *enteles* means 'complete' or 'perfect', and it is this connotation in particular that Leibniz trades on.

60. Leibniz's first use of the term to refer to a substance is generally

reckoned to be in a letter to the Marquis de l'Hospital of 1695 (M xxxvi). Loemker points out, however, that the term had been in use since Bruno (L 508).

61. 'They have that which is perfect.' See above, note 59.

62. 'In the beginning I readily agreed with those contemporary philosophers . . . such as Galileo, Bacon, Gassendi, Descartes, Hobbes and Digby, that in explaining phenomena we must not necessarily resort to God or to any other incorporeal thing, form, or quality' ('Confession of Nature against the Atheists' (1669): GP IV. 106; L 110).

63. *Recherche* VI, ii, 3: Malebranche 450.

64. Cf. F. Suarez, *Disputationes Metaphysicae* (1597), XII. ii. 4. For Leibniz's general attitude to occult qualities, compare his 'Metaphysical Consequences of the Principle of Reason' (c.1712): 'The fundamental principle . . . that there is nothing without a reason . . . disposes of all inexplicable occult qualities and other similar fragments' (CO 11; P 172).

65. *First Enquiry* (1748): Hume (2), sect. VII, pt. 2.

66. See further Cottingham (1) 143 ff.; for a recent collection of readings on rationality in modern science, see Hollis and Lukes.

67. Leibniz discusses the Democritean account in a paper of 1669, but argues that it cannot explain basic phenomena such as *cohesion*. If two bodies are said to stick together by some mechanism such as microscopic hooks, this presupposes that the hooks themselves must be hard and tenacious: 'But whence this tenacity? Must we assume hooks on hooks ad infinitum?' (GP IV. 108; L 112).

68. A version of the argument from contingency forms the third of Aquinas's 'Five Ways' of proving God's existence.

Chapter 4

1. Quotations from Descartes: AT VIII. 52; CSM I. 232; Malebranche: *Recherche* I, I (Malebranche 2); Leibniz: GP IV. 483; P 121.

2. See, for example, Churchland, ch. 8; Hofstadter and Dennett, ch. 23; Shoemaker 287 ff. See also Cottingham (2) 119 ff. For a recent defence of dualism (albeit a 'soft' variety), see Swinburne, ch. 8.

3. Compare Arnauld's strictures: 'as far as I can see all that follows is that I can obtain some knowledge of myself without knowledge of the body. But it is not yet . . . certain that I am not mistaken in

excluding body from my essence' (Fourth Objections: A T VII. 201; CSM II. 141).

4. Cf. Leibniz, *New System*: GP IV. 482; L 456.

5. Cf. T. Nagel, 'Brain Bisection and the Unity of Consciousness', in Nagel (1) 164.

6. For further discussion of the divisibility argument, see Cottingham (2) 116 ff.

7. For Descartes's view of the role of brain events in sensation and imagination, see further J. Cottingham, 'Cartesian Trialism', *Mind*, 1985.

8. For Descartes's views on immortality and the afterlife see Synopsis to the *Meditations*. AT VII. 13; CSM II. 10. For indivisibility in relation to Christian doctrine cf. Seventh Set of Replies: AT VII. 520; CSM II. 354. However, one central strand in Christian orthodoxy affirms the idea of *bodily* resurrection, thus making the doctrine of the afterlife independent of the thesis of the immateriality of the mind. For this, cf. Swinburne, ch. 15.

9. For modern versions of the claim that disembodied existence is at least logically possible, or conceivable, compare Sprigge 19–21 (though the author implicitly concedes that what is apparently conceivable may or may not turn out to be coherently conceivable).

10. Cf. Leibniz's critique of the ontological argument: pp. 99 ff.

11. N. Malebranche, *Méditations chrétiennes et métaphysiques* IX. 23; cf. Church 53 ff.

12. Locutions like 'X bumps into Y' seem to presuppose notions like force and resistance which take us far beyond the simple properties of geometry. Descartes, however, seems to have believed that a three-dimensional conception of extension implies solidity and impenetrability (AT VII. 442; CSM II. 298 and AT XI. 33; CSM I. 91). See further Cottingham (2) 86 ff. and Williams 229.

13. *Principles of Human Knowledge* (1710), para. 19: Berkeley 68 (italics supplied).

14. For Locke's support of the Cartesian framework, compare Locke II. xiii. 22 and II. xxiii. 31; for some of his criticisms see II. xix. 4 and II. xxiii. 29.

15. Locke IV. iii. 6.

16. Cf. Locke IV. x. 16: 'Unthinking Particles of Matter, however put together, can have nothing thereby added to them but a new relation of Position, which 'tis impossible should give thought and knowledge to them.' Compare Leibniz, Preface to *New Essays*: 'Sense and thought are not something which is natural to matter, and there are

only two ways in which they could occur in it: through God's combining it with a substance to which thought is natural, or through his putting thought into it by a miracle' (RB 67).

17. For the way in which the concept of matter developed even during the century immediately following Descartes, see Yolton.

18. Descartes also argues that, being situated near the conjunction of the optic nerves, the pineal gland is suited to serve as a locus for the unification of the two sets of optic stimuli into a single image (*Passions* I, 32).

19. See further *Treatise on Man*: AT XI. 143; CSM I. 102, and *Optics*: AT VI. 130; CSM I. 167.

20. For more on the 'arbitrariness' of the relation between brain movements and sensations, see Cottingham (2) 138 ff.

21. *Recherche de la vérité* V, 1 (Malebranche 338). In his *Comments on a Certain Broadsheet* Descartes himself talks of the mind forming certain representations on the *occasion* of certain corporeal motions (AT VIIIB. 359; CSM I. 304).

22. For more on the relation between Malebranchian occasionalism and the orthodox Cartesian view, see Watson 109–10. As regards the relation between sensations and brain-events, which appears to reduce, for Descartes, to an arbitrary conjunction of heterogeneous items, the only kind of explanation which Descartes seems willing or able to provide is an explanation of a kind which he resolutely avoids in the rest of his philosophy—one in terms of final causes or purposes: the sensations ordained by God are those that are 'conducive to the preservation of the healthy man' (AT VII. 87; CSM II. 80. See further Cottingham (2) 140 ff.

On the interaction issue, some commentators have recently argued that Descartes did *not*, after all, regard interaction between heterogeneous substances as problematic. See, for example, R. C. Richardson, 'The "Scandal" of Cartesian Interactionism', *Mind*, 1982. Certainly in the letter to Clerselier of 12 January 1646 (AT IX. 213; CSM II. 275) Descartes, in discussing sense-perception, does appear to say that the different nature of soul and body need not prevent their interacting. But it is dangerous to take this at face value. To begin with, Descartes readily concedes that he is not yet in a position to give a satisfactory account of the mind–body relation (so he is certainly not saying that there are no difficulties whatever for his view of the nature of the mind). Second, he goes on to observe, somewhat ruefully it seems, that his own views are no harder to accept than the scholastic account of sense-perception (an account which he of course regards as quite unintelligible). Compare a closely similar passage in the letter to 'Hyperaspistes' of August 1641 (AT III. 424; K 112), and see Alquié's comments at ALQ II. 362. I conclude that these texts provide weak evidence for the claim that Descartes saw no difficulty in the supposition of an interaction between heterogeneous substances. On the other side, there are many passages where Descartes, implicitly and even explicitly (see *Principles* IV, 198) seems to be telling us that such interaction is difficult if not impossible to comprehend (see also Ch. 3, note 15 above).

23. Cf. *Ethics* I, prop. 13: 'an absolutely infinite substance is indivisible.'

24. The distinction between the (often misleading) deliverances of the faculty of imagination and the clear and reliable perceptions of the intellect is taken from Descartes, cf. AT VII. 365; CSM II. 252.

25. '*Aquam quatenus aqua est dividi concipimus . . . at non quatenus substantia corporea*' (G II. 60; C 424). Spinoza's frequent use of the qualificatory term *quatenus* ('in so far as') has been criticized by some commentators as involving a kind of logical sleight of hand (cf. Scruton 116). But in the case under discussion Spinoza's argument can be seen as a development of the Cartesian idea that the things we think of as ordinary objects and parcels of matter are mere modifications of *res extensa*. And if *res extensa* is construed (as Descartes sometimes does construe it) simply as space, then there is at least some sense to the notion that it is not susceptible of division into parts. For this line of interpretation see Bennett 86.

26. An interestingly similar result (that extension and thought are compatible properties) was reached—though by a different route—by the Cambridge Platonist Henry More (1614–87). More at first supported Descartes—'that sublime and subtil Mechanick', as he called him—applauding his attacks on scholasticism, his conception of philosophy as a unified system, and his defence of the Christian doctrine of the immortality of the soul. But he criticized several aspects of Cartesian physics even in the exchange of letters which he had with Descartes in the late 1640s; and he later came to see the Cartesian distinction between thinking substance and extended substance as paving the way for atheism (since for More the denial of spatial location to spirits—what he called 'Nullibism'—implied that spirits were 'nowhere', and hence incapable of initiating movement). In his *Enchiridion Metaphysicum* (1671), More insists that extension is a property of *all* substances, whether spiritual or material; the fact that thought and extension are conceptually distinct does not show that they are incompatible. Though this accords with Spinoza's view,

More had little time for Spinoza's monistic metaphysics; like most of his contemporaries, he regarded it as impious and dangerous to the Christian faith. Spinoza himself was described by More as 'a Jew first, after a Cartesian, and now an atheist' (letter to Robert Boyle of 4 December 1671). For an illuminating account of More's hostility to Cartesian and allied systems of thought, see A. Gabbey, 'Philosophia Cartesiana Triumphata', in Lennon 171 ff. For the criticisms of Spinoza raised by More's fellow Platonist Ralph Cudworth (1617–88) see Cudworth, *The True Intellectual System of the Universe* (1678).

27. The doctrine of infinite attributes is the subject of a vast amount of speculation among commentators, much of it fruitless. Spinoza himself asserts (Letter 64) that 'the human mind cannot attain to knowledge of any attribute of God apart from Thought and Extension' (G IV. 278; W 307).

28. Hence the label 'attributive dualism', which is sometimes applied to Spinoza's system. For this term see Williams 293.

29. Henricus Regius, anticipating Spinoza, remarked in his Broadsheet (1647): 'Since the attributes of thought and extension are not opposite but merely different, there is no reason why the mind should not be a sort of attribute co-existing with extension in the same subject' (AT VIIIB. 343; CSM I. 294). Descartes's reply is instructive: 'this would be a contradiction since it would be tantamount to saying one and the same subject has two different natures' (AT VIIIB. 350; CSM I. 298).

30. The celebrated phrase 'the ghost in the machine', as a description of the Cartesian view of man, comes from Gilbert Ryle (Ryle, ch. 1). Spinoza acknowledges that many people are convinced that the mind does causally interact with the body, but argues that when unpacked this belief turns out to be radically confused (G II. 142; C 495).

31. For some of these see Delahunty 195. Thomas Nagel defines a dual aspect view of the mind as the view 'that one thing can have two sets of mutually exclusive essential properties, mental and physical' (Nagel (2) 31). This characterization could aptly be applied to Spinoza.

32. From a letter to Simon de Vries of March 1663. Spinoza's other example in this passage concerns colours: 'by a plane surface I mean whatever reflects all rays of light without any change; I also understand the same by *white*, except that it is called white in relation to a man looking at the flat surface.' This suggests that one and the same feature can be described in the objective language of science,

but also in terms of the subjective apprehension of that feature in the observer's consciousness. The difficulty here is that rather than being an explanatory analogue of the thought–extension relation, the example seems to involve an instance of the very phenomenon that is supposed to be explained.

33. See Parkinson (4) 43 (where it is readily admitted that what is involved is 'no more than a metaphor' for the mind–body relation).

34. Spinoza's actual example concerns 'a circle existing in nature' and 'the idea of the existing circle which is in God' (see p. 129).

35. For functionalist approaches to the mind see Dennett (I), pt. III, and Shoemaker, ch. 9.

36. For the difficulties involved in making Descartes's geometrical conception of matter generate notions like *solidity*, see above, note 12.

37. Bayle 368. As Bayle goes on to point out, the Cartesians tended to 'solve' this problem by recourse to the power of God as the 'sole and immediate cause of motion' (Bayle 369). Cf. Descartes, *Principles* II, 36: AT VIII. 61; CSM I. 240.

38. This objection is raised in Bayle's *Dictionary*: Bayle 359; quoted in Brown (1) 87.

39. For the phrase 'point particles of energy' see Ross 53. For the gradual progression in the seventeenth and eighteenth centuries away from the Cartesian conception of matter as inert towards a more energetic conception see Yolton, esp. ch. V.

40. For further discussion of Leibniz's reasons for rejecting the Cartesian doctrine of matter as *res extensa* cf. Jolley 98–9 and I. Hacking, 'Individual Substance', in Frankfurt 137 ff.

41. From a brief handwritten review found at the end of Leibniz's copy of Berkeley's *Principles of Human Knowledge* (1710). For a discussion of the importance of this review, see Brown (2) 42–3 and 147.

42. Letter of 28 April 1704, quoted in Jolley 102. It is important to notice, however, that Leibniz does not follow the Cartesians in supposing that the soul is *separable* from the body. See *New Essays*, Preface: 'I hold that all souls . . . are always joined to a body, and for this reason there can never be entirely separate souls' (RB 58; P 160). Cf. *Metaphysical Consequences of the Principle of Reason* (*c.*1712), para. 7: 'Every simple substance has an organic body which corresponds to it—otherwise it would not have any kind of orderly relation to other things in the universe . . .' (CO 14; P 175). In the

light of such passages Stuart Brown has argued that Leibniz came near to an 'Aristotelian' approach to the mind–body problem, regarding the soul as the *form* of the body (that is not a separate immaterial substance). On this view, Leibniz rejects dualism and maintains that 'God is the only immaterial substance' (Brown (2) 167). Leibniz certainly strove to close the Cartesian 'gap' between mind and matter (see above, p. 107); but passages like those cited in the text clearly show that Leibniz was never able to free himself entirely from a Platonic-Cartesian notion of an immaterial soul (and Brown himself acknowledges this, p. 201).

43. The term 'automaton' thus has a rather different sense in Leibniz from its sense in Descartes. For Descartes an automaton is a 'moving machine' whose operations can be specified in purely mechanistic terms (*Discourse*, Part V: AT VI. 55; CSM I. 139). For Leibniz it is an automaton in the strict etymological sense of a *self*-moving thing— something that carries within itself an active force or principle of motion. Thus Leibniz describes the soul of man as 'a kind of spiritual *automaton*' (*Theodicy* I, 52). This latter phrase occurs in Spinoza's *Treatise on the Purification of the Intellect* (G II. 32; C 37) though earlier in the same work Spinoza uses the term 'automaton' in the mechanistic Cartesian sense, to mean 'completely lacking in a mind' (G II. 18; C 22).

44. This was the thesis later advanced in Julien de la Mettrie's *L'Homme Machine* (1747).

45. Cf. the discussion by Maxwell and others in Maxwell and Savodik 319.

46. Cf. Descartes, *Description of the Human Body* (1647): 'I shall give such a full account of the entire bodily machine that we will have no more reason to think that it is our soul which produces in it the movements . . . not controlled by our will than we have reason to think that there is a soul in a clock which makes it tell the time' (AT XI. 226; CSM I. 315). Descartes's defence of reductionism, however, extends only to physiology and biology; it does not, of course, encompass the phenomena of consciousness.

47. He dismisses the argument from clear and distinct perception as question begging (*Remarks on Descartes's Principles*: GP IV. 364; L 390).

48. Cf. Hume (1) I. iv. 6: 'For my part, when I enter most intimately in what I call *myself*, I always stumble on some particular perception or other, of heat or cold, light or shade, love or hatred, pain or pleasure. I can never catch *myself* at any time without a perception, and never

can observe anything but the perception.' See also op. cit. at note 5, above.

49. Leibniz seems to have regarded the very notion of a substance as being derived from our internal experience of ourselves as individual subjects of consciousness: 'That we are not substances is contrary to experience, since we have no awareness of substance except from the . . . experience of ourselves when we perceive the *Ego*, and on that basis we apply the term to God and to other monads' (GG II. 558; quoted in Jolley 123).

50. For a full-blooded materialist-reductionist approach to mental states see Churchland, ch. 7. The Spinozan position falls short of this: though brain-states are identified with mental states, the Spinozan would regard mental properties as 'distinct' in the sense that they cannot be deduced from physical properties. See above, p. 132. Thomas Nagel, similarly, has argued that what is given in our subjective conscious experience is an irreducible feature of reality that cannot be captured by (and is not entailed by) the objective descriptions of physical science. Cf. Nagel (2), ch. 1.

51. In Descartes's system, the soul has the power to produce small movements in the pineal gland, which in turn produces changes in the motion of the animal spirits (*Passions* I, 34). To the objection that the physical movements described in this scenario must occur in violation of the principle of the conservation of motion, the Cartesians suggested 'that it was unnecessary to give the soul the power of increasing or diminishing the force of the body, but only that of changing its *direction* by changing the cause and direction of the animal spirits' (GP VI. 540; L 587). Compare the model Descartes offers in the *Treatise on Man*: the body is compared to a system of fountains and water pipes; the soul is like the fountain keeper, who by turning certain taps can direct the flow of water into various channels, as desired (AT XI. 131; CSM I. 101). Leibniz's apt reply is that to ascribe to the soul a power of changing the direction of motion is 'no less inexplicable' and contrary to the order of things and the laws of nature' (loc., cit.). For the principle of the conservation of motion in Descartes see *Principles* II, 37–40.

52. For influence or 'influx', see Chapter 3, p. 111.

53. In the *New Essays*, Leibniz describes his system as 'uniting Plato with Democritus, Aristotle with Descartes, the scholastics with the moderns, theology and morality with reason. It takes the best from all systems and then advances them further than anyone has yet done' (RB 71).

54. Simon Foucher, 'Response à Leibniz sur son nouveau système de la communication des substances', *Journal des Savants*, 12 September 1695; cited in Watson 137.

55. In his correspondence with Descartes in the late 1640s, Henry More had precisely questioned Descartes's use of this metaphor: 'motion being a mode of body, cannot pass from one body to another' (letter of 23 July 1649). Descartes's reply is not entirely satisfactory: he acknowledges that 'transmigration' of motion is a dubious notion, but invokes instead the scarcely less problematic language of 'force' and 'impulse'. Significantly enough, however, he seems to feel that a study of his mathematical formulae for the calculation of the speed and direction of bodies after impact will be enough to dispel More's worry (letter of 4 August 1649; A T V. 402 ff.; K 258).

56. For an elegant discussion of this point see H. Ishiguro, 'Harmony versus Constant Conjunction', in Kenny (2) 66 ff.

57. The traditional scholastic theory of sense-perception (developed originally by Aquinas) maintained that when we perceive an object, the intellect somehow apprehends its *form*, though without an actual transfer of matter taking place. Neo-Epicureans like Pierre Gassendi (1592–1655) argued that a purely formal account could not explain perception: there must be material items transmitted from object to observer (Gassendi proposed that these were configurations of atoms capable of impressing on the sense-organs an image resembling the external object: *Exercitationes Paradoxicae Adversus Aristotelicos*, 1624). In the writings of the seventeenth-century scholastics, the status of the 'form' (*species*) supposedly apprehended in sense-perception becomes distinctly obscure: it tends to hover between an immaterial form and some kind of flying image transmitted from object to observer. The contradictions involved here are a recurring theme in Cartesian writers of the later seventeenth century, notably Louis de la Forge (1605–79). For a useful account of these issues, see Watson 30–1 and 85–6.

58. For linguistic abilities as the crucial sign of the occurrence of genuine thought, see Descartes, *Discourse on the Method*, A T VI. 57; CSM I. 140. Despite Descartes's official 'all or nothing' thesis, there are passages where he appears very close to granting that non-human animals at least have *sensations*. See J. Cottingham, 'A brute to the brutes? Descartes' treatment of animals', *Philosophy*, 1980.

59. Several recent commentators on Leibniz have seen an anticipation of modern genetic theory here. G. M. Ross, for example, notes that Leibniz was 'not far removed from modern biology' in maintaining

that animal bodies 'included organic components which embodied the information required for generating future unborn individuals— in a word genetic codes' (Ross 107). For earlier variations on this theme cf. Van Peursen, ch. 3. There may, however, be a certain imprecision in Leibniz's talk of the monad as 'representing' or 'expressing' external things (cf. *Monadology*, paras. 56, 60). Something may be 'ensouled' in Aristotle's sense of possessing an intricate organizational structure, and in this sense we may speak of DNA as having a certain informational content. But informational content is not *eo ipso* representational content, and it is not clear in what sense a Leibnizian monad, which is 'conscious' only in a very attenuated sense (see Chapter 3, p. 113 and Chapter 4, p. 149), can be said to possess *representations* of the universe. For a mere mirroring or reflecting of patterns is not in itself enough to count as a representation in the sense in which a thought or a sentence may be said to express or represent something outside itself. (For this last point compare Putnam, chs. 1 and 2.)

60. Locke II. i. 10.
61. 'It may be said as a result of these minute perceptions that the present is big with the future and laden with its past, that all things conspire—*sympnoia panta* as Hippocrates said' (P 156; RB 55). The Greek phrase means literally 'all things breathe together' (and the same notion underlies the Latin root from which the English verb 'conspire' is derived).
62. Sometimes Descartes uses 'idea' to refer to a mental act, sometimes to an object; for this ambiguity see Kenny (1) 97 ff. Sometimes ideas are concepts (for example, the idea of a triangle); sometimes they are propositional (as when Descartes says I have ideas of 'common notions', that is, basic truths like the principle of non-contradiction); sometimes they have the role of sense-data or sense-contents, forming objects of awareness that are intermediate between me and the external world. Cf. Third and Sixth Meditations, *passim*.
63. Compare AT VII. 189; CSM II. 132, and see Chapter 2, p. 70.
64. *Recherche de la vérité*, III. ii. 4 (Malebranche 227.) Though the criticism quoted has force against any 'store-house' theory, Malebranche's actual target in this passage is the theory that even ordinary sense-perception of external objects involves the mind's utilizing a store of innate ideas. Descartes himself comes close to saying just this in the *Comments on a Certain Broadsheet* (1648): AT VIIIB. 359; CSM I. 304.
65. For more recent criticism of the view that consciousness is a process

that is transparently revealed in introspection, cf. Churchland, ch. 7.
66. *Recherche*, III. ii. 7 (Malebranche 238).
67. *Méditations chrétiennes et métaphysiques* ix. 15. Cf. Radnor 73–4; Church 49–50. Malebranche was not the only seventeenth-century writer to raise questions about the complexity of the mind. Compare Gassendi's apt criticisms of Descartes's view that the mind is better known than the body (Fifth Set of Objections: A T V I I. 276–7; C S M I I. 192–3).

Chapter 5

1. Quotations from Spinoza: G I I. 276; C 594; Leibniz: G P V I I. 89; L 427; Bayle: Bayle 314 (under 'Spinoza').
2. The separation is most apparent in the specialization of contemporary academic philosophy: it is comparatively unusual, for example, to find writers on the 'theory of knowledge' making substantial contributions to ethics, or vice versa. This division should not, however, be seen as an entirely modern phenomenon; compare Aristotle's distinction between theoretical and practical reasoning, for example in *Nicomachean Ethics* VI.
3. This orientation is perhaps most striking in Spinoza—see *Treatise on the Purification of the Intellect*: G I I. 15; C 7.
4. Descartes says, when introducing the hypothesis of universal deception: 'I will suppose that *not* God, who is supremely good and the source of truth, but rather some malicious demon of the utmost power and cunning has employed all his energies in order to deceive me' (A T V I I. 22; C S M I I. 15). For the impossibility of deception by a supremely perfect being, see Sixth Set of Replies: A T V I I. 428; C S M I I. 289, and *Conversation with Burman*: A T V. 147; C B 5.
5. For more on clearness and distinctness and their role in Descartes's metaphysics, see Chapter 2, pp. 49–50.
6. For more on Spinoza's critique of Descartes, see E. Curley, 'Spinoza and the Ethics of Belief ', in Freeman and Mandelbaum.
7. For more on this, see Chapter 2, note 43.
8. Sometimes called 'soft determinism', but misleadingly, since it does not involve any softening of the thesis of strict and universal determinism.
9. For the phrase 'freedom of enlightenment' (*libertée eclairée*) see A L Q I I. 461.
10. 'The spontaneity and freedom of one's belief were all the greater in

proportion to my lack of indifference' (AT VII. 59; CSM II. 41).
Writers on freedom have traditionally distinguished 'liberty of
indifference'—which means a 'negation of causes', as Hume put it—
and 'liberty of spontaneity', which is compatible with universal
determinism. As argued in the text, in spite of language which at
times suggests a contra-causal conception, Descartes typically
favours the spontaneity conception. His use of the term 'indifference'
is, however, confusing. Sometimes he seems to use it as a virtual
synonym of freedom: 'We are intimately aware of the freedom and
indifference which is in us' (*Principles* I, 41). But elsewhere he
equates indifference with the state which I am in when 'there is no
reason pushing me in one direction rather than the other'. Such
indifference is 'the lowest grade of freedom—not evidence of any
perfection of freedom but rather of a defect of knowledge or a kind
of negation' (AT VII. 58; CSM II. 40). For a detailed account of
Descartes's terminology in discussing freedom, see A. Kenny, 'Descartes on the Will', in Butler. For more on the question of Spinoza's
and Leibniz's interpretation of Descartes's views, see J. Cottingham,
'The Intellect, the Will and the Passions: Spinoza's Critique of
Descartes', *Journal of the History of Philosophy*, 1988.

11. A possible defence for Leibniz here is suggested by the recent work
    of D. Dennett, who has argued that the ability to do otherwise than
    we in fact do is irrelevant to the way in which the concept of
    responsibility actually operates: Dennett, ch. 6.

12. This holds good despite fashionable talk of the 'psychological
    determinants' of action which is sometimes used by modern writers
    in a way which suggests (tendentiously) that all choice is somehow
    illusory; see the examples given in Dennett 30.

13. Leibniz also talks of retributive punishment as giving satisfaction to
    the injured; and he also briefly mentions the idea that it may have the
    function of restoring the moral order, or compensating for the
    disorder that would otherwise 'scandalise the mind'. The various
    strands of retributivism hinted at here prefigure the more detailed
    retributive theories of Kant and Hegel. For a discussion of some of
    these strands see J. Cottingham, 'Varieties of Retribution', *Philo-
    sophical Quarterly*, 1979.

14. Leibniz is by no means alone in advancing a compatibilist account of
    the relation between freedom and determinism. Thomas Hobbes had
    argued in the *Leviathan* (1651) and in his treatise *Of Liberty and
    Necessity* (1654) that 'liberty and necessity are consistent, as the
    water that hath not only liberty but also a necessity of descending

downhill'. The Cambridge Platonist Ralph Cudworth (1617–88), writing later in the century, also took a reconciliationist line (though he criticized Hobbes on a number of points). In his *Treatise on Free Will* (edited posthumously in 1838), Cudworth rejects the notion of freedom of indifference—the view that freedom consists in the arbitrary exercise of a contra-causal power (cf. note 10, above).

15. The phrase 'in so far as it is in itself' (Lat. *quantum in se est*) refers back to the definition of substance as 'that which is in itself' (*id quod in se est: Ethics* I, def. 3). Spinoza's meaning, then, is that each thing, in so far as it is [a mode of] substance, strives to persist in its being. Against this interpretation, Edwin Curley has argued that in Spinoza's account of *conatus* at *Ethics* III, prop. 6, the phrase *quantum in se est* should be taken in its ordinary non-technical sense to mean 'as far as it lies in itself', or 'as far as it lies in its own power' (C 498, note). But it seems clear from passages such as the scholium at *Ethics* II, prop. 45 ('the force by which each thing persists in existing follows from the universal necessity of God') that the phrase *quantum in se est* does indeed bear its technical Spinozan sense: the attribution of *conatus* to individual things directly depends on their status as modes expressing an attribute of the unique substance, God (cf. Parkinson (4) 54–5).

16. Descartes's use of the phrase *quantum in se est* ('in so far as it can'), in formulating his principle of inertia, lends at least some support to Curley's interpretation of Spinoza's *conatus* principle (see preceding note).

17. The title reads *De potentia intellectus seu de libertate humana* ('Of the power of the intellect, or of human freedom'): G II. 277; C 594.

18. For the full list see 'Definitions of the Affects' at the end of part III of the *Ethics* (G II. 190 ff.; C 531 ff.).

19. Compare Delahunty 248; Bennett 339.

20. Many commentators have remarked on the negative view Spinoza takes of love (of the ordinary human variety). It is an exaggeration to say, as does for example Delahunty, that Spinoza 'repudiates' love (Delahunty 266); for while Spinoza roundly condemns excessive and obsessional love (cf. G II. 294; C 606), he does seem to allow that it can exist in a 'moderate' form that is compatible with the life of reason (cf. G II. 271; C 591). But it is true that Spinoza seems suspicious of that *particularity* of commitment which is, arguably, the essence of genuine human love. Thus in one passage where he talks of the need to 'overcome hate by love', the context makes it clear that what he has in mind is a kind of intellectual resolve—a

noble refusal to return hate for hate (*Ethics* IV, prop. 46, schol.). 'Love' in this context is explicitly equated with 'nobility', which is defined in fairly austere and universal terms: it is 'a desire by which each person strives *solely from the dictates of reason*, to aid other men and join them to him in friendship' (*Ethics* III, prop. 59, schol.).

21. For a seminal paper on the importance of 'reactive' attitudes see P. F. Strawson, 'Freedom and Resentment', in Strawson, ch. 1. For discussion of these themes in Spinoza, compare Bennett 324 ff. and Delahunty 260 ff.

22. For the Aristotelian account of the soul, see Chapter 3, note 24. For Aristotle's doctrine that virtue involves a disposition to have the right feelings in the right amount, and that it is an excess (or deficiency) that is bad, see *Nicomachean Ethics* II.

23. Compare the passage from *Ethics* V, Preface, quoted above, Chapter 4, p. 131.

24. For a more detailed account of Spinoza's critique of Descartes's theory of the passions, see Cottingham, op. cit. at note 10, above.

25. The dispositions characteristic of the virtuous person are neither innate, nor to be acquired simply by an intellectual decision: ethical behaviour, says Aristotle, is a matter of *habit* (*ethos*). *Nicomachean Ethics* I, 1.

26. The seventeenth-century writer Robert Sanderson speaks of 'a mere rationalist, that is to say in plain English an Atheist of the late edition' (*Ussher's Power Princes* (1670), quoted in the *Oxford English Dictionary* under 'rationalist').

27. Voetius of Utrecht, an implacable foe of the Cartesian philosophy, dubbed Descartes a papist, but also compared his arguments with those of a notorious atheist, Vanini, who had been burned for atheism at Toulouse in 1619. For Descartes's troubles at the hands of theologians, both Catholic and Protestant, cf. *Conversation with Burman*: AT V. 176 and 178; CB 46 and 49, and commentary at CB 115–16.

28. 'A rumour was spread everywhere that a book of mine about God was in the press, and that in it I endeavoured to show that there is no God . . . When I heard this from certain trustworthy men, who also said that the theologians were intriguing against me everywhere, I decided to postpone publication . . .' (letter to Oldenburg of September 1675).

29. Leibniz's secretary, J. G. Eckhart, reports in his biography of Leibniz (written in 1717) that the Hanoverian clergy reproached Leibniz for his infrequent attendance at church. He adds: 'die gemeinen

Leute hiessen ihn daher insgemein auf Plattdeutsch *Lövenix*, welches *qui ne croit rien* heisset' ('among the people he was generally known as "Lövenix", meaning "one who believes nothing"') (Eckhart 201).

30. Bayle 341 under 'Takiddin'. 'Pyrrhonism' in the seventeenth and eighteenth centuries was the term commonly used to denote extreme scepticism (after Pyrrho of Elis, *c.*365–275 BC, founder of the Sceptics). See further Popkin 11 ff. and 103 ff.

31. For Descartes's problems with the doctrine of transubstantiation, see Fourth Set of Replies: AT VII. 249 ff.; CSM II. 173 ff. For Genesis, see *Conversation with Burman*: AT V. 169; CB 36. See also letter to Mersenne of 1641 (AT III. 295).

32. Cf. *Principles* III, 29; see further Cottingham (2) 96.

33. Paracelsus 183.

34. A serious objection to Copernicus's heliocentric theory was the absence of stellar parallax; to meet this objection Copernicus proposed that the stars were vastly further away than had previously been thought. Empirical support for the notion of an extremely large universe had come with Galileo's telescopic observations of the Milky Way (which showed it to be composed of innumerable stars). Several sixteenth-century thinkers (among them Giordano Bruno (1548–1600)) had proposed that the universe was infinitely extended. Descartes's arguments for this thesis are largely a priori (cf. letter to Chanut of June 1647: AT V. 32), though he prefers to use the term 'indefinite' when describing the extent of the universe, reserving the term 'infinite' for God. Cf. *Conversation with Burman*: AT V. 167; CB 33.

35. Francis Bacon, *De dignitate et de augmentis scientiarum* (1623) III, 5 (Bacon 473).

36. Bacon, for example, maintained that the physicist's task was to uncover the inner structure of bodies, their *latens schematismus*: *Novum Organum* (1620), II, 6 and 7 (Bacon 305 ff.). Cf. Chapter 3, note 50.

37. 'The best system that could be devised is one where any given movement in the part of the brain immediately affecting the mind produces the one corresponding sensation that . . . is most frequently conducive to the preservation of the healthy man . . . So there is nothing here that does not bear witness to the power and greatness of God' (Sixth Meditation: AT VII. 87; CSM II. 60). See further Cottingham (2) 140–1.

38. Cf. Hobbes, chs. 13 and 14. There can be no doubt that Spinoza's

political theory was greatly influenced by that of Hobbes. For an account of some of the ways in which Spinoza diverges from Hobbes see H. Gildin, 'Spinoza and the Political Problem', in Grene 377 ff. Cf. also Scruton, ch. 6.

39. For Leibniz's attempt to reconcile the notions of efficient and final causation, see Chapter 4, p. 144.

40. This follows from the principle of the identity of indiscernibles. See Chapter 3, note 56. In the *Theodicy*, Leibniz defines 'metaphysical evil' as that which consists in 'mere imperfection'. There is an 'original imperfection in the creature before sin, because the creature is limited in essence' (I, 20–1). The underlying idea here is that God is, as Descartes put it, 'supreme and pure being' (AT V. 147; CB 5). A created thing can come into existence only by a process of negation or subtraction, as it were; to exist as a separate entity it must necessarily lack some of the positive perfections of God. 'Even before the fall,' says Leibniz in the *Discourse on Metaphysics*, 'there was an original imperfection or limitation connatural to all creatures . . . This, I believe, is what the opinion of St Augustine and others comes down to, when they maintain that the root of evil lies in nothingness . . .' (GP IV. 455; P 40). It should be added, however, that central to Leibniz's discussions of all the varieties of evil is the thesis that God is constrained by what is logically possible (a thesis denied by Descartes: AT VII. 432; CSM II. 291, cf. AT I. 145 and 152). Leibniz's God creates not a perfect world but the best *possible* world all things considered; Leibniz expresses this by saying that 'God wills antecedently the good and consequently the best' (*Theodicy* I, 23).

41. Voltaire, *Candide* (1759), ch. 5.

42. '*Le silence éternel de ces espaces infinis m'effraie*' (*Pensées*, no. 206: Pascal II. 127).

43. Cf. Matthew Arnold, *Dover Beach* (1867).

Reference List

Aiton, E. J., *Leibniz, a Biography* (Bristol: Hilger, 1985)

Alexander, P., *Ideas, Qualities and Corpuscles* (Cambridge: Cambridge University Press, 1985)

Aubrey, John, *Brief Lives*, ed. O. L. Dick (Harmondsworth: Penguin, 1962)

Bacon, Francis, *The Works of Francis Bacon*, eds. J. Spedding and R. E. Ellis, abridged J. M. Robinson (London: Routledge, 1905)

Baillet, Adrien, *La Vie de Monsieur Des-Cartes* (Paris: Horthemels, 1691); photographic reprint, Hildesheim: Olms, 1972)

Bayle, Pierre, *Dictionnaire historique et critique* (1697), tr. R. Popkin, *Pierre Bayle: Historical and Critical Dictionary, Selections* (Indianapolis: Bobbs Merrill, 1965)

Bennett, J., *A Study of Spinoza's Ethics* (Cambridge: Cambridge University Press, 1984)

Berkeley, George, *Berkeley's Philosophical Works*, ed. D. M. Armstrong (London: Macmillan, 1965)

Boyle, Robert, *Selected Philosophical Papers of Robert Boyle*, ed. M. A. Stewart (Manchester: Manchester University Press, 1979)

Brown, S. (1), *Leibniz* (Milton Keynes: Open University Press, 1983)

Brown, S. (2), *Leibniz* (Brighton: Harvester Press, 1984)

Butler, R. J. (ed.), *Cartesian Studies* (Oxford: Blackwell, 1972)

Church, R. W., *A Study in the Philosophy of Malebranche* (London: Allen and Unwin, 1931)

Churchland, P., *Neurophilosophy* (Cambridge, Mass.: MIT Press, 1986).

Clarke, D., *Descartes' Philosophy of Science* (Manchester: Manchester University Press, 1982)

Cottingham, J. (1), *Rationalism* (London: Paladin, 1984)

Cottingham, J. (2), *Descartes* (Oxford: Blackwell, 1986)

Cottingham, J. (3) (tr.), *Descartes' Meditations on First Philosophy with Selections from Objections and Replies* (Cambridge: Cambridge University Press, 1986)

Curley, E. M. (1), *Spinoza's Metaphysics* (Cambridge, Mass.: Harvard University Press, 1969)

Curley, E. M. (2), *Descartes against the Sceptics* (Oxford: Blackwell, 1978)

Delahunty, R. J., *Spinoza* (London: Routledge, 1985)

Dennett, D. (1), *Brainstorms* (Sussex: Harvester, 1978)

Dennett, D. (2), *Elbow Room* (Oxford: Clarendon, 1984)

Doney, W. (ed.), *Descartes, A Collection of Critical Essays* (London: Macmillan, 1968)

Drake, S., *Galileo* (Oxford: Oxford University Press, 1980)

Eckhart, J. G., *Lebensbeschreibung des Freyherr von Leibniz* (1779), repr. in J. A. Eberhard and J. G. Eckhard, *Leibniz Biographien* (Hildesheim: Olms, 1982)

Edwards, P. (ed.), *The Encyclopaedia of Philosophy* (New York: Macmillan, 1967)

Engfer, H. J., *Philosophie als Analysis* (Stuttgart: Frommann, 1982)

Frankfurt, H. (ed.), *Leibniz, A Collection of Critical Essays* (New York: Doubleday, 1972)

Freeman, E., and Mandelbaum, M. (eds.) *Spinoza: Essays in Interpretation* (La Salle: Open Court, 1975)

Friedmann, G., *Leibniz et Spinoza* (3rd edn., Paris: Gallimard, 1974)

Galileo Galilei, *Le Opere*, ed. A. Favaro (Florence: Barbera, 1889–1901; repr. 1968)

Grene, M. (ed.), *Spinoza: A Collection of Critical Essays* (Indiana: University of Notre Dame Press, 1973)

Hobbes, Thomas, *Leviathan* (1651), ed. C. B. Macpherson (Harmondsworth: Penguin, 1968)

Hofstadter, D. R., and Dennett, D. C., *The Minds I* (Harmondsworth: Penguin Books, 1982)

Holland, A. J. (ed.), *Philosophy, its history and historiography* (Dordrecht: Reidel, 1985)

Hollis, M., and Lukes, S. (eds.), *Rationality and Relativism* (Oxford: Blackwell, 1982)

Hooker, M. (ed.), *Descartes: Critical and Interpretative Essays* (Baltimore: Johns Hopkins, 1978)

Hume, David (1), *A Treatise of Human Nature* (1739–40), ed. L. A. Selby-Bigge (2nd edn. revised P. H. Nidditch, Oxford: Oxford University Press, 1975)

Hume, David (2), *An Enquiry concerning Human Understanding* (1748), ed. L. A. Selby-Bigge (3rd edn. revised P. H. Nidditch, Oxford: Oxford University Press, 1985)

Jolley, N., *Leibniz and Locke* (Oxford: Oxford University Press, 1984)

Kant, Immanuel, Critique of Pure Reason (*Kritik der Reinen Vernunft*, (1781, 2nd edn. 1787), tr. N. Kemp-Smith (London: Macmillan, 1929)

Kenny, A. (1), *Descartes* (New York: Random House, 1968)

Kenny, A. (2) (ed.), *Rationalism, Empiricism and Idealism* (Oxford: Clarendon, 1986)

Kripke, S., *Naming and Necessity* (1972; rev. edn. Oxford: Blackwell, 1980)

Lennon, T. M., *et al.*, *Problems of Cartesianism* (Kingston and Montreal: McGill-Queen's University Press, 1982)

Locke, John, *An Essay concerning Human Understanding* (1689), ed. P. M. Nidditch (Oxford: Clarendon, 1975)

Loeb, L. E., *From Descartes to Hume* (Ithaca: Cornell University Press, 1981)

Malebranche, Nicolas, *The Search after Truth* (*De la recherche de la vérité*, 1674–5), tr. T. M. Lennon and P. J. Olscamp (Columbus: Ohio State University Press, 1980)

Marion, J.-L., *Sur le prisme metaphysique de Descartes* (Paris: Presses Universitaires de France, 1986)

Maxwell, G., and Savodik, I. (eds.), *Consciousness and the Brain* (New York: Plenum Press, 1976)

Nagel, T. (1), *Mortal Questions* (Cambridge: Cambridge University Press, 1979)

Nagel, T. (2), *The View from Nowhere* (Oxford: Oxford University Press, 1986)

Pappus of Alexandria, *Collectiones*, ed. F. Hultsch (Berlin: 1785–8)

Paracelsus, *Selected Writings*, ed. J. L. Jacobi (London: Routledge, 1951)

Parkinson, G. H. R. (1), *Spinoza's Theory of Knowledge* (Oxford: Oxford University Press, 1954)

Parkinson, G. H. R. (2), *Logic and Reality in Leibniz' Metaphysics* (Oxford: Oxford University Press, 1965)

Parkinson, G. H. R. (3), *Leibniz on Human Freedom* (Wiesbaden: Steiner, 1970)

Parkinson, G. H. R. (4), *Spinoza* (Milton Keynes: Open University Press, 1983)

Pascal, Blaise, *Oeuvres*, ed. L. Brunschvicg (3 vols., Paris: Hachette, 1904)

Popkin, R. H., *The High Road to Pyrrhonism* (San Diego: Austin Hill Press, 1980)

Putnam, H., *Reason Truth and History* (Cambridge: Cambridge University Press, 1981)

Radnor, D., *Malebranche* (Amsterdam: Van Gorcum, 1978)

Rescher, N., *The Philosophy of Leibniz* (Englewood Cliffs: Prentice Hall, 1967)

Reference List 229

229

Ross, G. MacDonald, *Leibniz* (Oxford: Oxford University Press, 1984)

Russell, B. (1), *A Critical Exposition of the Philosophy of Leibniz* (Cambridge: Cambridge University Press, 1900; 2nd edn., London: Allen and Unwin, 1937)

Russell, B. (2), *A History of Western Philosophy* (London: Allen and Unwin, 1961)

Ryle, G., *The Concept of Mind* (London: Hutchinson, 1949)

Scruton, R., *Spinoza* (Oxford: Oxford University Press, 1986)

Shoemaker, S., *Identity Cause and Mind* (Cambridge: Cambridge University Press, 1984)

Sorell, T., *Descartes* (Milton Keynes: Open University Press, 1981)

Sprigge, T. L. S., *Theories of Existence* (Harmondsworth: Penguin, 1984)

Strawson, P. F., *Freedom and Resentment and Other Essays* (London: Methuen, 1974)

Swinburne, R., *The Evolution of the Soul* (Oxford: Clarendon, 1986)

Van Peursen, C.A., *Leibniz* (London: Faber, 1966)

Voltaire, *Candide*, tr. J. Butt (Harmondsworth: Penguin, 1970)

Watson, R. A., *The Breakdown of Cartesian Metaphysics* (Atlantic Highlands: Humanities Press International, 1987). This incorporates Watson's earlier *Downfall of Cartesianism 1673–1712* (Nijhoff: The Hague, 1966)

Williams, B., *Descartes, The Project of Pure Enquiry* (Harmondsworth: Penguin, 1978)

Wilson, M., *Descartes* (London: Routledge, 1978)

Yolton, J. W., *Thinking Matter: Materialism in Eighteenth-Century Britain* (Oxford: Blackwell, 1984)

Index